MOVIE CRAZY

To my parents

MOVIE CRAZY

Fans, Stars, and the Cult of Celebrity

Samantha Barbas

palgrave

Movie Crazy: Fans, Stars, and the Cult of Celebrity
© SAMANTHA BARBAS, 2001

First published 2001 by
PALGRAVE
175 Fifth Avenue, New York, N.Y.10010 and
Houndmills, Basingstoke, Hampshire RG21 6XS.
Companies and representatives throughout the world

PALGRAVE is the new global publishing imprint of St. Martin's Press LLC Scholarly and Reference Division and Palgrave Publishers Ltd (formerly Macmillan Press Ltd).

ISBN 0-312-23962-9 hardback

Library of Congress Cataloging-in-Publication Data

Barbas, Samantha.
    Movie crazy : fans, stars, and the cult of celebrity / Samantha Barbas.
        p. cm.
    Includes bibliographical references and index.
    ISBN 0-312-23962-9
        1. Motion picture audiences. 2. Fans (Persons) I. Title.

PN1995.9.A8 B37 2001
302.23'43--dc21

                                                                    2001021889

A catalogue record for this book is available
from the British Library.

Design by planettheo.com

First edition: November 2001
10 9 8 7 6 5 4 3 2 1

Printed in the United States of America.

CONTENTS

ACKNOWLEDGMENTS

I am deeply grateful for the many kind and brilliant souls who have helped this project to fruition. Professor Paula Fass, my dissertation advisor at the University of California at Berkeley, generously shared her time, enthusiasm, and extensive historical knowledge, and to her I am greatly indebted. Professors Michael Rogin and Kerwin Klein, members of my dissertation committee, offered insightful comments while Professor Ruth Rosen gave me a crash course in women's history, as well as an invaluable peek into the world of book publishing. I am thankful also to Professor K. Scott Wong of Williams College, and for the unfailingly helpful and cheerful advice of Professor Jim Kettner, who assisted me in numerous ways throughout my graduate school career.

In Los Angeles I relied on the expert assistance of Ned Comstock at the Cinema Television Library at the University of Southern California and the extraordinarily resourceful librarians at the Academy of Motion Picture Arts and Sciences in Beverly Hills. In Austin, Steve Wilson of the Harry Ransom Humanities Research Center at the University of Texas answered questions and guided me through the institute's extensive collection. Deborah Gershenowitz, my editor at Palgrave, has helped me see American history, and my own work, with much clearer vision.

I owe special thanks to the friends and colleagues who have sustained me with wisdom, compassion, and encouragement. Much love and gratitude to my friends and fellow faculty in the Interdisciplinary Studies Program at Arizona State University, especially to Paul Fotsch. Marco Louisse graciously hosted me in Los Angeles, and David Goldweber has been a perfect friend and traveling companion. Above all, I thank my parents, Louis and Mie Barbas, for escapes to Seattle, Hawaiian days, and a lifetime of love and learning.

INTRODUCTION

BETWEEN THE FIRST AND SECOND WORLD WARS, the American cinema flourished. With opulent theaters, lavish screen productions, and beautifully gowned film goddesses, the movies were more than just entertainment. For millions of Americans, Hollywood was a dream factory, turning out elaborate fantasies of glamour, success, and romance.

During those years marked by tremendous social and cultural change, movie stars became America's most visible celebrities. Newspapers, magazines, newsreels, and radio dutifully chronicled the comings and goings of famous actors and actresses. So entranced were Americans that the press often devoted more attention to stars than to traditionally newsworthy items. In 1926, critics complained that Rudolph Valentino's funeral received far more media coverage than the passing, on the same day, of Harvard president Charles Eliot. In 1935, the divorce of Mary Pickford and Douglas Fairbanks was reported on the front page of the *New York Times*.

In this movie-crazed climate, Americans voraciously consumed anything having to do with Hollywood. They eagerly scanned magazine articles that explained how films were directed, stunts performed, and costumes made. They perused countless ads that claimed to reveal the beauty secrets of glamorous actresses. They even read about movie fans, those zealous devotees of the motion picture, who somehow managed to receive their own share of the spotlight.

Between 1910 and the 1950s, movie fans frequently appeared in the popular media. Films, magazine articles, and novels showcased their passion and enthusiasm with descriptions that tended, not surprisingly, toward the sensational. As if to reassure average moviegoers that their love for the cinema had not yet reached a fanatical extreme, writers and filmmakers generally portrayed movie fans as naive, overeager, and a little off-kilter.

In 1916, for example, *McClure's* magazine told readers about a new illness that had taken hold of countless Americans—movie fandom or "filmitis." Disease soon became a popular metaphor for fandom, one that was repeated endlessly in the press. Overtaken by the movie bug, fans allegedly lost control of their senses. According to the *New York Times,* the quintessential display of movie madness took place at Valentino's funeral, where thousands of unruly admirers crowded the streets to get a glimpse of his coffin. Even Hollywood satirized the movie fan. In 1924, it produced *Merton of the Movies* about an awkward young man who loves the movies so much that he decides to pursue an acting career. In 1931, a similar film was made under the title *Movie Crazy,* with Harold Lloyd performing the antics of the sincere but ridiculous Hollywood aspirant.

Perhaps the most dramatic and frightening portrayal of movie fans of this era came in Nathanael West's *The Day of the Locust,* a biting, satirical novel written in 1938. In the final chapter of *The Day of the Locust,* the protagonist, struggling artist Tod Hackett, accidentally stumbles upon a crowd of fans waiting outside a Hollywood film premiere. Immediately he is overwhelmed by a sickening sensation of loneliness and desperation. These celebrity watchers, Tod realizes, are seeking in film fandom compensation for the emptiness of their lives. "It was a mistake to think them harmless curiosity seekers," West wrote. "They were savage and bitter, especially the middle-aged and old, and had been made so by boredom and disappointment."[1]

When the stars arrive at the premiere, the crowd turns violent, aggressively grabbing at the celebrities' hair and clothing. "At the sight of their heroes and heroines, the crowd would turn demoniac," West narrated. "Individually the purpose of its members might simply be to get a souvenir, but collectively it would grab and rend." Growing more and more frenzied, the crowd soon erupts into a raging mob. Although he tries to escape, Tod is swept into its center, carried forward and backward by the pushing, screaming, pulsating mass. Fans are buried, bruised, and trampled; Tod, bewildered and injured, is carried off by a wailing ambulance. In the meaningless, unreal context of Hollywood, the violent, fanatical possibilities inherent in film fandom are pushed to frightening realization.[2]

That same year, the Metro-Goldwyn-Mayer studio gave Americans a completely different portrait of the movie fan. In a cheery, light-hearted musical, *The Broadway Melody of 1938,* Judy Garland plays a sweet but giddy adolescent in love with her favorite star, Clark Gable. Pen in hand, preparing to write a fan letter, she stares at a portrait of the actor and sings passionately of her infatuation—how she fell in love with Gable while watching him in *It Happened One Night* (1934), how Gable smiled at her during a personal appearance at a movie theater, how he seemed to her "the nicest fellow in the movies." As the scene fades out, she croons dreamily into the camera and vows to adore her handsome idol forever.

The frenzied mob and the silly schoolgirl; the jaded celebrity watcher and the infatuated adolescent—these two popular stereotypes of film fandom would coexist throughout much of the twentieth century. Although MGM's teenage star worshiper was far less threatening than West's middle-aged washouts, both figures existed at society's margins. Never a truly "normal" activity, film fandom as depicted in popular culture seemed to attract the lonely, the naive, and the immature. Any fan behavior that seemed to confirm this image—crazed fans who tried to attack celebrities, frenetic young bobbysoxers who swooned over handsome actors in the 1940s and 1950s—would be duly reported by the press as evidence.

But as West penned his satire and Judy sang to Clark, thousands of movie fans, neither teenagers nor bitter, engaged in activities too mundane for the press. Somewhere in New York, a businessman developed a crush on Greta Garbo. In Nebraska, a mother of four discussed her love for Fred Astaire with the next-door neighbor. In Texas, a schoolteacher quietly dreamed of becoming a movie star. Near

Chicago, a 70-year-old grandmother clipped photos of Joan Crawford from the latest edition of *Photoplay* magazine.

Film fandom in the classical era of the Hollywood cinema—from the beginning of the motion picture star system in 1910 to the decline of the studio system in the late 1940s—is far less dramatic and sensationalistic, and far more complex and interesting, than it has typically been portrayed. Far from the marginal discontents they were made out to be, movie fans came from a broad cross section of society. Moreover, they participated in a wide range of activities. More than just celebrity watchers and letter writers, fans contributed to magazines, joined fan clubs, and dispensed advice to film studios. Some made fan activity a central part of their lives, devoting hours each day to their passion. For others, fandom was only a casual pastime, pursued occasionally or sporadically.

Yet despite their differences, fans had one thing in common. Not satisfied merely to watch films, they tried constantly to influence, control, and become directly involved in the filmmaking process. Sometimes this took the form of letter-writing campaigns. In an attempt to earn their idols better publicity and more prominent roles, fans inundated studios with thousands of insistent missives. Others sent studios scripts and story ideas for films. Some ambitious fans even tried to become actors. From 1910 until about 1930, thousands of fans flocked to Hollywood in the hopes of launching film careers. The story of film fandom, in large part, is the story of the way that fans refused to accept mass culture passively and, instead, became actively involved in their entertainment.

It is also the story of the way that fans significantly influenced Hollywood. Fearing the wrath of angry fans—in particular, potential box office losses and negative publicity—studios frequently changed casting and publicity decisions in response to fans' complaints. Sometimes studios even altered stars' appearances and personalities when they received enough requests. In the 1930s, for example, when fans wrote to MGM demanding a tough-talking hero, the studio created a personality to fit the bill. Through careful casting and a skillful publicity campaign, Clark Gable, an undistinguished, unassuming stage actor, was transformed into a rugged, charming, and phenomenally popular star. Fans, to a great extent, actually created their idols.

But the dynamic often went the other way. Just as fans sometimes controlled Hollywood, Hollywood also controlled fans. Capitalizing on fans' interest in stars, the film industry, with the help of publishers and advertisers, sold fans a variety of consumer products. They urged fans to see consumption as a form of participation: rather than become personally involved in the movies, fans might vicariously participate by purchasing the cosmetics and clothing endorsed by the stars. Between 1910 and 1950, a passion for the movies drew Americans not only into fan culture but also into a rapidly expanding consumer culture and into a burgeoning celebrity culture centered around the exploits and personalities of the most popular actors.

Perhaps the most significant way that fans became involved in the movies concerns what I call a search for authenticity. Since the earliest days of motion pictures, fans have been both fascinated and frustrated by the cinema's ability to create a realistic illusion of life. Though thrilled by the sight of photographic images in motion, fans often wondered whether they should trust their eyes. What if the stunts and chases they saw on the screen were faked? What if movie stars were only images and did not exist in person? Unless they were present when the movies were made, there was no way to know—and this lack of verification, for many fans, was frightening. In an attempt to confirm that the movies had a basis in reality, fans tried to learn as much as they could about the world behind the screen. Fans wanted to know: were stars as charming in real life as in the movies? What were actors and actresses really like?

In the years before 1910, these questions were often difficult to answer. Because movie star publicity was not yet a widespread film industry practice, fans had to barrage studios with questions and letters in order to learn detailed information about actors. By 1915, however, the situation had changed. Both established mainstream publications—such as *Collier's* and the *New York Times*—as well as a host of new movie fan magazines—*Photoplay, Motion Picture,* and *Shadowland,* among others—filled pages with facts about Hollywood stars. Although fans were delighted with the proliferation of information, at the same time they were skeptical. Often based on gossip or unconfirmed rumors, the new celebrity journalism seemed to raise as many questions as it answered. How could readers know whether the articles were true? With so many competing accounts, which ones should they believe? In another aspect of their search for authenticity, fans often tried to out-scoop journalists. Some fans tried to uncover the truth about actors by directly corresponding with them. Others trekked to Hollywood and camped out in front of celebrities' homes. Many fans would not be content until they had learned for themselves the facts about the stars.

Conceiving fandom as a quest for authenticity, influence, and involvement—in other words, an attempt to understand, control, and participate in the movies—sheds new light on a number of important issues in twentieth-century American culture. To begin, it contradicts the claims of critics who see the fan phenomenon as purposeless and trivial. It also adds another dimension to the many insightful studies of fan behavior that have been published in the last 20 years. As John Fiske, Janice Radway, Henry Jenkins, and other scholars of popular culture have written, fans not only consume mass culture but also appropriate and manipulate it. Aware of the impersonal, commercial nature of popular culture, fans nonetheless subvert it to serve their own personal interests. Many fans, for example, have used their passion for a particular singer or genre of film to find strength and self-esteem. Fan club members, too, speak of the closeness and camaraderie that have resulted from their shared interests. Some fans even use their favorite films, television programs, or fictional characters as inspiration for their own novels and short stories. When viewed in the context of the search for authenticity, influence, and involvement, these efforts at cultural appropriation might be seen as more than just attempts to inject personal meaning into mass entertainment. By becoming closely and actively involved in their entertainment, fans may be attempting to make more real and immediate the simulated reality presented by the movies, television, and other mass media.[3]

But not only movie fans have been concerned with these issues. Many casual moviegoers have wondered about the relationship between cinema and life; television viewers and fans of popular music, too, have raised questions about the people behind the images and voices. In other words, the growth of a mass-mediated culture, in which simulations of reality often substitute for genuine experiences, has not been smooth and flawless. Contrary to what many scholars have suggested, Americans have not passively accepted these images and representations. We do not desperately and unquestioningly consume them but actively question and investigate them.[4]

After nearly 100 years of motion pictures, Americans are still fascinated by the cinema. Although most of us feel quite sure about the way the movies work—that the camera depicts a distorted, constructed version of reality—we still engage in acts of verification. Although most of us accept that we cannot take part directly in the filmmaking process, we still want to feel a part of the movies by learning about the inner workings of film studios and the details of stars' lives. As long as we go to the movies, we will probably always be fascinated by questions of authenticity and involvement. And as twenty-first-century technology provides us with more—and more lifelike—forms of entertainment, the more urgent these issues may become.

CHAPTER ONE

FROM REEL TO REAL: THE FIRST MOVIE FANS

IN 1902, A COUNTRY FARMER named Uncle Josh embarked on an adventure: he decided to go to the movies. Josh had never been to the cinema before and eagerly anticipated his first show. But what he discovered far surpassed his expectations. The images on the screen, he found, were incredibly realistic—they were so lifelike that he mistook them for reality. When an attractive woman appeared on the screen, Josh jumped out of his seat to dance with her. When a train whizzed by in the next scene, he leaped back in terror. Josh was so engrossed that he started shouting when he saw a film of a man and woman embracing; the young woman, it seemed, was being seduced, and he was determined to stop the affair. Hoping to attack the lecherous villain, he lunged toward the screen, which collapsed under his weight.

But Uncle Josh's adventures did not take place in an ordinary movie theater. Instead, they happened in a film studio. Uncle Josh, the main character of the 1902 film *Uncle Josh at the Moving Picture Show*, was an imaginary moviegoer concocted by the Edison Film Company, a figment of director Edwin S. Porter's imagination. But Josh's experience was not entirely fictional. Like the befuddled moviegoer, many Americans worried about mistaking the movies for reality. How would they know what was real and what was filmed? Did the people and places in films really exist or were they mere images? At the turn of the century, these questions loomed large in the minds of many. As audiences watched the flickering images on the screen, they could not help but wonder: what was reel and what was real?

Early audiences were fascinated by the movies. Most Americans had never seen an onrushing train hurtling toward them in black and white. They had never seen technology that could so vividly mimic life, or that could so convincingly blur the boundaries between fantasy and reality. During the first decade of the twentieth century, Americans were both fascinated and curious about the enigmatic new medium and worked diligently to unravel its mysteries. Newspapers and magazines sold thousands of copies by promising to teach moviegoers how to distinguish between the cinematic and the real.

Perhaps the greatest enigma facing early audiences concerned the new motion picture actors and actresses. Charming, funny, and incredibly lifelike, these "picture players" were so enchanting that they seemed to cast a spell over all who watched them. "I have seen you so many times that I feel like I know you," confessed a fan to actress Florence Lawrence. "Sometimes when I see you in the moving pictures I feel like running up to the screen there and kiss you," wrote another. Not surprisingly, these players sparked as much curiosity as affection. Who were these actors? fans wondered. Why did they seem so intimate?[1]

From 1908 until 1910, film studios were barraged with inquiries from movie fans. In particular, because most studios at the time did not publicize their players, they were flooded with questions about actors. Fans wanted to know the name of the fat comedian, the dark-haired hero, and the "girl with the curls." They also hoped to uncover something even more important. By learning the identities of their favorite actors, fans hoped to confirm that they were real people, not Celluloid phantoms.

In response to the flood of questions, the head of the Independent Moving Picture Company, Carl Laemmle, at last publicized the names of his actors, and in 1910 the movie star system was born. Movie fans would no longer have to search for actors' identities. But the curiosity did not end there. Now certain that their favorite actors were real, fans wanted to know more. Were they the same in life as they were on the screen? Were they really as charming as they appeared? Once again, fans wrote letters—this time, to the new movie fan magazines—asking about stars' offscreen personalities. The responses they received were reassuring. "You may worship Lillian Gish for her fragile loveliness. Or Mabel Normand for her quick wit. If you like them for these qualities you will not be disappointed upon meeting them," assured *Photoplay* magazine. Fans could feel secure: they had fallen in love with an image, but that image happened to be very much like the real thing.[2]

Although the first movie fans were enthusiastic about the cinema, they were equally curious. They not only wanted to watch movies, but to understand them—to know how films were made, what actors were really like, and the relationship between the cinema and life. Ultimately, their letters and questions about the world behind the screen led to much more than they had ever dreamed: a powerful, glamorous Hollywood star system supported by a network of studios, publicists, advertisers, and fan magazines. Far from passive consumers, fans played an active role in creating the celebrity culture that would so passionately engage them.

THE TRICKS OF THE MOVING PICTURE MAKER

At the end of the nineteenth century, film manufacturers addressed audiences with a bold claim: their new technological novelty, the moving picture, did nothing less than duplicate life. The Phantoscope, an early projection machine, was advertised as a "perfect reproduction of living originals"; the Vitascope offered a "magnificent reproduction of living forms." "You won't see marionettes," explained the *New York World* in 1895, "You'll see people and things as they are."[3]

Spectators responded to these new "life-pictures" with great enthusiasm. The first public exhibition of motion pictures, at Koster and Bial's vaudeville theater in New York in 1896, was met with "the heartiest kind of applause," according to the *New York Dramatic Mirror.*

Later that year, audiences at Coney Island were delighted by the "almost perfect simulation of moving scenes in real life." Audiences were less interested in the subject matter of these early films—images of a woman dancing, a burlesque boxing match, and waves crashing into a pier—than in the fact that they presented images *in motion*. As one observer recalled, "We were primarily fascinated with movement itself. It did not make very much difference what moved or why; the important thing was that movement occurred."[4]

Since the vast majority of films before 1905 consisted of documentary footage—scenes of foreign lands or footage of sporting and other newsworthy events—filmmakers could convincingly advertise their products as newsreels. These views, they claimed, depicted nothing less than unadulterated reality. But as audiences soon learned, many of these films were not all they were promised to be. Quite a few, in fact, were faked.

Moviegoers who went to see footage of the famous Corbett-Fitzsimmons boxing match in 1897 found out the hard way. "The views are decidedly on the fake order, being unrecognizable by the people who are familiar with the ring and who know pictures of Corbett and Fitz. The first round was so tame that lovers of the manly art could not restrain the disgust they felt at the palpable fakeness of the alleged representation," read one description in the *Little Rock Gazette*. Audiences in that city became so angry that they stormed the box office demanding a refund. In the end, the theater manager turned over the evening's receipts to a state senator, who refunded the patrons' money.[5]

For viewers of the phony boxing match, the trickery was easy to detect. The faces of the actors did not resemble Corbett or Fitzsimmons; the audience's knowledge of the real boxers made the attempts at deception into a mockery. In the wake of the public outrage against the phony boxing film, studios ran full-page ads in New York newspapers decrying the "fake picture scheme" and claiming the authenticity of their own productions. The American Mutoscope and Biograph Company warned viewers, "DO NOT BE DECEIVED and DO NOT INVEST IN FAKES when the only real pictures . . . are those of the American Mutoscope and Biograph Company." The Edison studio similarly urged exhibitors not to be "fooled by fake pictures" when they could get "the real thing at a reasonable figure" from Edison.[6]

The Spanish-American War provided another opportunity for audiences to hone their skills in the detection of deception. Although many war films were shot on location in Cuba, others were filmed using miniatures or staged battles. Film companies advertised their phony footage as "accurate" and "authentic," and many observers, tricked by the skillful reenactments, could not tell the difference. One of the most popular war films, depicting a naval battle in Santiago Bay, used toy boats, a bathtublike ocean, and smoke from several cigarettes. Other studios tried to pass off scenes from travel films as authentic war footage. As the *New York Dramatic Mirror* described one film, "Queen's Jubilee scenes masqueraded as troops departing for Cuba; a dock view of the Orient, with Turks and fezes, was labeled 'Fugitives Leaving Havana.'" Audiences were apparently convinced. "The people cheered all of [the scenes]," the newspaper reported. "Business was large."[7]

Some moviegoers did not mind being deceived. As a Harlem cigar-store clerk commented, "I know a lot of the pictures are fake, but what of that? It only costs five cents." Others were less tolerant. "It hurts me and other fans as well to see a big, reputable film concern do anything that at all looks like and approaches faking," wrote a self-described "picture fan" to film industry trade journal *Moving Picture World*. "A short picture, recently released and called 'Among the Japanese' was incorrectly labeled. It should have read 'Among the Japanese in Chicago.' 'Orientals Tramping Around the Studio' would have been another good and appropriate title."[8]

In some cases, audiences went to the movies in the hopes of being deceived. At the turn of the century, the "trick films" of French magician-turned-filmmaker George Méliès were phenomenally popular in the United States. Méliès used the power of the camera to create spectacular illusions: men and women exploding in clouds of smoke, vanishing into thin air, or traveling into outer space as in his famous 1902 *A Trip to the Moon*. But because Méliès's movies made no claim to reality, most audiences perceived them as harmless. Critics never complained that Méliès faked his films.

Between 1904 and 1907, however, a new trend in filmmaking intensified the audience's concern with cinematic deception. In response to a growing lack of interest in documentaries, studios began to produce narrative films. One might have thought that the fear of being tricked would decline. After all, how could fiction be faked? As audiences discovered, however, skillful storytelling required a good deal of trickery. In response to widespread confusion surrounding the new narrative films (some were so difficult to follow that they required lecturers to explain them), several filmmakers, including D. W. Griffith, developed a set of techniques that would clarify cinematic storytelling—parallel editing, point-of-view shots, and close-ups. These innovations, sometimes dubbed "tricks" by journalists, allowed audiences to gain insight into characters' thoughts and emotions; complex stories could now be told from multiple points of view.[9]

Audiences found themselves deeply involved with the stories and characters of these new narrative films. As a reviewer from *Variety* noted in 1909, the dramatic realism that Griffith achieved in his films seemed like a kind of magic. "In this [film] a situation is worked up to a tremendous pitch of suspense . . . and the tension of suspense tightens almost painfully," he claimed. "The Biograph studios have a producer who is a wonder at dramatic trick work." That year, reporters from *Moving Picture World* noted audiences' reactions to D. W. Griffith's film *The Lonely Villa* in which a wife and child are rescued from invading burglars by a heroic husband: "'Thank God, they're saved!' said a woman behind us at the conclusion of the . . . film. Just like this woman, the entire audience was in a state of intense excitement as this picture was being shown." Owing to the artful tricks of the camera, many fictional films seemed more lifelike to viewers than documentary films.[10]

Given the power of this "dramatic trick work," it is not surprising that the public discourse on cinematic deception *increased* with the advent of narrative film. By 1908, story films outnumbered actuality films, and the establishment of cheap nickelodeon theaters around the country enabled millions of Americans to become familiar with the camera's capacity for illusion. In response, journalists boldly took up the challenge of demystifying what one magazine called "the tricks of the moving picture maker." In 1909, *Scientific American* warned readers of the camera's ability to perform "miracles utterly inexplicable to the uninformed spectator" but offered a technical explanation of "the more important of these mysteries." For example, characters could be made to appear and disappear by stopping and starting the film so flawlessly that "the spectator fails to realize the manner in which he was deceived."[11]

A similar article in *Current Literature,* "How Miracles are Performed in Moving Pictures," explained that cameras did not perform miracles but merely used "applied science." William Allen Johnston assured readers of *Harper's Weekly* that film actors rarely performed their stunts: "Of course the performers do not go through all the disastrous experiences attributed to them on screen. The man does not jump from the cliff, is not ground to pieces under the railway, is not crushed flat by the heavy steam roller. These are tricks of the camera."[12]

However, articles claimed, the camera did not always deceive. Sometimes it actually did depict the truth. A popular anecdote from 1908 told the story of a man watching a film of a New York crowd, only to see his own image on the screen.

> He was still more surprised to see a valuable watch-charm which he had always worn . . . drop and disappear from sight. Then out of the moving throng appeared a young lady, who stooped and picked up the charm from the pavement. The man gasped and dropped back in his seat when he recognized the features of the woman. . . . A few weeks later he recovered his watch-charm after he had cabled the woman to be certain if there was any truth in the strange coincidence or whether it was all fiction.[13]

Do not be deceived, warned magazines. What seems real may be faked, and what seems faked might be real. And when at the movies, be careful what you do—you may lose control of your senses. In 1907, it was reported that a Chicago audience watching a film of a man eating raw onions began sneezing and coughing. "The crowd in the gallery was imitating the picture on screen," *Moving Picture World* explained. Later it was discovered that a joker had sprinkled snuff around the seats. On a more serious note, in 1906 *Variety* claimed that a woman committed suicide after she saw a film that depicted the suicide of a criminal. The same year, it reported that three London boys committed a robbery after watching a film about burglars.[14]

By 1909, Americans had become aware, both through popular literature and their own experiences, of the motion picture's ability to confuse fantasy and reality. Images and stories that appeared to be real were often only tricks of the camera. But these tricks held an unusual power. They might cause viewers to become intensely involved in a narrative, to imitate actions on the screen, or to fall deeply in love with a Celluloid image called a motion picture actor.

WHAT'S IN A NAME?

Movie fans may have felt most deceived when it came to the subject of film actors. Unknown, unpublicized, and intentionally kept anonymous by film studios, actors seemed like yet another cinematic enigma. According to some film scholars, the studios' policy of anonymity was designed to control their employees. If actors remained unknown to the public, they could never become stars and demand high salaries. Others have claimed that it was the actors themselves who shunned publicity. Many members of early studio stock companies were theater actors who were either out of a job or seeking work between shows. Fearing that their stage careers would be ruined if they were associated with the lowbrow motion picture, actors chose to remain anonymous.[15]

Moviegoers were incredibly curious about these actors and with good reason. Living in a culture that placed great importance on demystifying the cinema, movie fans were eager to discover the true identities of their favorite players. From 1908 until 1910, fans wrote hundreds of letters to studios asking for actors' names, but the studios did not respond. "I wrote to the [studio] asking for your name and address but received no answer to my first letter," a disappointed fan wrote to Florence Lawrence, the beautiful star of many of D. W. Griffith's films. "I wrote again . . . and the answer was that it was against the rules of the company to give out the names of either actor or actress taking part in their films." In desperation, fans bombarded local theater managers with questions. "You have no idea of the amount of interest our patrons take in the players they see in these pictures," commented one manager. "I am approached for new information every day."[16]

But movie fans had an even more pressing reason to learn actors' names: they had fallen in love with them. By 1909, as a result of the innovations in film narrative pioneered by Griffith and other directors, many moviegoers experienced strong feelings of intimacy with actors. Since narrative films, through point-of-view shots, often allowed viewers access to characters' thoughts and perspectives, audiences were able to identify and sympathize with the men and women they saw on screen. Acting had also become increasingly realistic, shifting from an exaggerated pantomime to a more natural, subtle style based on facial expression. Some fans, who watched movies nearly every night in inexpensive nickelodeon theaters, began to feel as if they knew, quite personally, the characters in films and the actors who played them.[17]

For these early audiences, this sense of intimacy must have come as a shock. Many of the fans who corresponded with Florence Lawrence between 1909 and 1911 explained that they felt awkward about writing to her, but that they were moved to do so by surprisingly intense feelings of familiarity. "Dear Miss Flo," wrote Mabel Hilton of Hartford, "I know you will think I am bold—very bold—but I just can't help it. You see, I have seen you in so many moving pictures that it seems as though I should naturally speak to you if ever I met you on the street." Another fan begged, "Please dear don't be cross with me for writing informally to you without ever having met you. I feel that I almost know you."[18]

On the surface, these fans appeared to be making the mistake that countless articles had described: they seemed to blur the cinematic and the real. But what these passionate letters really reveal is a desire to clarify the relationship between the movies and reality. By writing to Lawrence, fans hoped to receive some sign—a return letter, a comment, a photograph—that would confirm that she had a real-life identity distinct from her fictional characters.

One way to do this was to probe the distinction between the real Florence Lawrence and her cinematic characters. "Miss Lawrence dear I would never on earth write to you unless I knew you were too sweet to scorn this letter. Anyone could tell you were the best hearted, sweetest little woman just by looking at you in a moving picture," wrote 16-year-old Edith Crutcher. "Won't you answer this letter? Please don't disappoint me because I want to hear from you so much." Mrs. T. L. Wheelis of Philadelphia wrote Lawrence for a photograph. "It would be a great honor, besides, I should know then that you are the pure-minded, noble-hearted girl I think you are," she explained.[19]

Others hoped to verify Lawrence's existence by meeting her in person. One young woman urged the actress to visit her in Boston;

another invited Lawrence to spend the summer with her in Portland. Some fans sought correspondence in lieu of face-to-face contact. "I can only see your pictures, I may never see you in person, so won't you please, please write," begged Elmer Jones. "This card is from a young girl whose greatest desire is to become acquainted with you," wrote May Woelfel in 1910. "As it is impossible to do so personally, she sends this little message hoping you will answer it and fulfill her wish."[20]

But what fans wanted more than anything else, prior to 1910, was to learn actors' names. A name would provide an actor with a clear offscreen identity; it would confirm that actors were real people, not "tricks of the moving picture maker." Many fans recounted that the first thing they did once they fell in love with Florence Lawrence was to try and discover her name. Stephen Horsky explained that the first time he saw the actress, he felt an impulse "to write the [studio] and find out your name and address because I could not forget you." Other fans hoped to bypass the studio by questioning the actress herself. In letters addressed to "the lady who played the lead in the film 'Love's Stratagem'" or "the lady who appeared in 'The Ingrate' and 'The Reckoning,'" fans begged Lawrence to reveal her identity. "Dear Stranger," wrote Leland Ayers, "Will you please answer this letter . . . just telling me your name, your real name not a stage one? I promise I won't tell no one."[21]

When letters failed to yield a response, fans invented names of their own. Fan Etta Ward confessed to Lawrence, "In order to have some kind of name for you we called you 'The Queen of Sheba.'" Lawrence was also widely known as "The Biograph Girl," after the name of her studio. In late 1909, when Lawrence moved from the Biograph studio to the Independent Moving Picture Company (IMP), the nickname was transferred to her replacement, Mary Pickford.[22]

In early 1910, fans' prayers were at last answered. The public cry for actors' names had become so loud that it was impossible for the studios to ignore them. "Every film manufacturer . . . can testify to the numerous demands from picture theater spectators for information in reference to the members of their stock companies," the *New York Dramatic Mirror* explained in January 1910. *Moving Picture World,* which had urged studios to release actors' names, also reported that film companies were "burdened by correspondence." In response to the pressure, in March 1910, IMP studio head Carl Laemmle revealed the name of his new leading actress—Florence Lawrence. The silence was broken, and the movie star system was born.[23]

A STAR IS BORN

Given the public's concern with cinematic trickery, it is ironic that the event that first widely publicized the name of a film actor was a ruse. During the first week of March 1910, Laemmle stunned movie fans throughout the nation by issuing, as a publicity stunt, a phony report claiming that Florence Lawrence had been killed in a streetcar accident. The report of Lawrence's death was published in several newspapers, along with a photograph of the actress and her name. But Laemmle did not keep the nation mourning for long. On March 6, the *St. Louis Post-Dispatch* published an announcement, most likely planted by Laemmle, that the report of Lawrence's death had been "a canard," allegedly sent out by a rival of the IMP studio. The following week, Laemmle printed a similar account, along with a photo of Lawrence, in an advertisement in *Moving Picture World:*

> The blackest and at the same time the silliest lie yet circulated by the enemies of the "Imp" was the story foisted on the public of St. Louis last week to the effect that Miss Lawrence (the "Imp" girl, formerly known as the "Biograph" girl) had been killed by a street car. It was a black lie because so cowardly. It was a silly lie because so easily disproved. Miss Lawrence was not even in a street-car accident, is in the best of health, will continue to appear in "Imp" films, and very shortly some of the best work in her career is to be released.[24]

In early April 1910, Laemmle sent Lawrence to St. Louis to reassure fans that she had not been killed. According to *Moving Picture World,* it was fans who demanded to see Lawrence: "The newspaper report of the death of Miss Lawrence . . . so upset her many admirers in St. Louis that nothing short of seeing her in the flesh would satisfy them." Indeed, some fans seemed to have been genuinely worried by the phony announcement. "A great many of our patrons have been attracted by your personality in the Imp pictures and the rumor of your death caused considerable depression among our patrons," wrote one theater manager to Lawrence. "I had to write and tell you how glad I was that the report of your accidental death proved untrue," explained another fan. Whether or not moviegoers actually believed that Lawrence had been killed, they were thrilled at the chance to see the actress in person. When Lawrence arrived in St. Louis, she was nearly crushed by a mob. "The crowd surged toward her like a wave, and for a moment it looked as if the young woman would be drowned in a human sea," wrote one reporter. Fans "demonstrated their affection by tearing the buttons from her coat, the trimmings from her hat, and the hat from her head."[25]

As her visit proved, Florence Lawrence was not dead. And for fans who had fallen in love with the actress, Lawrence's appearance in St. Louis—and perhaps most important, her name—confirmed her real, offscreen existence. Lawrence's fans expressed great relief when they at last learned the identity of their favorite actress. "Oh, I am so glad I know your name and address now, for I certainly love you," Edith Crutcher wrote. "Miss Florence I found out your name at last— two of them!" another fan wrote gleefully. Fans prized this information dearly. Before star publicity became a widespread industry practice, many fans felt that an actor's name was a privileged kind of knowledge, available only to dedicated admirers. "All the girls here are crazy about you," wrote Virginia Kramer and Helen Wood, "but we are the only ones that know your name."[26]

Knowing Lawrence's name, commented many fans, gave her a real identity distinct from her characters onscreen. George Armstrong revealed to Lawrence that although he had been familiar with the actress for a long time "through the pictures," he felt that he did not really know her until he learned her name. A more impassioned fan, Dick Shields, explained that learning Lawrence's name put his "relationship" with her on an entirely new level. "Well I remember the first time I saw your face and name connected," he wrote. "From an enlarged photo in the lobby of a theater your bright eyes looked out at me and beneath them was the name 'Florence Lawrence.' At last my dream girl had a name!" Shields confessed that from that point on, he carried on mental conversations with Lawrence about her life and her acting, praising good performances and chastising her for "wretched" ones. Although this ardent fan engaged in flights of fancy, he had clearly managed to separate Lawrence's real-life existence from her cinematic image. He was in love with Florence Lawrence the actress, not Florence Lawrence as "Mrs. Jones" or any of her other fictional characters.[27]

Technically, Florence Lawrence was not the first actress appearing in motion pictures whose name had been printed. In 1908, the Pathe company publicized the names of well-known stage actors who were appearing in the studio's "Films D'Art" series. And in January 1910 *Moving Picture World* began a column called "Picture Personalities" that featured the names, photographs, and career highlights of actors, many of whom had worked on the stage. Even Florence Lawrence's name may have been released prior to March 1910. In February of that year, an advertisement for an IMP film claimed that "in this picture, Miss Lawrence, known to thousands as 'Mrs. Jones,' does the most excellent work of her remarkable career."[28]

But it was not until Laemmle's stunt that the name of a popular actress, and one who worked exclusively in motion pictures, became widely known among the public. And it was only after the stunt that film studios became aware of how profitable names could be. Realizing that audiences were often more interested in actors than in films, studios soon initiated the infamous motion picture star system, which dominated the industry for decades.

By 1912, nearly all film studios, with the exception of D. W. Griffith's Biograph studio, had revealed the names of their leading actors. Stars began making regular appearances at theaters around the country, and newspapers and magazines featured glamorous photos and lengthy articles on these "picture personalities." Fan magazines even began offering readers "the latest novelty in motion picturedom," large portraits of actors with their names emblazoned across the frame. Some commentators thought that this widespread publicity would surely put an end to the insistent letters of inquisitive fans. Little did they know that the real outpouring of curiosity had only begun.

PICTURE PERSONALITIES

In 1912, Laemmle tried another stunt, this time with actor King Baggott. Because Baggott's name had already been well-publicized,

Laemmle resorted to another tactic: assuring the public that Baggott behaved in real life as he did on screen. "King Baggott is not dead," read the advertisement. "The rumor started in Kansas City this time. Last time it was St. Louis. King Baggott is not only very much alive but is just as good a fellow off the stage as on."[29]

Once again, Laemmle had his finger on the pulse of the moviegoing public. Now that they no longer had to search for names, fans turned their interests in another direction. One journalist explained in 1911 that readers were simply not interested in actors' names anymore; their "desire was to learn . . . whether they were married, where their respective home towns were located, etc., etc." Hundreds of fan letters began pouring into studios and magazines, asking similar questions. Was King Baggott really as "good a fellow" in real life as he appeared on screen? Was Florence Lawrence as charming as she seemed? As columnist Lux Graphicus of *Moving Picture World* explained, fans wanted to know about "the personalities—the corporeal personalities—of the good people who make those 'shivery shadows' for our entertainment." In their continuing quest to connect cinematic images to their offscreen roots, fans delved into the realm of the personal.[30]

To understand just how important this was—how new and unprecedented was the intense curiosity about stars' private lives—we need to turn back to the days before the movies. By the time the motion picture made its debut, the concept of celebrity fandom had existed for decades. Throughout the nineteenth century, Americans had become passionate admirers of popular actors, singers, and dancers; in the 1840s, for example, audiences were so captivated by touring Austrian dancer Fanny Elssler that some critics declared the nation in a state of "Elsslermaniaphobia." Eager fans not only chased her after performances, but purchased Elssler-endorsed shoes, stockings, garters, and soap. Popular stage actors like Harry Montague and Kyrle Bellew also won huge followings. Some admirers formed fan clubs; others collected photos and autographs of their idol or wrote passionate fan letters. And all theater fans made a ritual out of attending their favorite star's latest performance, where they sat in the front row—called "rush seats," since fans rushed to get them—and waved and cheered in the hopes of catching his attention.[31]

But for the most part, these fans were never gripped by the questions of reality and authenticity that played such a central role in film fandom. Unlike film actors, who appeared as images, stage stars were obviously real, living humans. In addition, the very nature of the theater made questions about actors' real selves less important. Enticed by the cinema's illusion of intimacy, moviegoers were encouraged to probe into stars' personal lives; theatergoers, however, generally cared far less about actors' offscreen characteristics. A good actor, fans knew, did not present himself to the audience but masked his qualities in a carefully crafted stage persona. His offstage personality, for the most part, was irrelevant.[32]

Moreover, if theater fans were curious about what their idol did off the stage, it was not difficult to find out. During the late nineteenth century, fans became notorious for waiting outside the stage door to catch a glimpse of their favorite actor. Unlike movie fans, theater fans who wanted to communicate with a star could often do so—if not in person, with cheers and applause in the theater. Although stage stars sparked a great deal of enthusiasm and interest, they never generated the kind of curiosity that surrounded film actors.[33]

So when movie fans wrote to magazines and newspapers hoping to learn about stars' private lives, editors were taken aback. This kind of intense curiosity was unprecedented, even shocking. In 1911, the *New York Dramatic Mirror* initiated "Letters to The Spectator," a weekly column that responded to letters from curious fans. "The Spectator," drama critic Frank Woods, answered a variety of questions ranging from the identities of actors—particularly extras or minor actors, who were often not publicized by studios—to the best way to break into a motion picture career. But what most fans requested, and what the Spectator adamantly refused to answer, concerned actors' private lives—in particular, their marital status. When fans became too inquisitive, Woods reminded them of the *Dramatic Mirror*'s strict "rule about matrimonial information." When *Moving Picture World* initiated a similar column in 1911, it also adopted a policy of silence. "Inquiries to the private affairs of photoplayers will not be answered," it warned. "This includes the question as to whether or not they are married."[34]

One reason for this policy may be linked to actors' earlier desires for anonymity. Just as many film actors had not wanted their names publicized, they similarly refused to have their private lives revealed. Another may be that the Spectator and other columnists simply did not know the answers to the many personal questions posed by fans.

But the most likely reason, given the cultural and social climate of the era, is that revealing such information might mark a publication as a "scandal sheet" catering to the sensationalistic desires of uneducated readers. Because motion picture studios and film publications feared the attacks of critics and censors who associated the movies with delinquency and vice, they refused to divulge any information that might be considered improper or morally questionable. Journals like *Moving Picture World* hoped to establish themselves as respectable publications dedicated to the scientific and professional aspects of the motion picture—not to gossip and scandal.[35]

The first movie fan magazine, *Motion Picture Story Magazine,* which debuted in February 1911, also adopted this attitude. Originally the magazine's founder, J. Stuart Blackton, head of the Vitagraph studio, had not intended the magazine to discuss actors at all. He initially envisioned a publication that would feature novelized versions of motion picture plots—from the Vitagraph studio, of course, and from other members of the film alliance known as the Motion Picture Patents Company—along with still photos from films. What Blackton and editor Eugene Brewster did not realize, however, was that fans were far more interested in stars than in stories. When fans wrote thousands of letters to the magazine asking for information about actors, Blackton and Brewster were forced to change their approach. By 1912, *Motion Picture Story* had become a hybrid of short stories, star publicity, and technical information about filmmaking, mixed with advertisements for face creams and screen-writing schools—in short, a good representation of the varied interests of Americans who were rapidly becoming motion picture fans.

During most of its first year, *Motion Picture Story* offered readers much the same fare as *Moving Picture World* and the *Dramatic Mirror.* In April 1911, for example, the magazine gave readers curious about actress Mabel Trunnelle one sentence: "One of Miss Trunnelle's latest successes was as the fiancée in 'The Doctor,' which interesting story will be found in this magazine." The magazine's "Answers to Inquiries" column similarly avoided any mention of the personal. "We do not answer inquiries as to the matrimonial or other personal affairs of the players," the column's "Answer Man" repeated. When fans failed to heed this warning, the magazine placed a formal announcement at the top of each month's column: "This department is for the answering of questions of general interest only. Involved technical questions will not be answered. *Questions concerning the marriages of players will be completely ignored.*"[36]

In 1912, the Answer Man claimed to receive letters from 2,500 of the magazine's estimated 500,000 readership. Many of these letter writers, of course, continued to ask about forbidden topics—hobbies and habits, marriages and divorces. One reader satirized these overly eager and inquisitive admirers:

> They'll ask "Oh where is [John] Bunny?"
> Is Florence Lawrence dead and when
> was Billy Quirk most funny?
> Is Alice Joyce a suffragette?
> Where's Mary Leonard gone to?
> Has Arthur Johnson married yet
> and do you think he'll want to?[37]

Occasionally the Answer Man responded to these questions with sarcasm. To a Chicago woman he answered: "'Is Maurice Costello married?' We will give you three guesses. Such information is not furnished."[38]

Although the Answer Man maintained his strict policy of silence until 1915, the magazine's feature stories took another direction. In December 1911, *Motion Picture Story* initiated "Chats with the Picture Players," a column that printed interviews with popular actors. For the first time, fan magazines began to address the question that had consumed fans for years: were stars the same in real life as they appeared in the movies?

In some cases, the answer was no. "Listen, fans. Demure Florence Lawrence, who looks so utterly feminine on the screen, used to be a baseball star before she became a luminous planet of the photoplay," an article explained. On the other hand, Owen Moore was not as bold as he appeared: "You wouldn't believe that a good looking young chap, who can make love all over the screen and cause girlish hearts to thump terribly, could turn the color of a ripe red beet just because these same girlie girls want so much to have a peek behind the screen and see him for a moment in real life," wrote *Photoplay* magazine, *Motion Picture Story's* rival that debuted in 1912.[39]

Fans may have actually been relieved to learn that certain actors were different than they appeared on the screen. As a writer for *Photoplay* explained, "I have never had such a surprise in my life as I did when I met George Periolat face to face. You remember how he looks in pictures—all whiskers, or old and feeble, sometimes ragged too. . . . Imagine my surprise when a young, extremely good looking, rather chubby faced man rose to greet me." Alice Hollister, too, was nothing like the villains she portrayed. "Now the first thing you must do, if you would learn to know her, it to forget the 'reel' Alice Hollister. For truly they are very little alike. The Alice Hollister of the films is cruel [and] designing; the Alice Hollister of her own home is clever and sweet," *Photoplay* commented.[40]

The vast majority of early fan magazine articles, however, insisted that actors were similar if not identical to their roles. "Miss Lawrence off the stage is exactly like Miss Lawrence upon the stage— the same charmingly expressive face, the same dainty, natural yet finished manner," *Motion Picture Story* proclaimed. Similarly, the reporter who wondered whether Howard Missimer was "half as funny off the screen as on it" was not disappointed: the comedian performed as many antics in person as he did in his films. Without delving too deeply into actors' personal affairs (by 1914, both *Photoplay* and *Motion Picture Story* revealed whether actors were married, but wrote little about the specifics), fan magazines assured readers that stars shared the same qualities as their characters. Pearl White, for example, was as "impulsive, generous, and fearless" as her adventurous heroine in *The Perils of Pauline;* Blanche Cornwall was as "jolly and vivacious" on the screen as in life.[41]

Fans were thrilled to learn that they had not been deceived— their favorite actors were really as charming as they had imagined. Throughout the rest of the century, moviegoers would continue to turn to fan magazines for such confirmation. Although many fans demanded that magazines reveal genuine, proven facts about the stars, others sought more limited information. By mid-decade, fans were splitting into two camps: those determined to uncover the truth about actors, and those who only wanted to confirm what they saw in movies. Determined to maintain their positive image of their favorite stars, many fans avoided, shunned, or denied any information that presented them in an unflattering light.

In fact, many fans urged magazines *not* to publish information about the stars that was too revealing, fearing that it would completely destroy their impressions. As one fan wrote to movie columnist "Mae Tinee" of the *Chicago Tribune*, "I would prefer to know nothing of their real life history. . . . When we know our hero is a fond daddy and another married to a dowdy wife and the leading woman is working to earn money to buy a divorce, it certainly does not add to my interest in them." Ben Lewis wrote a similar letter to *Photoplay* in 1915: "Your interviews with movie stars are interesting, because a fan enjoys learning the intimate facts about his favorites. But why stick to facts? I see my stars through a haze of romance. The fact that they wash dishes in a bathtub does not impress me as being one of their characteristics." A poem in *Photoplay* satirized the disillusionment that fans felt when reality diverged too greatly from the movies:

> He was so very handsome
> We girls all lost our hearts,
> And we would sit and worship him
> In nice heroic parts.
>
> His eyes were dark and soulful,
> His smile an ardent plea
> Whene'er he hugged the heroine
> We wished that we were she.
>
> But then the idol tumbled
> They told us he ate *cheese*
> And cabbages—and someone
> Had even *heard him sneeze.*
>
> So now we go to movies
> With hearts of molten lead
> The cause: Obituary—
> One Movie hero—DEAD.[42]

"The private life of Charlie Chaplin, as recently exposed in one or two publications, brings the reader a sense of disappointment," wrote one magazine in 1916. "To find that the hero of so many knockdown and lay-out comedies is, in his own home, an ordinarily sane and intelligent citizen is disillusioning." In jest, it imagined an alternative vision of Chaplin's home life, one that suited his screen image. At breakfast his routine might go something like this: "Tears off half loaf of bread and stuffs it in mouth with both hands. Spears seven buckwheat pancakes with fork and douses them with maple syrup. Washes face with largest pancake. Eats napkin by mistake."[43]

But not all fans could be so lighthearted after learning about the differences between stars' on- and offscreen personalities. In some cases, fans reacted strongly when they learned that their favorite star was not all he appeared to be. In 1921, when popular actor Fatty Arbuckle was accused of rape and murder, vengeful fans, feeling that they had been misled by Arbuckle's boyish, innocent roles, urged studios to ban the actor from films. Not surprisingly, Arbuckle's career was destroyed. In the wake of the Arbuckle scandal, the film industry hired infamous movie czar Will Hays to ensure that the cinema and real life would never diverge so greatly again.

By 1920, movie fan magazines had undergone a noticeable change. Once cautious about revealing personal information, magazines began to address more freely the private lives of stars. *Photoplay* devoted increasing attention to actors' homes, vacations, cars, and, in particular, their romances. In 1917, the magazine printed a full-page article on actress Anita Stewart's engagement; the following year, it featured Clara Kimball Young's thoughts on "the techniques of good lovers." *Motion Picture Story* also underwent a similar transformation. In 1915, Eugene Brewster, its editor, renamed the magazine *Motion Picture* and ended its focus on novelized plots. *Motion Picture,* along with its new sister publication *Motion Picture Classic,* would be devoted almost entirely to articles about actors' fashions, marriages, and offscreen exploits. In 1919, a third Brewster-edited publication, *Shadowland,* tried to attract a sophisticated upper-middle-class readership with poetry and art photography in addition to the latest news about the stars.[44]

As these changes attest, many fans, like the film industry itself, began to perceive films merely as an excuse to see famous actors. As one fan explained to *Motion Picture,* "it has come to the point that we no longer go to see the pictures, but the players." These changes also reveal that publishers had radically changed their attitude about actors' offscreen lives. When editors sensed that fans were far more interested in the personal than the professional, they were happy to oblige—and to sell more copies. In 1919, the three Brewster-edited publications reached approximately 750,000 readers a month; in 1922, *Photoplay* boasted a circulation of two million.[45]

Editors may have also realized that a positive portrayal of stars' personal lives could help the film industry in its ongoing quest for respectability. Threatened by social reformers and censorship advocates during the decade beginning in 1910, the film industry set out to prove that the movies did not promote sex and violence, and that film stars were not promiscuous and immoral like their allegedly debauched counterparts on the stage. Studios sent out hundreds of press releases that portrayed movie stars as compassionate, honest, and virtuous. Fan magazines, too, ran articles that depicted actors at home with their families, hard at work in the studio, or helping friends in distress. Unlike stage actors, who spent their lives on the road, claimed actress Mary Fuller in 1915, "a motion picture player is located in one neighborhood and is recognized as a permanent and respectable citizen." Movie stars were not eccentric artists or sexual renegades, but "a whole-souled, generous, sympathetic and honest class," wrote a columnist for *Motion Picture*.[46]

During the 1920s, fans would continue to use the private lives of stars as a means of verifying and authenticating what they saw on the screen. But these increasingly intimate details also had another function. Many fans found themselves using their knowledge of stars' lifestyles as a guide for their own personal behavior. Fans wanted to dress, shop, and look like stars, and magazines showed them the way. Stars helped Americans make the transition from a culture based on a producer ethic to a modern consumer society concerned with style and personality. The discourse that emerged from fans' pursuit of reality would eventually lead Americans into a celebrity culture based on the worship and emulation of movie stars.

SEARCHING FOR REALITY

By 1920, many film audiences may have thought themselves full-fledged movie experts. At last they understood the cinema's relationship to reality: motion pictures presented an enhanced, dramatized version of life. Although movies were firmly grounded in the real world, they were nonetheless still an illusion; they presented a world that was similar but distinct from reality. Only the naive thought the movies were pure fantasy—or, as a poem in an early *Motion Picture Story* magazine had suggested, believed that the movies and reality were identical:

> "How did you like them" asked his friend,
> When lights were turned on at the end;
> Then Hiram gazed hard at the sheet,
> While getting slowly to his feet;
> "Huh! Movin' Pictures! Caint fool me!
> Why them was people, I could see!"[47]

Indeed, by the 1920s, movie fans were much clearer about the motion picture's powers of representation than they had been ten years before. They knew, for the most part, that film actors were real, living people, and that their offscreen qualities often resembled their screen characteristics. Yet their curiosity about stars' private lives remained. From 1910 to 1930, fans sent thousands of letters to actors, filled with detailed questions. "How old are you and when is your birthday?" wrote a fan to Betty Marsh. "What kind of books do you like? What are your favorite colors?" In 1916 one fan begged Buster Collier, "Won't you please write me a letter and answer these questions. What are your latest plays? What are your favorite hobbies? What is your height? What is your age? What color is [sic] your eyes? Now please answer these questions." Some stars became frustrated with the never-ending flood of inquiries. Betty Blythe was so annoyed that she published in a fan magazine a list of "Don'ts" for correspondents: "Don't ask what a star does with her old clothes. Don't ask if she is married. Don't ask a star's age!"[48]

Fans also hoped to learn about their favorite stars by meeting them in person. "If there was ever a person who wanted to see you, it is me," wrote one fan to cowboy star William S. Hart in 1917. "You don't know how disappointed I am at not being able to see you and hear you," he wrote. "I would like you to come to our house for dinner," wrote one woman. "I would just like to look into your face, so come, please come."

One woman working at Marshall Field's department store urged Hart to visit her. "I wish you'd come," she wrote, "but don't come between eleven and twelve, because that's my lunch hour."[49]

Stars eventually received so many letters of inquiry and so many requests for personal appearances that they were forced to hire secretaries. In 1920, Antonio Moreno reportedly spent hundreds of dollars a week on secretaries, stationery, postage, and photographs. Mary Pickford sent out so much mail that the Los Angeles post office required her to use canceled stamps, "thus saving Uncle Sam the expense of hiring several extra clerks just to cancel the Pickford postage." Film studios began establishing their own fan mail departments to respond to the thousands of letters sent to their contracted stars.[50]

Fan magazines also continued to answer questions about stars' personal lives. "Are they the same on and off screen or have they dual personalities?" wrote Photoplay in 1922. The answer was hardly surprising. "Viola Dana plays herself on the screen," it wrote. Norma Talmadge "is herself very much like her screen personality—warm and genuine." And, "You would not be disappointed in James Kirkwood were you to meet him outside the studio. The same qualities which he shows on the screen are apparent in real life. He's a man's man; he takes his work seriously, but he refuses to take himself seriously." Photoplay encouraged fans to trust their eyes: the reason why stars were so similar to their roles, it explained, had to do with the nature of the motion picture. Because the movie camera "penetrates all artifice and exaggerates what it sees," fans could "read character through the screen." But if readers wanted confirmation, they could turn to Photoplay, which "mirrors the personality of the players as truthfully as it is humanly possible."[51]

In a marketing ploy that still continues, movie magazines used fans' intense curiosity about actors to raise interest in articles—and to sell thousands of copies. "Is Myrna Loy's bizarre screen personality a pose, or is she actually the strange, fantastic being that she appears to be?" asked Picture Play magazine. Readers who wanted to know would have to purchase the latest issue to find out. In 1923, Pictorial Review promised to reveal the world "behind the screen." "Do you know what Adolph Zukor really paid Mary Pickford? Do you know why Mack Sennett nearly fired Charlie Chaplin? Do you know why Mary

Pickford left David Griffith?" it asked. Curious fans could read the *Review*'s interview with producer Samuel Goldwyn, who "tells intimate stories of the great personalities of the screen that no one else could tell. And they're all true."[52]

Of course, interest in stars' offscreen lives and, more generally, curiosity about the relationship between the movies and reality were not the only reason why moviegoers wrote fan letters and read movie magazines. Many fans wrote to stars to compliment them on their beauty or talent. Others hoped to initiate friendships or correspondence with their idols. Some bought fan magazines not to read the articles but to look at the pictures. To many moviegoers, it was passion more than inquisitiveness that compelled them to participate in fan activity.

Moreover, fans were attracted to stars not merely for their onscreen charm and beauty. Many fans found that stars provided comfort in times of struggle. One teenager believed that Florence Lawrence, whom she saw in the movies each night, was her only friend. "I am having an awful hard time with Dad, he chases us at midnight when he gets drunk. I am afraid you won't like me, but I thought you was [sic] the only friend I could write," she explained. Others fell in love with stars because they reminded them of friends or relatives. "Some pictures in which you appear I could almost believe that it was my dear sister speaking to me," an ardent fan wrote Lawrence. Several fans believed that their idols could find them jobs or lend them money. A down-and-out stage actress begged Lawrence to help her find work in the movies; another fan asked William S. Hart for $500 for an operation.[53]

But in spite of their many reasons for writing fan letters, in spite of the different motivations behind their passion for movie stars, all fans confronted the same predicament. They could never know whether the images on the screen were authentic. They could never know whether film stars were real, living people, and whether they were all that they seemed. For casual moviegoers, the need to verify the movies did not seem so pressing. But for fans, it was tremendously important. Because they desired to connect personally with stars, to interact and correspond with actors away from the camera, fans had to know that the people on the screen were not only images. They wanted to confirm that the movies had a connection to real life.

In the late nineteenth century, as primitive film projectors displayed flickering black-and-white images to a nation of first-time moviegoers, no one predicted how captivated and inquisitive many of those spectators would become. Curious about the cinema's ability to mimic reality, thousands of fans sent letters to film studios and publications begging for information about the world behind the screen. When the film industry, beginning in 1910, responded by revealing and publicizing actors' identities, fans' prayers were answered. From their curiosity and vigilance, the motion picture star system was born.

This first episode in the history of film fandom established a lasting feature of movie fan culture: stars, rather than films, became the primary focus of fans' interest in Hollywood. It also initiated a dynamic between audiences and the film industry. Although studios ultimately determined the content of films as well as the methods of star publicity, their decisions were often guided by fans. Concerned with profits and public opinion, they frequently altered casting, production, and marketing decisions in response to fans' requests and complaints.

Throughout the twentieth century, fans would use their power as consumers and activists to significantly control the film industry. And film studios would use their prestige, visibility, and financial resources to change the decisions, buying habits, and aspirations of fans. Contrary to what is often assumed, fans and the film industry shared a relationship of mutual power and influence. They sometimes cooperated with each other but more often struggled in an attempt to determine the content of films, star publicity, and American popular culture.

CHAPTER TWO

THE CULT OF PERSONALITY

BY THE END OF THE DECADE FOLLOWING 1910, the prestige, visibility, and influence of movie stars had significantly expanded in American society. No longer confined to the movie theater, stars were everywhere. Their faces adorned advertisements for cosmetics and clothing; their exploits filled newspapers and magazines; their names appeared regularly in everyday conversation. It was almost as if someone had forgotten to stop the film at the end of the show, as if actors had spilled off the movie screen into the realm of everyday life.

The increased prominence of the movie star can be traced directly to the growing popularity of film. In 1912, 16 million Americans went to the movies each week; by the early 1920s, the figure had jumped to 40 million. The growth of celebrity journalism also pushed stars to center stage. By 1915, articles about the personal lives of movie stars began to appear in national publications ranging from *Photoplay* to *Collier's* to the *Saturday Evening Post*. But perhaps the most significant reason for stars' sudden popularity concerned their changing role in American society. By the 1920s, stars were more than just actors. To many Americans, they had become models of modern selfhood. They seemed the perfect embodiments of charm, style, and most of all, personality, an important individual trait seen as crucial for success.[1]

Personality entered American culture during the first two decades of the century as part of an ongoing dialogue on the nature of the self in a rapidly modernizing culture. The growth of the city, the development of the mass media, and the expansion of consumer culture between 1900 and 1930 sparked pressing concerns about individual behavior and the relationship of self to society. How would Americans adjust to the new mass culture? How would they define themselves as individuals in the crowded modern metropolis?

The answer, according to many scholars and journalists, lay in personality. Unlike nineteenth-century self-help writers, who advocated character, morality, and sincerity, the new gurus of personality preached the value of charm, friendliness, and flawless self-presentation. In a mobile mass society, in which faces and first impressions mattered more than ever, a stylish, charismatic appearance, they claimed, held the key to prosperity and social success. The individual with personality stood out from the crowd because she had created a striking public persona, one that made an unforgettable impression on those around her.

As Americans searched for living examples of this important trait, they turned, not surprisingly, to film actors. On the screen, stars were dashing, funny, lovable, and charming. It was not long, in fact, before many Americans began to see stars as the reigning experts of personality. And it was not long before corporations, Hollywood, and the growing advertising industry realized how easily this perception could be exploited. In popular advice columns and self-help books, stars shared their tips for self-presentation. In advertisements, they claimed that the right toothpastes, lotions, stockings, and automobiles helped them create their charm. By the 1920s, the movies and movie stars had become firmly entrenched in America's growing consumer culture.

More than just performers, more than celebrities, stars by the 1920s had become educators. To millions of Americans, they provided concrete lessons in personality, style, and good grooming. They reaffirmed the value of entertainment, pleasure, and sensual freedom in an increasingly leisure-oriented, youth-oriented consumer culture. Wealthy and charismatic, successful and adored, they became the nation's most prominent spokespeople for modernity.

MAKING THE MOVIES MAINSTREAM

In the first decade of the twentieth century, the movies were undeniably a lowbrow affair. Although "respectable" men and women occasionally sneaked into picture shows, claimed *Moving Picture World,* they "looked around to see if [they were] likely to be recognized by anyone before entering." The movie theater was largely a working-class domain; thus, in order to expand its market, the film industry knew that it would have to sell the movies to the middle class. But this was impossible unless it cleaned up its reputation, unless it convinced the public that movies were not cheap entertainment but a respectable and intelligent art.[2]

Beginning around 1910, the film industry embarked on a full-scale mission to dignify the motion picture. The first part of the campaign involved transforming the exhibition environment. Up to that time, movies had been shown primarily in nickelodeons, spare storefront theaters that hardly conjured up images of taste and class. Determined to link the movies with luxury, studios and local entrepreneurs constructed lavish movie theaters known as "picture palaces." In 1910, the nation's first such palace, the Princess Theater, was built in Milwaukee. Boasting a seven-piece orchestra, mahogany doors, and an electric fountain, the Princess accommodated over 900 viewers. In 1914, Samuel "Roxy" Rothapfel opened "the cathedral of the motion picture," the Strand Theater in New York, which featured a symphony-sized orchestra, plush curtains, and oil paintings. In its opening week, the Strand entertained over 40,000 viewers, who paid between ten and twenty-five cents for admission.[3]

By no means did nickelodeons disappear. With their flashy ornamentation and garish displays of electric lights, cheap theaters continued to turn profits in working-class areas. But the movie palaces did something that the nickelodeons had never been able to achieve— they drew millions of middle-class viewers to the movies. "Respectable" patrons were also attracted by films based on well-known novels or stage plays, such as *Queen Elizabeth* (1912), *The Count of Monte Cristo* (1912), and *The Birth of a Nation* (1915). By linking the cinema to literature, filmmakers tried to convince Americans that the movies were not vulgar and frivolous but tasteful, serious, and meaningful.[4]

By about 1915, the cinema, once a pariah institution, was gradually winning a solid place in middle-class culture. It had also become an important part of many Americans' lives. Millions went to the movies each week; some even went every night. For some moviegoers, the cinema continued to provide entertainment even after the show was over. One woman admitted in 1912 that she spent hours "discussing the moving pictures and their players"; another reported that she and her neighbors gave each other nicknames after the stars they resembled.[5]

Not surprisingly, the movies and movie stars also began making frequent appearances in the mainstream press. In 1914, actress Kathlyn Williams shared her offscreen adventures with readers of *Sunset* magazine; that same year, *Literary Digest* published "The Real Perils of Pearl White," on the star of the *Perils of Pauline* film series. Like typical fan magazine fare, these articles gave readers a look behind the scenes into stars' private lives. Kathlyn Williams, *Sunset* explained, was a "nervy movie lady" who performed all her stunts; Pearl White was a "daredevil" who was as bold and adventurous as her screen character.[6]

Major newspapers also began to devote space to the movies and stars. By 1915, the *New York Times* printed film reviews and the *Chicago Tribune* ran a daily column, "Photoplay Stories and News," that featured portraits and career histories of popular actors. In 1916, it was replaced by "The Latest News from Movie Land," a more intimate gossip column that competed with the *Chicago Herald*'s "Seen on the Screen" written by Louella Parsons. With her chatty style, Parsons responded to readers' questions about actors' lives. "Has Crane Wilbur been hiding the true state of his matrimonial affairs from his worshipful movie fans? For many a day hundreds of fans have been writing to ask whether [he] was married or single. To all the anxious ones: Crane Wilbur is not married. He is divorced," she explained in a column in 1915.[7]

Advertisers, too, capitalized on the growing public interest in the movies. In 1915, the Coca-Cola company published a series of advertisements based on an endorsement by Mary Fuller; the actress also lent her name to Mary Fuller Perfume. In one of the most famous campaigns of the decade, Mary Pickford became the spokeswoman for Pompeian skin cream. In addition to product samples, for ten cents customers could receive a color portrait of Pickford, suitable for framing. Pickford's ads for Pompeian appeared between 1916 and 1921 in several fan and general interest magazines, including the *Ladies' Home Journal*. Her image could also be found on special cards included in cigarette and chocolate boxes.[8]

By the time America entered World War I, stars had gained a prominent place in American culture. Part of this can undoubtedly be attributed to the rising popularity and accessibility of the cinema. While the population of New York doubled between 1910 and 1930, as historian Lary May has noted, the capacity of movie theaters increased more than eight times. But there was another reason for the widespread public fascination with movie stars. More than just entertainers, stars had become models of a new, modern mode of self-presentation: personality.[9]

To understand the connection between movie stars and personality—and why stars came to be seen as the quintessential embodiments of this characteristic—we must turn back to the earliest years of the motion picture, when viewers made a stunning observation. Film stars seemed not to act but to behave naturally in front of the camera. Rather than depict characters, they seemed to portray themselves—wonderful, spontaneous, captivating selves who exuded grace and charm for all the world to see.

A PERFORMING SELF

In the first few years of the century, when the motion picture functioned as a newsreel, the men and women who appeared in films were said to pose in pictures, as one would sit for a photograph. But when directors began creating narrative films, dubbed "photoplays," around 1906, the people appearing in movies were renamed "photoplayers." Like stage actors, these men and women did not merely pose but performed in front of the camera.

Since many of these early photoplayers had been trained on the stage, they brought to the movies a traditional pantomimic style of acting. In the late nineteenth century, Frenchman François Delsarte had popularized the Delsarte system, a set of poses and gestures that corresponded with different emotions. In Delsarte's code, recorded and circulated in a series of illustrated manuals, the right hand raised to the forehead symbolized woe, the wringing of hands equaled despair, and the clenched fist, anger. Although pantomime had begun to decline in popularity by the turn of the century, actors realized that it was perfectly suited for silent film. "Moving pictures are pantomime," *Moving Picture World* explained in 1909. "To please the eye, you must know how to use your hands and arms."[10]

Before long, however, filmmakers noticed that pantomime seemed out of place in the movies. Audiences, too, complained that actors' "wild gestures and agonizing expressions" seemed artificial. "Weeping, sighing, and the other extreme emotions cannot be faked for the screen, as they can be for the stage," explained the *Weekly Movie Record*. "In pictures the audience demands direct visual evidence of the emotions." Pantomime not only seemed unrealistic, it was growing increasingly unnecessary. Between 1908 and 1911, a series of technical innovations pioneered by D. W. Griffith and his contemporaries enabled the camera to take on many of the responsibilities of storytelling. Through the new point-of-view shot, for example, viewers could see how a situation looked from a particular character's perspective. With the close-up, audiences could read emotions from an actor's face, rather than just his or her movements. Moreover, because the camera recorded slight movements and changes in facial expression, subtlety rather than exaggeration became the key to convincing screen portrayals.[11]

As a result, by 1915, the criteria for good film acting had entirely changed. Skilled actors did not dramatically enact a role, but seemed spontaneous and relaxed on screen. The best movie stars were so natural, fans claimed, that they appeared simply to be playing themselves. "Thomas Cummerford displays a charming manner of acting," wrote one woman to *Motion Picture Story Magazine* in 1915. "Or should I say living, not acting, for [he seems] to have acquired such an easy grace before the camera." "Miss Pickford is wonderful," wrote another fan. "One cannot call her work merely acting. She goes beyond that stage. Her portrayal of characters is real, lifelike. She does not smirk or look into the camera. Hers is a natural, graceful manner that seems to belong to her alone."[12]

The mark of a truly talented performer, fans claimed, was not only the ability to act naturally but to bare one's soul before the camera. "The wonderful fact of Blanche Sweet is that she does not act; instead, she lives through the stories with such fervor that the audience believes that it is not witnessing the illusion of life but life itself," explained a fan magazine in 1915. "She has in her beautiful face a mirror of what passes in soul or brain." One fan put it more poetically. To her idol she wrote, "Thy soul shines in thine eyes, and thy face thy heart, without disguise."[13]

After seeing so many convincing performances, many fans were sure that film actors were not acting at all. Fan magazines did their part to enforce this belief, insisting that stars' on- and offscreen qualities were identical. One reason for such striking similarities, explained *Photoplay,* had to do with directors' casting preferences. Directors tried to cast only those "persons who are the characters portrayed, rather than those who may be able to enact them." It was also a function of the movie camera. Stars had no choice but to be themselves in films, because the camera exposed all pretense and artifice.[14]

By 1915, many fans were convinced that actors' roles mirrored their true characteristics. Fans told each other that they loved "Mary Pickford's sweetness and childishness" and "Dorothy Gish's sense of humor." These qualities, of course, really applied to characters rather than actors. But that mattered little. In the eyes of fans, actor and character shared the same charisma, the same magnetism, and the same captivating personality.

MAGNETIC PERSONALITIES

At the beginning of the twenty-first century, the word "personality" is so familiar that it hardly needs to be explained. But a hundred years earlier, the term was only beginning to come into use. Although common today, phrases like "a shy personality" or "she has lots of personality" might have been meaningless in 1900. The concept had not yet been invented.

Personality was a product of modernity, the result of vast cultural and technological changes that transformed American society in the early twentieth century. Urbanization, the development of national communication and transportation networks, the decline of religion as a social force, and a growing cultural emphasis on consumption and entertainment had created a mobile, leisure-oriented mass society—and as a result, the need for a new way of conceiving the individual self. Traditional exhortations to lead moral, frugal, self-sacrificing lives seemed distinctly out of place in the new culture of consumption. So, too, was the earlier emphasis on family honor and reputation, which mattered little in a city of strangers. Americans desperately needed a new vision of selfhood, in particular, one that addressed the difficulty of individual recognition and distinction in a crowded mass society.

The solution came, in part, through the concept of personality. Using popular psychology, religious thought, and common sense wisdom, scholars, writers, and journalists created a concept of the ideal self—the individual with personality—that was uniquely suited to the modern age. For our study of the connection between movie stars and personality, it is important to note that the term was used in two different though related ways. In some cases, it described the sum total or dominant quality of an individual's traits: "he has an outgoing personality" or "her personality is friendly," for example. But often personality was used as a description by itself for a particular set of characteristics: charm, attractiveness, magnetism.

As historian Warren Susman has written, unlike the nineteenth-century man of character, who cultivated such internal traits as "honesty, truth, nobility and sincerity," the man with personality devoted himself primarily to the art of self-presentation. In a culture based increasingly on appearances and first impressions, he cultivated a pleasing, well-groomed appearance. In tune with the growing importance of leisure in American culture, he was also a skilled performer and entertained others with his poise and charm. In short, the individual with personality was in many ways like a movie star. He impressed others not with the force of his character, but with his looks, style, humor, and charisma.[15]

In 1919, *Film Fun* magazine told the story of one successful businessman who used personality to his advantage. The president of the company had recently announced that he was looking for an executive assistant, and "all the office was wondering which one of us would be the lucky man," wrote the author of "The Secret of Making

People Like You." "The main requisite, as we understood it, was striking personality." When the president selected Mr. Peters, a man who had once been shy and awkward, the author was stunned. What had enabled Peters to develop so much personality in such a short amount of time? Unbeknownst to everyone, Peters had been following a regime of "personality development." Every time Peters interacted with a fellow employee, he showed complete, undivided attention. He tried diligently to be cheerful and went out of his way to help others. "You can make an instant hit with anyone if you say the things they want you to say, and act the way they want you to act," the author concluded. "You can do this easily by knowing certain simple signs. Written on every man, woman, and child are signs which show exactly what to say and do to please them. Knowing these signs is the whole secret of getting what you want out of life—of making friends, of business and social advancement."[16]

As Peters proved, the key to personality lay in charming and pleasing others. His success also reinforced what experts had been claiming for years—that men and women without inborn personality could cultivate it. From 1910 on through the 1920s, writers penned hundreds of self-help books that shared with readers strategies for developing memorable personalities: *Personality as a Business Asset, Masterful Personality,* and *Personality in the Making,* among others. Some "personality experts" even offered correspondence courses. In 1920, the Gentlewoman Institute of New York promised to transform students into "glorious, magnetic women radiating charm and personality, captivating hearts of men and women alike . . . sparkling with the attraction that draws friends like a magnet." One correspondence course promised students their money back if they did not attain "magnetic personality" within a month.[17]

In many ways, this obsession with personality might be characterized as a shift from depth to surface. The value once placed on internal qualities, such as honesty and integrity, was transferred to external traits, such as charm, friendliness, and good looks. In spite of the emphasis on appearance, however, Americans were not instructed to hide their true selves under a mask of glamour. Instead, a major component of personality, said experts, involved sincerity, honesty, and authenticity. "'Be yourself' is the first commandment of personality, and 'act yourself' the whole law of it," explained journalist French

Strother in *American Magazine*. "Letting one's own natural inner self show on the outside is the real secret of personality."[18]

To many Americans this may have seemed contradictory, and rightly so. How could one be charming, pleasing, and completely uninhibited at the same time? Didn't a charismatic and well-groomed appearance require effort? To these questions the experts had a simple answer: personality involved a balance of control *and* spontaneity. The first step in developing personality involved perfecting one's inner qualities, a process requiring hard work and discipline. It was only after one had achieved a degree of inner perfection that he or she could indulge in freer, less inhibited behavior. After "acquiring knowledge with regard to your outward appearance and expression," explained self-help writer Imogene Wolcott, "you must dare to be yourself." Personality, in other words, was a carefully orchestrated yet seemingly spontaneous externalization of self.[19]

Who were the new models of personality? Which Americans were most adept at externalizing perfectly pleasing selves? The answer was obvious. Movie stars, more than any other figures, seemed to have mastered the art of personality. They were beautiful and charismatic. They projected kindness and friendliness. And rather than act, they seemed spontaneous and natural. With little effort, they displayed their sincere and charming selves to a nation of captivated moviegoers.

PERSONALITY AND PERFECTION

The connection between film actors and personality dates back to the beginning of the star system. In 1910, film industry trade journal *Moving Picture World* published a weekly column, "Picture Personalities," that praised the work of popular film stars. These skilled performers, the journal explained, were so natural that they seemed not to act. Instead, they simply exuded personality in front of the camera. Mabel Trunnelle was "dramatic, humorous and spontaneous. In the first picture in which she worked her personality stood out prominently." Mary Pickford was so blessed with personality that it "pervades her work and carries over into the audience. It seems as though she was not acting at all, but was simply having a good time."[20]

Before long, personality was widely acknowledged as the key to screen success. According to director Fred Niblo, "the greatest necessity" for a film career was "to register personality on the screen." "Don't assume any affectations. Be out and out who you are. Affectations are fatal in Hollywood because they weaken and eventually destroy personality, the one quality which carries a person to success on the screen." Speaking of his ingenue Lucille LeSueur (later known as Joan Crawford), Metro-Goldwyn-Mayer executive Harry Rapf told *Movie Weekly* magazine, "When she came into my office, I knew that she had that rare thing—personality. She is beautiful, but more essential than beauty is that quality known as screen magnetism." MGM even initiated an advertising campaign in the 1920s that promised audiences "Pictures with Personality."[21]

Many film critics feared the growing importance of personality in the movies. Instead of becoming a respectable art, the movies might simply be a showcase for charismatic selves. "Does the American public want to see its favorites of the stage and screen only as themselves?" asked one writer in 1922. "Is it personality and not impersonation that the average motion picture fan enthuses over?" The American obsession with personality, she lamented, had forced many character actors to seek work in other countries, where the "personality bug" had not yet arrived. "The thing for which a motion picture actress must create a demand is her personality—spelled with a capital P," satirized writer Esther Lindner. "Don't worry if you can't act. That isn't necessary. Your personality is more important."[22]

To an extent Lindner was right. From 1910 to 1929, fans seemed genuinely fascinated if not obsessed with stars' personalities. In fan club journals and correspondence with movie magazines, they praised their favorite actors for their charm and magnetism. "I am in love! My sweetheart is the most wonderful member of my own sex—Agnes Ayres," proclaimed a fan in 1922. "You will probably say, 'because she is beautiful.' However, there is something else about her that has fascinated me. I think truly it is her personality." "I cannot repress my desire to say a few words about my favorite moving picture actress, Viola Dana. Her winning personality is remarkable," wrote one fan. One woman summarized the sentiments of many when she confessed that she fell in love with actors not for their ability or talent but solely for their charm. "To me *personality is the whole thing*," she explained.[23]

Personality, in fact, may have been one of the most common words to appear in fan letters during those two decades. Close behind were a series of related terms—magnetism, sincerity, charm, and perhaps more than anything, ideal. Many fans saw their favorite stars not merely as talented actors, but as exemplars of grace, poise, and sociability. "Dear Billie Dove, Here is what I think of you. B is for beautiful, I is for ideal, L is for lovely, L is for ladylike, I is for *my* ideal, E is for ever-charming," wrote Alice Hare to her favorite actress. "Mary Pickford has been my ideal," claimed one fan. "I think she has the sweetest personality of the screen." William S. Hart, according to one fan, was the embodiment of "real manhood." "He brings to the screen a sincerity and personality that cannot be equaled anywhere," he explained.[24]

Not only did fans praise stars' personalities and mannerisms, but they often tried to imitate them. One fan told *Picture Play* magazine that she had spent years trying to be like Mary Pickford. "If I could grow up to be one hundredth part as sweet and lovely as Mary Pickford, my dearest wish would be fulfilled," she wrote. After one of Pickford's movies, admitted another, "I'd find myself walking up the aisle with that certain little bent knee, toe turning in walk. I went so far as to dress up like [Pickford's character] the Poor Little Rich Girl and have my picture taken." According to fans, imitating the stars had many benefits. Adopting his idol's "easy-going air," explained one fan, enabled him to cope with "many tight situations." Friends and family members, however, were often less enthusiastic. Charles Dolista, writing in the fan magazine *Movie Weekly,* explained that the movies had "terrible consequences":

> I'm never going to take my wife to the movies any more
> The movie habits she's acquired I really quite deplore
> My life is ruled by standards of the moving picture screen
> The moods my missus cultivates depict a movie queen
> She wears her hair like Pickford and she has a [Theda] Bara stare
> She dresses like Barriscale and has Mae Murray's air.[25]

More than any other star, it was Mary Pickford, America's most celebrated actress in the first star decade, whom fans most often linked with personality and cited as an ideal. Pickford, claimed admirers, was "absolutely perfect." She was blessed with charm, sincerity, and "magnetic personality—that so called indescribable something— which colors and vitalizes everything she does." Believing the actress to be the same on the screen as in life, fans praised Pickford for her sincerity and kindness. "We sense [the] character of our favorites through the medium of the screen," wrote one fan. "We know that persons such as Mary [Pickford] . . . are real persons, possessed of a fine balance and worthy of a lasting regard." "I don't suppose a day has ever passed in all these years that I haven't thought of her at least once," confessed Betty Rosser. "She has never been a movie star to me—but a person, a friend, an ideal."[26]

In dozens of dramas and comedies between 1910 and the mid-1920s, Pickford thrilled viewers with her energetic, charismatic performances. When she lent her name to self-help books and advice columns, she assumed another function, that of a teacher. The acknowledged master of self-expression and self-presentation, she shared tips with readers eager to develop their own magnetic charm.

AMERICA'S SWEETHEART

In 1892, one of America's most influential actresses was born in Toronto, Canada. One of three children in a strict working-class family, Gladys Smith had a normal childhood filled with school, games, and mischief. But when her father died in 1898, her world forever changed. As the Smiths faced poverty, Gladys, her mother, brother, and sister looked for work in the theater. Fortunately, Gladys was blessed with dramatic talent and soon became a stage success. In 1909, however, Gladys found herself out of a job, and in desperation she turned to the movies for a quick source of income. She was soon hired by D. W. Griffith to work as an extra in his Biograph studio.

But Gladys, renamed Mary Pickford, did not remain an extra for long. By 1910, she had earned a number of starring roles and was known among fans, in the days before the star system, as "The Girl with the Curls." In the next four years she reached even greater heights with a series of powerful performances, including the highly acclaimed *Tess of the Storm Country* (1914). As Tess, a girl battling a corrupt sheriff, Pickford established what would become her screen persona—an honest, innocent, yet willful young woman determined to fight for justice.

By 1915, Mary Pickford was the "best known girl in America," according to the *Ladies' Home Journal.* Throughout the country, writers, critics, and moviegoers praised her grace, talent, and youthful beauty. A writer for the *New York Review,* captivated by Pickford's waiflike charm, called her "the wistful, butterfly-like, elusive quality of supreme Innocence." Poet Vachel Lindsay was so moved that he composed an ode in her honor, proclaiming her his "valentine." To many moviegoers, Mary Pickford was more than an actress. Her nickname said it best: she was "America's Sweetheart."[27]

Part of the fascination with Pickford can be attributed to her tremendous talent. Unlike many stage performers who went into film, Pickford adapted easily to the cinema's subtle, natural acting style. With "the appeal of a glance, the crook of an arm, the twist of a smile," wrote *Motion Picture Classic,* she conveyed a range of powerful emotions. Perhaps even more important than her acting skill, however, may have been her ability to embody—and negotiate—conflicting conceptions of womanhood. With her golden locks, girlish clothing, and petite frame, she seemed the ultimate embodiment of the chaste Victorian maiden, still the reigning feminine ideal in the first two decades of the century. Yet Pickford's characters pursued remarkably emancipated goals. In *Behind the Scenes* (1914), she portrayed a young wife struggling for equality with her husband; in *The Eternal Grind* (1916), she was a sewing machine operator fighting for the rights of working women. Other films show her rebelling against her elders in order to pursue a career or enjoy such leisure activities as dancing and the movies. By fusing modern aspirations with a youthful, innocent appearance, Pickford may have helped Americans adjust to women's rapidly changing social roles. She assured viewers that women's increasing independence did not strip them of their traditional purity and femininity, but instead might enhance their charms.[28]

As Lary May has noted, Pickford's personal life also merged tradition and modernity. Though one of the wealthiest working women in the world, who spent lavishly on automobiles and clothes, her finances were controlled by her mother, who managed her career and constantly chaperoned her. Though an ardent advocate of women's employment and suffrage, she distanced herself from the movement for greater female sexual freedom. She refused to play suggestive roles, to drink or smoke in public, and until the late 1920s, to wear bobbed hair, a style associated with women's social and sexual liberation. Both on and off the screen, Pickford merged elements of the Victorian past and the modern future.[29]

But to her many fans, Mary Pickford's amazing popularity stemmed from one single factor: her personality. More than any other screen star, they claimed, Pickford embodied the art of successful self-presentation. She was beautiful, graceful, and poised. Moreover, she seemed sincere and unpretentious, and infused every role with her inner warmth and integrity. "Mary Pickford is pretty, you say. But her ornamental attributes, including her curls, are only the garnishings of something far more durable and profound—a magnetic personality," wrote one fan. "Her personality made such an impression on me that I can never forget it," confessed another. By 1915, Mary Pickford had become such a national icon of personality and of the modern working woman that she was hired by the McClure newspaper syndicate to write an advice column. "Mary Pickford's Daily Talks," ghostwritten by screen-writer Frances Marion, dispensed beauty tips, workplace advice, and Pickford's secrets for happiness and success. Between November 1915 and October 1916 the column appeared in the women's pages of over 150 newspapers from coast to coast.[30]

An advice column written by an actress was not new. For years, singer and stage actress Lillian Russell had published a daily column, "Lillian Russell's Beauty Secrets," in the *Chicago Tribune*. As a successful theatrical performer, Russell shared her expertise in the arts of costume and makeup. Columns with bylines of screen actresses, however—"Daily Talks," and similar pieces by Beverly Bayne, Ruth Stonehouse, and Anita Stewart—took a different approach. As embodiments of both beauty and personality, movie stars guided readers not only on their appearance but their behavior. Beverly Bayne's column, for example, told readers "how to keep beautiful, how to greet your friends, how to entertain company, how to walk gracefully and how to act at all times."[31]

Like the personality experts, Pickford preached the gospel of beauty, sincerity, and individuality. Good grooming was important for success, she admitted, and should be maintained at all costs. "Keep [your hair] clean, brush it well, and never curl it with an iron," she wrote. But the real key to a stunning appearance was "inner beauty"—compassion, authenticity, spontaneity. The most attractive men and women, she claimed, were those who had learned to "be themselves." "Self-consciousness steals your beauty and individuality," she warned.[32]

Pickford urged readers to think of themselves as film stars, under constant visual scrutiny. "If we make a mistake the merciless camera catches it and it is there, registered and held against us. That is why the smallest details must be perfected in costume and manner." Inner flaws, too, manifested themselves through outward appearances. "No woman can be a success on the screen if she dissipates even one little bit," she wrote. "The slightest excess shows unmistakably in the face and its expression." But if one did commit the occasional excess, "rice powder and olive oil on the skin" could conceal wrinkles or blemishes, she added. In the true spirit of personality, Pickford told fans that charisma derived from external *and* internal beauty—and that both kinds of perfection could be achieved through a combination of spontaneity and self-control.[33]

Reinforcing the connection between her on- and offscreen personalities, Pickford frequently drew on her own life to illustrate her points. It was not luck, but patience, friendliness, and hard work that made her a star, she claimed. And though her charm may have seemed natural, it required constant effort. Everything in her life, from hobbies to work habits to her diet, contributed to the Pickford personality. "A reason why I have always had [success] is that I have always lived on simple, wholesome food," she claimed. Even housecleaning, an activity requiring creativity and "individuality," enabled her to perfect her talent at self-expression. Although Pickford encouraged greater independence for women, she also preached stereotypical feminine virtues: physical perfection, good housekeeping, submission to the scrutinizing gaze of others.[34]

Through her "Daily Talks," as well as countless articles that appeared in national publications between 1915 and 1918 (including the *San Francisco Chronicle, Los Angeles Times, New Republic, Everybody's Magazine,* and *American Magazine*) Mary Pickford used her charm—that is, the charisma associated with her on-screen persona—to educate Americans in the art of modern living. Considered one of the most prominent national experts on personality, she received hundreds of letters each day from fans curious about the best ways to dress, win friends, or succeed in a career. No one could challenge Pickford's expertise, it seemed, except for one rising young star. His name was Douglas Fairbanks, and he was fast establishing himself as a guru of pep and personality.[35]

Like Pickford, Douglas Fairbanks came to the cinema by way of the stage. Born in 1883 to a well-off Denver family, he had little interest in the expensive education that his parents offered him and dropped out of college to pursue stage acting. Fairbanks was never particularly talented or handsome. But he was amazingly athletic and remarkably charming, two qualities that kept him employed. After 14 years on and off the stage, in 1915 Fairbanks moved to Hollywood, where he starred in a series of successful comedies scripted by the famous screen-writing team of John Emerson and Anita Loos.[36]

Like Pickford, Fairbanks's characters combined the modern impulses of leisure, consumption, and pleasure with traditional exhortations to rugged masculinity and disciplined labor. In *Wild and Wooly* (1917) and *The Mollycoddle* (1920), Fairbanks fought his Victorian elders, who preached self-sacrifice instead of enjoyment. A champion of physical exercise, he also urged men to counter the softening effects of modern life through strenuous workouts and rugged living.

With his stunning physique and charming screen presence, Fairbanks was the perfect embodiment of personality. He was also a perfect candidate to write advice columns and self-help books. Between 1916 and 1924, with the help of personal secretary Kenneth Davenport, Fairbanks composed a series of success manuals— *Making Life Worthwhile, Taking Stock of Ourselves,* and *Wedlock in Time,* among others—that became instantly popular. Davenport also penned a monthly column, "Douglas Fairbanks' Own Page," that appeared each month in *Photoplay.* Each piece was advertised as an authentic extension of the famous Fairbanks charisma, each page "full of his personality."[37]

Like Pickford, Fairbanks told readers that the key to success lay in a combination of moral perfection and good grooming. At the same time that he preached the value of exercise and physical hygiene, he urged readers to develop patience, initiative, honesty, and compassion. By developing "sturdy qualities" and expressing them sincerely, by working diligently to please and entertain others, claimed Fairbanks in *Laugh and Live,* one could attain a stunning personality, "the ultimate fulfillment of self-development—physically, mentally, spiritually."[38]

Through their interviews, books, and advice columns, Douglas Fairbanks and Mary Pickford successfully united the screen and life. By conflating their on- and offscreen traits, "Doug and Mary" reassured Americans that the camera did not lie—movie stars were really as charming as they seemed. The magnetism they exuded in movies was simply an extension of the personality they cultivated in their private lives. When Fairbanks and Pickford fell in love and married in 1920, the connection between the movies and reality was complete. The king and queen of personality would now become the monarchs of another domain, Pickfair, a palatial mansion in Beverly Hills. Like true royalty, they would preside over a nation of devoted followers, who read voraciously about their luxurious lifestyle, envied their wealth and prestige, and eagerly awaited their latest advice.

"IT"

With their advice columns and self-help books, Douglas Fairbanks and Mary Pickford started a national trend. By the early 1920s, countless other film stars, capitalizing on the widespread interest in personality, began to write advice columns and dispense tips on beauty and charm. In 1921, film heartthrob Wallace Reid authored a series of articles that preached the value of the "smiling habit." "The way to make friends is to cultivate cheerfulness, and not only to look but to feel cheerful," he wrote. "Acquire the smiling habit—make it genuine!" Constance Talmadge even endorsed a "personality correspondence course" that promised to make students as graceful and charming as the actress herself.[39]

Stars also promoted consumption as a way to cultivate personality. By the early 1920s, dozens of actors were paid to claim that a variety of products, from lipstick to cookies to automobiles, were responsible for their charms. Gladys Leslie allegedly gained "magnetic personality" through the use of Tokio Beauty Cream. "Thousands of women and girls are actually wearing the wrong shade of face powder," said one actress in a cosmetics advertisement. "They quench their personality, destroy what ought to be their glamor and charm." In an expanding consumer culture, movie stars helped legitimate shopping as a means of self-improvement. And judging from the results of several government and sociological reports from the 1920s, Americans took these encouragements seriously. According to one magazine study, the movies had created a "revolutionary change" in buying habits at major department stores in northern cities. Middle-class Americans were increasingly patterning their purchases on the images they saw in celebrity advertisements and in films.[40]

Hollywood's ability to influence Americans' buying habits would not have been possible without the significant increase in national wealth that occurred in the early 1920s, and the increase in consumer spending it triggered among the middle class. Between 1909 and 1929, average household expenditures tripled, and in 1924, middle-class Americans spent eight times as much on cosmetics, beauty aids, and home decorations than they had ten years before. Fueling this craze for goods was a rapidly expanding advertising industry. Between 1914 and 1929, manufacturers increased their advertising expenditures fourfold; during this period, the total volume of magazine advertising increased 600 percent.[41]

As historian Roland Marchand has written, advertising techniques also changed dramatically. Rather than extol the virtues of the featured item, a common strategy in previous decades, advertisers of the 1920s shifted the focus from the product to the user. Ads told consumers less about the quality and price of a product than its social and psychological benefits: toothpaste-whitened teeth made one likeable, deodorants offered self-confidence. Celebrity endorsements fit perfectly with this scheme. The proper ensemble of clothing, toiletries, and accessories, ads claimed, made one as popular and charismatic as Hollywood stars.[42]

But as Mary Pickford, Douglas Fairbanks, Constance Talmadge, and other celebrities dispensed advice and purchasing recommendations, powerful forces were working to dethrone these monarchs of personality. Before long, a new group of actors would become America's leading experts on charm. The first inkling of the new order was the arrival of British author Elinor Glyn in Hollywood. A well-known writer of racy novels, including the scandalous *Three Weeks* (1907), Glyn was hired in the early 1920s by the Paramount studio to write scripts for its top stars. After working on successful screenplays for Rudolph Valentino and Gloria Swanson, Glyn penned a novel that would forever change film history: *It*. The story of a charismatic young woman who triumphs over obstacles to win a man, *It* was turned into a film of the same name, starring flapper actress Clara Bow.

"It" was not a person or a thing, but a quality—a very important one, said Glyn—that made men and women instantly attractive. "One of the rarest gifts in the world," It could be found in stars like John Gilbert and Gloria Swanson, who appeared relaxed, natural, and uncommonly charming. "The person who possesses 'It' is always utterly unself-conscious and unaware of anyone's interest in him. The moment self-consciousness enters into the affair, 'It' departs," Glyn explained. Although It was often inborn, the quality could also be cultivated. "You must remember to be simple and not affected at all. You must try to be natural and dignified and never make yourself cheap," she advised.[43]

With its focus on spontaneity, magnetism, and self-expression, It seemed a lot like personality. Actor Lewis Stone called it "a jazz name for personality." But Glyn's trait was different in one crucial respect: It was openly sexual. "It," she told *Photoplay* in 1926, was a good deal like "animal magnetism." One of its foremost bearers, in fact, was a stallion named Rex in film westerns. Although Glyn typically protested when writers equated It with sexuality—the quality was far more complicated, she claimed—its sexual roots were undeniable. "'It' is a hypocrisy to cover up the honest phrase, sex magnetism," commented one critic. Another suggested that an appropriate synonym would be "S.A.," or sex appeal.[44]

Clara Bow's performance in *It* (1927) told the true story. In the film, Bow, known to America as the It girl, exudes passionate playfulness and erotic energy in every scene. An energetic department store clerk, she wins the love of her handsome boss with revealing dresses and coy come-ons. In one scene, she even lies across his desk to catch his attention. It, it seemed, required more than just the poise and sincerity preached by the personality experts, more than the physical and moral perfection advocated by Fairbanks and Pickford. True charisma now seemed to be frankly sexual in nature.

Given the changed social climate of the 1920s, this shift is hardly surprising. Though Americans had been gradually loosening the strict bonds of Victorian sexuality—the decade following 1910 saw increased public discussion of birth control and prostitution, increased use of cosmetics among women, and decreased use of the corset—during the 1920s, the signs of transformation became significantly more pronounced. A visible feminist movement, the growing popularity of Freudian psychology, increased national wealth, and a pervading sense of postwar restlessness had created a somewhat adventurous middle class fascinated with the possibilities of sexual expression, particularly for women. From secretaries to college coeds, young women donned shorter, more revealing dresses, danced, drank, smoked, and engaged in more premarital sexual experimentation than the women of any previous generation. Hollywood both depicted and accelerated this trend by starring glamorously gowned movie queens and short-skirted young flappers in "sex comedies" depicting the joys and struggles of sensual freedom. Though committed to matrimony, monogamy, and female domesticity—indeed, most sex comedies ended with the heroine's marriage—Americans saw in the new sexual ethics distinct possibilities for excitement, personal fulfillment, and liberation.[45]

Glyn's discovery of It, and Clara Bow's stunning, sexually charged performance sparked a national craze. Before long, advertisers used It to sell everything from lipstick to cars to shirt collars. Journalists, too, capitalized on the fad, with articles and questionnaires testing the It of readers. Although some moviegoers criticized Glyn and her "foolishness" ("she may go on giving the public this trash just as she has been giving us her stories, which are more or less trash," wrote one fan), many others took It seriously. "Oh, to possess what Miss Bow has—that elusive little thing called 'It'! After seeing her picture by that name, I immediately went home to take stock of my personal charms before the vanity mirror," said one fan. "I'll admit I have watched Clara Bow to a great extent to see how she develops 'It', and I'll also admit I've done my best to have 'It', too," said one young woman.[46]

Not surprisingly, the rise of It—and, in general, the movie star as an icon of glamour and sexuality—corresponded with the demise of Mary Pickford, Douglas Fairbanks, and their brand of wholesome, clean-cut personality. To many Americans, Mary Pickford's girlish purity began to seem outdated, and her popularity plummeted. In

1928, in an attempt to reinvent her image, she cut her trademark curls into the short bob hairstyle preferred by young flappers. Many of her remaining fans felt betrayed. The vast majority of moviegoers, however, were uninterested. "*Photoplay* readers were singularly calm in the face of the news that Mary Pickford had bobbed her curls," wrote editor James Quirk. Five years before, readers would have been stunned, "but today Mary's bob is of no . . . interest. Poor Mary is facing a new public that no longer believes in 'America's Sweetheart,' a public that thinks the word 'sweetheart' is a little ga-ga," he wrote.[47]

Although Pickford would continue to work in film, her career by the late 1920s was clearly crumbling. Fairbanks's fortunes had also declined; by the early 1930s starring roles were few and "Old Doc Cheerful," as he was once known, succumbed to depression. In a fitting conclusion to their reign as movie monarchs, Douglas Fairbanks and Mary Pickford separated and eventually divorced in 1935. Their magical spell over the nation had been broken. But their legacy continued. As America entered the age of sound, a new crop of actors and actresses followed in their footsteps, offering stunning film performances and important lifestyle secrets to a nation of curious moviegoers.

THE HOLLYWOOD CULT OF CELEBRITY

The merger of the movies and modernity truly revolutionized American popular culture. When the growth of an urban mass society placed new demands on the self, when performing skills rather than character became the means to social recognition, Americans looked to Hollywood for inspiration. Before long, movie stars had become America's ideal models of personality, and their tips for good grooming, self-presentation, and conspicuous consumption filled advertisements and advice columns. By the 1920s, stars were widely seen as America's foremost experts in the art of modern living.

The cultural impact was tremendous. Now vested with a potentially educational function, movies and movie stars gained greater popularity and national attention than ever before. Not only did film attendance continue to rise—in 1930, 90 million Americans went to the movies each week—but film stars became widely respected public figures. By the early 1930s, the *Nation* and *Saturday Evening Post* regularly discussed stars, *Time* magazine began featuring film actors on its covers, and even the *New York Times* regularly reported on Hollywood, with the divorce of Mary Pickford and Douglas Fairbanks making the front page. Once a marginalized, working-class institution, the movies had become mainstream, and film stars had become national if not international celebrities.[48]

The new movie star cult of celebrity also transformed film fandom. As stars became increasingly visible and popular, fan culture grew exponentially. By 1930 over a dozen movie magazines appeared on newsstands each month, top Hollywood stars received thousands of fan letters each week, and fan club membership reached into the millions. Influenced by the continued association of film stars with consumer products, fans also began increasingly to center their activities around purchasing. For many fans, worshiping a star meant not only watching her films but buying the items she endorsed, the styles she wore, and the magazines that chronicled her latest adventures.

In an era of profound cultural and social transformation, movie stars became not only entertainers but idols, models, and teachers. With their magnetic personalities, sumptuous lifestyles, and extravagant spending habits, they assured Americans that modernity held the keys to fulfillment, that success, affection, and popularity could be attained through leisure, consumption, and meticulous attention to appearances. Watched, imitated, and adored by millions, stars celebrated and legitimated the new modern order in which they would play an increasingly powerful role.

CHAPTER THREE

THE CHANCE OF A LIFETIME

IN 1916, WRITER ANNA STEESE RICHARDSON of *McClure's* magazine wrote of a dreaded disease that was rapidly spreading across the nation. It was not a plague or a flu, but something infinitely more dangerous. It was called filmitis, and it attacked the brain; it transformed level-headed young men and women into crazed, star-struck movie maniacs. "The germs of infection lurk in every moving picture theater," she explained. "The first symptom is a vague sensation in the region of the Ego. The patient murmurs: 'I could do it just as well.' The second symptom is pronounced unrest in the lobe of the brain occupied by self-esteem. The patient begins to argue that in suppressing his natural comedy or dramatic talents, he is doing the Great American Public a grave injustice. The third and most dangerous symptom," Richardson continued, "is a sharp pain generally in the palm of the hand or directly under the pocket in which the patient carries his purse." Under the spell of the movie bug, the "patient" becomes so delirious that he is willing to spend his last dollar to go to Hollywood to pursue an acting career. "Filmitis counts its victims by the millions," she concluded. "If you do not believe this, ask any moving picture producer or director."[1]

Richardson's article was intended to amuse, but she may have been only partially joking. Between 1910 and 1930, thousands of movie fans, especially female fans, made their way to the movie capital. Entranced by the glamour of Hollywood, eager for a life of wealth and fame, or simply searching for a way to make a living, fans actively pursued their dreams of stardom on the silver screen. But they were often disappointed. As scores of young hopefuls soon learned, their talents were not needed. They wandered from studio to studio, took odd jobs, or went back home, impoverished and dejected.

The movie-struck girl, as she was called, nearly caused a crisis in Hollywood. Unprepared to deal with the flood of aspirants—and the potential scandal that so many unaccompanied young women might create—the film industry used every possible means to keep them away. It tried to channel their energies into less risky pursuits, like screen-writing and costume designing. It tried to scare them with lurid tales of white slavers and drug dealers who preyed upon aspiring actresses. Throughout these decades, film studios spent as much time trying to keep women out of Hollywood as it did trying to get them into movie theaters.

But as the film industry learned, there were also benefits to be reaped from the female fans' interest in stardom. Rather than entirely stifle their passions, the industry found that it could turn them toward its own ends. No, you cannot find work in Hollywood, it told fans, but you can achieve your own kind of stardom at home. You can copy the looks and fashions of the stars. You can go to the movies and envisage yourself on the screen. And you can read and watch the stories of the lucky women who made it, who transformed themselves from small-town girls into movie queens. In their ongoing quest for the dollars and loyalties of female fans, film studios, fan magazines, manufacturers, and advertisers encouraged women to experience the Hollywood dream vicariously, through consumption.

This chapter explores the world of the movie-struck girl from 1910 through 1930—why she went to Hollywood, what she found there, and perhaps most important, how the film industry tried to control and channel her desires. More than an interesting story in itself, it sheds light on two very important aspects of movie fan culture.

The first is the issue of participation. Fans wanted not only to watch but to participate in movies, as actors, writers, publicists, and costume designers. The second has to do with the high level of female involvement in movie fan culture. Women loved the movies not only for the glittering fantasies they offered, but also for their potential work opportunities. For many female fans, Hollywood was a place where they might earn the income, power, and respect denied them through other channels.

The story of the movie-struck girl also gives us insight into the ways that Hollywood dealt with fans during much of the studio era. From the studios' perspective, many fans' demands—to visit the studios, meet film celebrities, and act in films—seemed unrealistic and unreasonable. Yet upsetting or alienating fans could have disastrous consequences at the box office. The challenge for the studios, then, was to appease fans at the least possible cost, to give them the semblance of participating in the movies without actually allowing them to do so. In the case of the movie-struck girl, it meant substituting consumption—buying fan magazines and movie-related products—for actual participation. Although many women undoubt-edly went along with the studios' plan and exchanged their Hollywood dreams for the consumer version, one wonders how many were actually satisfied with the bargain.

Women have always had an intimate relationship with the movies. More likely to imitate star styles, more likely to join fan clubs, and generally more open about their passion for the cinema than men, women formed the backbone of movie fan culture. This can partly be attributed to Hollywood's courting of female audiences—studios, pub-lishers, and advertisers promoted movies and movie-related products as the key to women's happiness. But women's enthusiasm for the cinema was not simply the product of careful advertising. Underlying their interest was often the dream of direct and passionate participation.

THE FEMINIZATION OF MOVIE FANDOM

Since the earliest days of the motion picture, women have been among the movie theater's best customers. Women went so frequently to the movies, trade journal *Moving Picture World* reported in 1910, that "a very large part of the constituency of the moving picture theater are women and children, especially women." In some urban areas, this actually turned movie theaters into female social centers. During the afternoons, observers noted, women filled nickelodeons, often using the theater as a place to rest during rounds of downtown shopping. The theater was "much more comfortable than to take street-car rides to rest, and they don't have to pay the return nickel," reported *Moving Picture World*. Busy mothers, too, found the movies convenient. As Barton Currie wrote in 1909, "Mothers will tell you that the cinematograph has a peculiarly hypnotic or narcotic effect on an infant. You will visit few of these places in Harlem where the doorways are not encumbered with go-carts and perambulators." And for students and working women, the nickelodeon was often an ideal destination for inexpensive entertainment. "After 4 o'clock the audiences were largely composed of schoolgirls, who came in with books or music rolls under their arms," noted the *Chicago Tribune* in 1907. "Around 6 o'clock audiences were largely composed of girls [working at] the big department stores, who came in with bundles under their arms."[2]

Sensing a tremendous opportunity, the film industry quickly mobilized to court, cajole, and ultimately expand the female audience. In 1910, *Moving Picture World* urged filmmakers to dress their actresses beautifully so that "women would go to see the dress" as well as the movie. Some studios created films aimed directly at women; in 1912, for example, the Rex Studio produced *The Fashion Review*, guaranteed to be "a terrific hit with the ladies." Advertisements in women's magazines also piqued women's interest in films. In 1912, the popular magazine the *Ladies' World* printed a novelized version of the film *What Happened to Mary*, and the results, it claimed, were tremendous. "Mrs. Jones of Buffalo buys Ivory Soap, Queen Quality Shoes and Corticelli Silk because she has seen them mentioned for years in her favorite magazines. Just so with pictures. Mrs. Jones learned something about moving pictures when she began reading 'What Happened to Mary' two years ago in the *Ladies' World*, and she has been going to see the pictures ever since," explained the editor.[3]

By 1915, the film industry had successfully forged a strong connection with female moviegoers. Ads, contests, and other marketing gimmicks were often pitched directly at women; cosmetics companies used actresses to sell products, and films frequently featured glamorous costumes and popular women's fashions. Films were being promoted as a woman's form of entertainment, and nowhere was this more evident than in movie fan magazines. Initially geared toward a mixed-sex audience, by the latter part of the decade they had become an almost exclusively female domain. Gone were the ads for men's underwear and hair tonics that had been a constant presence in *Photoplay* and *Motion Picture Story* between 1910 and 1915; advice from male stars on clothing and body building had also disappeared. Instead, beauty tips, articles on women's fashions, and female advice columns took their place. Once a venue for the discussion of a wide range of movie-related issues, fan magazines centered increasingly around women's interests and concerns.

This dramatic change in fan magazine content did not mean that movie fan culture had become completely feminized. As letters to the editor and reader contributions make clear, fan magazines continued to attract a large and dedicated body of male readers. But it was obvious that the film industry's campaign had achieved its purpose— women were flocking to the movies and participating in movie fandom in droves. Moreover, the film industry's wooing notwithstanding, it seemed that the movies had a genuine appeal to many women. Carolyn Van Wyck, *Photoplay's* advice columnist in the 1920s, received dozens of letters from women who were inspired by the movies to improve their lives: to find a job, to go back to school, or to improve their relationships with their husbands or children. Many women confessed that the movies helped them through difficult times. As one woman told *Photoplay,* when she and her husband moved to a faraway city, she turned to the movies for much-needed comfort and companionship. "This little letter cannot express what a desolate void [the movies] have filled in my life as well as thousands of other members of the Lonely Sisterhood," she wrote. To another woman, movies meant "rest to my tired body and comfort to my troubled soul":

> I am the mother of four children. We are too poor to hire help, so I am obliged to run both the day and night shift of the home. . . . Tired, tired, tired, that is I. Evenings when hubby toasts his feet by the fire and has his nose in the newspaper, I ask him for the price of the movies and away I go to find rest. Through the excitement and thrills that follow I forget my cares, my body relaxes and I am rested.

Many others admitted that imitating actresses' styles and mannerisms gave them poise and self-confidence. For many women, the movies and movie fandom became a way to address specifically female concerns about work, family, and physical appearance.[4]

One issue of interest to many women that was covered extensively in fan magazines concerned employment. For many single working- and middle-class women, who often pursued factory labor or clerical positions prior to marriage, work in Hollywood had obvious appeal. "Women in need of money," explained *Film Fun* magazine in 1919, would do better "at a studio than in an office or factory." "There is assuredly a fascination about the studios, an air of romance . . . and possibilities for big money for those who make good," it concluded. *Moving Picture World* agreed that "women's chances of making a living" had been significantly increased by the movies. "Every year there has been an increased demand for women to act, and indications are that the demand will go on increasing," it explained. Not only was film acting lucrative, but it seemed to require little experience or training. Movie star Mae Marsh, said one fan publication, held a job as a telephone operator in a hotel when she was discovered by D. W. Griffith. Another young woman with little acting experience was so determined to appear in movies that she waited in front of a film studio for days. Just as she was about to give up, she caught the eye of director Cecil B. DeMille, who made her into a star.[5]

By 1920, motion picture fan magazines had become not only a source of information about stars and films but a guidebook to stardom. Countless women perused the advice about making it in the movies, wrote to studios and actors for further suggestions ("each day my mail is weighted down with letters written to me by young women who want to go to the moving picture studios," claimed Mary Pickford in 1915), and dreamed of seeing their names in lights. Fandom had become not only a form of entertainment, but a way of potentially staking out a future in films.[6]

Fan culture, too, had taken on a distinctly female bias. Enticed by images of beauty and glamour, inspired by stories about powerful actresses, and intrigued by the opportunities that Hollywood seemed to offer women, thousands of female moviegoers were drawn deeper and deeper into the movies. Men, of course, continued to participate in film fan culture. Throughout Hollywood's studio era, male movie fans made regular contributions to fan magazines, corresponded with actors, and joined or formed fan clubs. In the 1920s and 1930s, *Film Fun* magazine even targeted an explicitly male audience with men's advice columns, advertisements, and revealing pinup photos of actresses. In spite of men's enthusiasm, however, it was largely women who were the most dedicated fans. Women seemed to have the most invested in the movies, and perhaps the most to gain.

GONE HOLLYWOOD

For some women, the idea of seeking fame and fortune in Hollywood was just that—an idea. Countless women who read the testimonies, articles, and advertisements had no intention of making the journey to the movie mecca. But thousands of others seemed to take the enticements seriously. Actress Florence Lawrence, for one, knew that many young women wanted to star in films. "I would like to know if a girl of 16 without any experience can [act in movies]. I have never had any experience at all, but I can roll my eyes every which way," Betty Melnick wrote to Lawrence in 1910. "I am anxious to join some [film] company and I have no experience whatever. Would you please tell me how to go about it?" pleaded movie fan Rose Forte. "Miss Lawrence have you a protege?" asked another fan. "I would like very much to act and I am going to act. You know that when a stubborn young person gets his or her mind on a thing that thing soon comes to pass. The very soul in me seems to cry out for the chance to express what it has concealed for years," she wrote in 1914.[7]

Fan magazines were flooded with similar questions. "How can I get into a moving picture company? That's a letter the *Motion Picture Story Magazine* gets in every mail," wrote the editor in 1912. "If there is no such letter we send the carrier back to the post office to get it, because we know there must be one there, and there most always is." *Photoplay's* "Answer Man" became so tired of the inquiries that in 1917 he composed a satirical "Owed to the Ambitious":

Oh doctor, bring the hemlock quick;
My mind is tired, my brain is sick;
The letters pile up six feet thick;

Here's what they say:
"My friends declare I am as cute
As Pickford and six more to boot
How can I be a movie star?"

"For the lovva Mike, quit askin me how to be a movie star. If I knew
how, I'd go be one myself," he concluded.[8]

Although the film industry knew that female fans were fascinated with the idea of acting in the movies, no one anticipated that
they would actually make the journey to Hollywood. But thousands
over the decades did. Fueled by their ambitions, they spent their last
pennies on train fare, then stood in front of the studios "waiting for
a director to summon them," reported *McClure's* in 1916. Some of
these women, said *Moving Picture World,* had been lured by economic
considerations. With families to support or bills to pay, film acting
was a potentially lucrative way to make ends meet. Others, like the
protagonist of the 1913 film *The Moving Picture Girl,* were lured by
the promise of fame and glamour. In the comedy, a woman is so
entranced by the idea of becoming a movie star that she deserts her
wealthy husband and speeds to the nearest film studio. Regardless of
their individual dreams and motivations, however, in the eyes of the
film industry, they all looked the same. They were a menace who
potentially meant only hassles, headaches, and trouble.[9]

To understand why the film industry seemed so hostile to the
movie-struck fans, it is important to look at the tremendous opposition Hollywood faced in the second decade of the twentieth century.
To social reformers and religious groups, the movies, with their often
frank depictions of romance and violence, seemed like a distinct
social menace. One reformer, Wilbur Crafts of the Protestant-led
International Reform Bureau, likened the movies to "bad beef" that
poisoned "not the bodies only but the minds and souls of our dear
youth"; another compared it to toxic waste that tainted entire
communities. Some organizations, such as the Women's Christian
Temperance Union, felt so strongly against the movies that they
campaigned for official film censorship. By 1915, over a dozen cities
and states had enacted official censorship laws, and the possibility of
federal censorship was being seriously debated in Congress. News of

young women running away from home to act in films would only strengthen the case against Hollywood.[10]

Part of the stigma surrounding the movie-struck girl stemmed from her scandalous predecessor, the stage-struck girl. During the first decade of the century, hundreds of young middle-class women, lured by the bright lights and glamour, went to seek their fortunes on the New York stage. The public outcry was tremendous. Parents complained that Broadway had ruined their daughters, while actors and theater managers deplored the amateurs who crowded around auditions. In 1906, famed actress Ethel Barrymore issued a warning to all stage-struck women. "Ninety-nine out of a hundred girls with theatrical ambitions may expect Failure spelled with the largest capital in the type-setter's outfit," she told *Cosmopolitan* magazine. Another well-known actor put it more bluntly. "To the young woman who comes home breathless and tremulous from some matinee that has inspired her with a wish to go on stage, I can only cry out in earnest warning: Don't."[11]

At some level, these writers and critics were trying to save the stage-struck women from dejection and disappointment. It was true, as they claimed, that the majority of aspiring actresses never attained the stardom they desired. But the critics' real concern may have been of a sexual nature. Rather than aspire to proper middle-class womanhood, the stage-struck girl might set her sights on the unstable, uncouth, and sexually adventurous life of an actress. Unlike the respectable woman, who was supported by her husband, the actress worked for a living, often becoming the breadwinner of her family.

Moreover, the nature of her work, critics claimed, made her indelicate and immodest. Since actresses were in constant contact with men—living on the road, changing costumes in mixed-sex quarters, enacting love scenes on stage—they were assumed to be promiscuous. As a result, they were prey for stage-door johnnies, male fans who provided fancy dinners and gifts in return for sex. In a 1910 article in the *Ladies' Home Journal,* an anonymous actress warned readers of the male mashers who crowded around the stage door after performances. "Behind the smiling mask of the men who approach," she claimed, lay "the fangs of the wolf." What may have frightened parents most, however, was not that their daughters might be corrupted, but that they *wanted* to be seduced. For a middle-class girl to seek an acting career was a strong assertion of will, independence, even sexual desire. The writers who set out to discourage the stage-struck girl tried to protect her not only from others but from herself.[12]

So in 1910, when *Moving Picture World* columnist Lux Graphicus announced that "the stage struck lady has entered the moving picture field," there was cause for alarm. Fearing for its reputation, the film industry immediately sent out announcements and press releases that dispelled the myth of easy money in the movies. It commissioned writers to pen articles describing the hard life of an actress and columns warning young women of the dangers they faced. "Friendly Talks with Screen-Struck Girls," a regular column by actress Beatriz Michelena in the *San Francisco Examiner*, told readers that movie-struck fans often ended up "broken in spirit," saddled with shattered expectations and "bitter disappointment." "The world is movie mad. I feel like telling every girl to stay home," wrote popular actress Ruth Stonehouse in her nationally syndicated advice column in 1915.[13]

But the warnings seemed to have little effect. As the flood of aspirants swelled by mid-decade, the film industry realized that discouraging the movie-struck was no easy task. Casting about for solutions, it turned to the fan magazines. A staple of movie fan culture that reached readers by the thousands, perhaps they could help Hollywood keep the movie-struck girl at home.

THE WOMAN SCREEN-WRITER

The film industry's efforts to enlist the help of the fan magazines met with mixed results. As some magazine editors realized, encouraging readers to seek acting careers piqued their interest and sold more copies. Fans wanted to hear that they had a chance to make it big in Hollywood and that opportunities for acting were plentiful. One fan magazine, however, seemed willing to risk dissuading fans from going to Hollywood: *Photoplay* saw in the crisis of the movie-struck girl an opportunity to win a measure of prestige and respect.

Although *Photoplay* emerged in 1912 as a rival to *Motion Picture Story Magazine,* which debuted in 1911, it had hardly the respect or circulation of its more powerful competitor. With few advertisements. and even fewer feature articles, the magazine was on the verge of bankruptcy when James Quirk, former ad agent, reporter for the *Washington Times,* and editor of the magazine *Popular Mechanics,* took over the editorship in 1914. Determined to raise the magazine's reputation and readership, Quirk launched a crusade to endear the magazine—and the movies—to the middle class. He hired professional writers, prohibited ads from acting schools, and demanded that films be treated as art rather than cheap entertainment. He also made every effort to convince his readers, largely young women, to abandon their dreams of stardom.[14]

In a typical article from 1914, "Breaking Into the Game," *Photoplay* told the story of a young woman's ill-fated attempt to make it in the movies. After waiting for hours in a casting office, she was finally given a few minor roles. But the days were long, the work unsatisfying, and the pay negligible. She finally met a director and begged for a chance in his upcoming film. He replied cruelly, "Yes, you can be a bench in a park scene." Crushed, she went back to her apartment, where she was told she would be called when needed. "That was four weeks ago," she miserably concluded, "and I am still waiting for that call." The magazine also alluded to the sexual dangers that might befall the movie-struck girl. After spending all their money on a fake acting school, said *Photoplay,* a group of young women literally wandered the streets of Hollywood. It was only when a charitable organization took up a collection to send them home that they were saved from certain ruin. "What chance has a girl . . . to break into the movies?" asked *Photoplay.* "There is only one answer: 'No chance in the world.'"[15]

Although Quirk tried diligently to keep female fans away from the studios, he was also wary of completely stifling their ambitions. He was astute enough to observe one of the most important aspects of film fandom: that fans wanted not only to watch movies but to participate in them. As a result, he offered his readers a safer, more reputable way to work in film. Writing screenplays, said *Photoplay,* involved no sexual threat. It was challenging, creative, and crucial to the filmmaking process. Moreover, like acting, it offered ample possibilities for fame and fortune. As *Photoplay* presented it, writing for the movies was the opportunity of a lifetime.

Championing screen-writing as an alternative to acting was not as farfetched as it might seem. By 1915, movie fans throughout the nation had engulfed themselves in a screenwriting mania, sending scripts or scenarios to studios by the thousands. Even in 1913, *Moving Picture World* reported that "if a census were made of all who had written one or two scenarios, the number would approximate twenty thousand." Dozens of screen-writing schools cropped up throughout the nation, and scenario advice books, like Louella Parsons's popular *How To Write for the Movies,* published in 1915, had become a genre in itself. As *Photoplay* joked, "scenarioitis in its most malignant form" had overtaken America. Many of these aspiring screen-writers, it noted, were women.[16]

Between 1915 and the early 1920s, *Photoplay* took every opportunity to convince women that their futures lay in scripts rather than stardom. To encourage movie-struck girls to pick up their pens rather than their suitcases, Quirk promoted screen-writing as the ideal pursuit for women of all backgrounds and aspirations. Women seeking extra income could write screenplays in their leisure time and sell them to studios. Those who wanted to pursue a profession could parlay screen-writing into a career. Writing for the movies even promised fame and wealth. "The field of scenario writing," *Photoplay* assured its readers, "is unique in its possibilities for women."[17]

One of *Photoplay*'s strategies to sell screen-writing to female fans involved sponsoring script contests, often in conjunction with film studios, and then lauding the virtues of their invariably female winners. To assuage fears that women screen-writers were unladylike, *Photoplay* assured readers that they were "normal, regular women, not short-haired feminists, not temperamental '*artistes*.'" Ida Damon, a stenographer and winner of a ten-thousand-dollar screen-writing prize awarded by the Thanhouser Film Corporation, was actually "very feminine and winsome, notwithstanding her business devotion," claimed the magazine. Cordelia Ford, winner of *Photoplay*'s own 1915 screen-writing contest, was also a "typical" woman who was found "trimming the flowers in her yard" when a *Photoplay* representative arrived with the 250-dollar prize. Helen O'Keefe, who won a contest sponsored by the American Film Company, worked on her script each night after she had put her children to bed.[18]

For these women, *Photoplay* explained, screen-writing was a hobby, something done in their spare time. But there were many opportunities for women, if they wanted, to transform script-writing into a career. In 1914, *Photoplay* hired Elaine Sterne, winner of the Vitagraph studio's International Scenario Contest, to oversee a monthly column, "Writing for the Movies as a Profession." The magazine also tried to inspire readers with monthly biographies of women who had succeeded as professional screen-writers. Marguerite Bertsch, it reported, was in charge of editing and approving all scripts for the Vitagraph studio. The Essanay studio also had a female editor, Louella Parsons (of later gossip column fame), who spent her days reading, writing, and revising screenplays. Paris-born Alice Guy Blache, *Photoplay* explained, was not only a screen-writer, but a director. "Madame Blache is a striking example of the modern woman in business who is doing a man's work. She is doing successfully what men are trying to do. She is succeeding in a line of work in which hundreds of men have failed."[19]

For its time, *Photoplay* took a relatively progressive stance on women's employment. During the early decades of the twentieth century, many conservative critics feared that rising levels of female employment—in particular, growing numbers of middle-class married women entering the workforce—would destroy the family and the institution of marriage, and women were dissuaded from seeking paid labor. *Photoplay*, on the contrary, encouraged both married and single women to pursue careers and compete with men in skilled occupations. Part of this attitude may have had to do with the magazine's largely female readership. Working women, who used their wages to go to movies and buy fan magazines, were among *Photoplay's* most loyal supporters. Another influence may have been Quirk's own attitude toward female employment. The majority of *Photoplay's* writers were women, including the well-known reporters Ruth Waterbury, Adele Whitely Fletcher, and Adela Rogers St. Johns. Kathryn Dougherty, Quirk's assistant, was also responsible for important editorial decisions and eventually took over the editorship when Quirk died in 1932.[20]

The short stories that *Photoplay* published each month also supported the working woman. "Dolly of the Dailies," a short story that had also been made into a film, featured a strong-willed female reporter; "The Evil Eye" chronicled the adventures of a woman physician, Doctor Katherine Torrance. In 1914, a serialized short story, "Laura Leonard, Heart Specialist," told readers about a beautiful and talented actress who played matchmaker to her friends but chose to remain single. As the ultimate sign of her independence, Laura was a successful screen-writer. "Laura wrote almost all of the scenarios of the pictures she was in. She'd write up a synopsis, and then someone else would do the work of fixing it up for production."[21]

But sometimes the truth was even more impressive than fiction. As *Photoplay* reminded readers, a handful of women screen-writers were so brilliant and successful that they had been assigned to write scripts for the most popular actors and directors in the nation. It was a woman named Jeanie MacPherson, readers learned, who put the drama in Cecil B. DeMille's epic films and the spice in his popular sex comedies. Precocious Anita Loos scripted dozens of screen adventures for Douglas Fairbanks. Lois Weber was not only a writer but a prominent director. And June Mathis, who wrote Rudolph Valentino's scripts, was so important that a film company insured her life for one million dollars. "These women," wrote *Photoplay*, "are essentially the brains of the motion picture business, making good equally with men."[22]

But it was Frances Marion, young, bright, and attractive, who quickly became the most prominent figure in *Photoplay*'s campaign for the woman screen-writer. In 1917, the magazine ran a four-page article, complete with glamorous photos, that celebrated Marion and her stunning looks—her "fair skin, soft, golden-brown hair and youthful-looking dark brown eyes." Although she had previously been an actress, *Photoplay* explained, Marion found the greatest satisfaction in her "absorbing and interesting" work as a writer. The creative force behind Mary Pickford's films and the author of dozens of successful screenplays, she was living proof that intelligent, beautiful, and respectable women *chose* to be screen-writers rather than actresses.[23]

If readers needed further encouragement, *Photoplay* often featured biographies of young women who found success in Hollywood as editors, writers, and designers. Of one woman the magazine wrote, "Her profile is like Norma Talmadge's. Daintily patrician, with the faint touch of arrogance that distinguishes beauty of that type. No, she is not an actress, nor does she aspire to be one. She writes for her daily bread!" Another beautiful woman, Kathleen Kay, chose to become a costume designer instead of an actress. "To the uninitiated this waste of beauty and distinction sounds appalling," it concluded. "But we of Hollywood applaud her wisdom."[24]

In spite of its efforts to steer women toward screen-writing, *Photoplay* had to admit that its campaign was failing. By the early 1920s, the flood of aspiring actresses had increased rather than abated, and social reformers, journalists, sociologists, and film studios had all declared the problem an urgent crisis. Moreover, as films became longer and more complex, and as studios hired professional writers, *Photoplay* could no longer, in good faith, encourage amateurs to send in their scripts. "The street car conductor, the plumber, the stenographer who could never differentiate between a comma and a semicolon, the woman who believed she was literary . . . have been left behind as the trained writer has been brought into the scenario field," it announced. Coming soon, lamented another fan magazine, was the day of the professional, "the million dollar scenarioist."[25]

Photoplay and the film industry were faced with a dilemma. According to some estimates, over a hundred young women were arriving in the movie capital each week, and the number seemed only to be increasing. The Hollywood Public Library reported that dozens of young women sought shelter in the facility each day; others slept on the street. The mounting crisis required a swift solution, and in desperation, the film industry turned to more extreme tactics. With grim statistics and terrifying tales of poverty and failure, it set out to so thoroughly scare female fans that they would never think about going to Hollywood again.[26]

THE CRISIS DEEPENS

The 1920s started ominously in Hollywood. In 1921, popular film comedian Roscoe "Fatty" Arbuckle was accused of having raped and murdered a young actress at a party in a San Francisco hotel room. As news of the scandal spread, Americans were treated to a host of unsettling images: drugs and bootleg gin, scantily clad women, and a gluttonous, sex-hungry actor. For a nation that had grown to idealize film actors, this first star scandal came as a shock. As if the Arbuckle case was not enough, in 1922 director William Desmond Taylor was mysteriously murdered, and film heartthrob Wallace Reid, one of Hollywood's most popular actors, died of a drug overdose. Religious groups, social reformers, and censorship activists seized upon this opportunity to prove their point. Behind the bright lights and glamour lay unspeakable debauchery—exploitation, promiscuity, addiction.

At the center of Hollywood's evils, they claimed, were two figures: the conniving actor and the naive, desperate movie-struck girl, sometimes called the "extra girl," because she tried to launch her career by working as a film extra. In 1921, *Literary Digest* warned readers of the thousands of gullible girls who went to Hollywood each year. Short on money but filled with ambition, these young women quickly became the victims of "men of ill omen." One young woman, unable to find work, became so desperate that she agreed to share lodgings with an actor. "I guess I know what that means," she told a friend, "but I'm tired of being hungry." "Of the hundreds who chase the rainbow only a few find the pot of gold at the end," the magazine concluded. "The others either crawl back to the family . . . or end up in some blind alley."[27]

Marilyn Conners, the author of a 1924 advice book for women, *What Chance Have I in Hollywood?*, told a similar tale. Hungry and alone in Hollywood, a young woman named Mamie Swemp met two men claiming to be film directors. When they offered her the lead part in a movie, she gladly accepted. Little did she know that the "directors" were actually "procurers from Tijuana." The article continued, "Records show that more than five thousand persons, mostly young and innocent women, disappear through the mysterious gateway of missing persons in Hollywood. Where they go to, few know, but most of them, ruined, heartbroken, sick, degraded, sink into the corruption of border towns, are swallowed into the oblivion worse than death, which is the clutch of the underworld."[28]

Parents had become so worried about their daughters that they ran urgent ads in newspapers, such as this notice printed in *Moving Picture World* in 1920: "Ethel Palmer Leake, 22 years old, has been missing since April 29 and is supposed to have gone with a moving picture company. Communicate with Bureau of Missing Persons, Police Department, West Philadelphia."[29]

In response to the negative publicity surrounding Hollywood and the extra-girl problem, fan magazines, the film industry, and the city of Hollywood quickly mobilized. While the Chamber of Commerce zealously defended itself—"Hollywood is the most lied about place on earth!" one pamphlet claimed—film executives hired former

Postmaster General Will Hays, a Presbyterian elder from Indiana with an impeccable reputation, to clean up Hollywood's image. Immediately Hays turned to the Studio Club, a rooming house for actresses that was established in 1916. For years, the Club had been publicized as a place where extra girls could live together and share "clean fun, with no aftermath of sorrow or regret," according to *Photoplay*. The only problem, however, was that it was simply not large enough for the dozens of women seeking shelter. In 1922, in response to prodding by Hays, the YWCA announced plans to open a new facility for 100 women. The 150,000-dollar cost would be raised through donations from studios, actors, and the Hollywood community.[30]

After countless benefit dinners and performances, by May 1923 the Studio Club Committee had raised 100,000 dollars—46,000 dollars from national corporations and 54,000 dollars from studios and actors. The major film studios contributed between 3,000 and 5,000 dollars each; Mary Pickford and Douglas Fairbanks, and directors Howard Hughes, Thomas Ince, and Hal Roach each donated 1,000 dollars. By late 1923, the Committee had finally reached its goal, and three years later the new facility was complete. Quiet and clean, the new Studio Club, run by the Hollywood YWCA, offered women a private room and "two wholesome meals" for 2.75 dollars a day.[31]

But the expansion of the Studio Club was not intended to lure more women to Hollywood. At the same time that Hays worked to expand the facility, he embarked on a drastic campaign to scare fans away from the city. Between 1923 and 1925, he dispatched a series of advertisements and announcements to newspapers throughout the country. One ad showed a huge crowd of men and women milling around an employment agency:

> DON'T TRY TO BREAK INTO THE MOVIES in Hollywood until you have obtained full, frank and dependable information from the Hollywood Chamber of Commerce. IT MAY SAVE DISAPPOINT-MENTS. Out of 100,000 persons who started at the bottom of the screen's ladder of fame ONLY FIVE REACHED THE TOP.

Studios hired extra staff, including policemen and detectives, to help turn away the applicants. The city of Hollywood also pledged its support. "I think you know of the Hollywood Chamber of Commerce's plan of constructive cooperation with the motion picture industry to relieve the studios of the nuisance of disposing of the scores of applicants who daily besiege the studios," wrote the head of the chamber to the Mack Sennett studio.[32]

Photoplay, too, stepped up its campaign. Dozens of articles, beginning in 1923, warned women of the "gold-crazy, sex-crazy, hard-boiled" city that had become a "port of missing girls." Interviews with judges revealed lurid tales of prostitution and disease; investigative reports publicized the gangsters and addicts who called the city their home. The centerpiece of *Photoplay*'s efforts was a four-part series in 1927, "The Truth About Breaking Into the Movies," in which reporter Ruth Waterbury attempted to find work as a film extra. The series, which described a harrowing ordeal ending in failure, was prefaced by a warning from editor Quirk. "Read on, little movie aspirant, who believes work in the movies to be romantic, easy, and golden. Here is a graphic report of the [life] of extra workers. Study it thoroughly before you buy your ticket to Hollywood." Waterbury, too, concluded with an urgent plea. "I have no words to express it strongly enough! Stay away! I saw things, heard them, learned them . . . that I want to forget." Waterbury related,

> It was explained to me how many a disillusioned girl reaches home by acting as a chaperon to a corpse. The dead are not supposed to travel alone. So when a body must be shipped from Hollywood, the railroad lets the Chamber of Commerce know and some girl gets a free ticket for performing this job. Adventure cannot end more abjectly than this. Don't go to Hollywood![33]

Were the scare tactics actually necessary? From Hollywood's standpoint, they were absolutely vital. Any more negative publicity surrounding the extra girl would only further damage the film industry's already tarnished reputation. And dealing with the aspirants, either by screen-testing them or trying to drive them off the studio lots, was troublesome, costly, and time-consuming. Moreover, life really was difficult for the extra girl. Central Casting, the agency created by Hays in 1926 to coordinate work for film extras, regularly turned out grim statistics. In 1926, every day 9,690 extras registered with Central Casting but only 1,000 were employed. In 1927, 14,000 had registered and only 700 found work each day. Decades later, fan magazine writer Cedric Belfrage recalled how dim and desperate those years were. "People were really going hungry. With the sun shining down, and everything so beautiful and all the glamour, there were actually people down the street going hungry," he reminisced.[34]

It is difficult to say how many women actually took the warnings seriously and stayed away from Hollywood. Undoubtedly there were more than a few. Some fans wrote to *Photoplay* thanking them for their warnings. Thanks to "your plain, honest, solid facts," wrote one reader, "you [have shown] that an amateur has got as much chance to get on the screen as I have to become president of the USA." One young woman confessed that *Photoplay* helped her channel her energies away from an acting career and into her job as a stenographer. "She once thought she was on the way to be a great actress. But she wasn't. She was on her way to be a good stenographer. And she was happy—happier than she had ever been," the magazine explained.[35]

But countless others refused to be talked out of their dream. As trains continued to bring dozens of aspiring actresses to Hollywood, it was clear that many fans were undaunted. For these persistent young women, the film industry had another plan. Rather than make the risky trip to the studios, they could pursue an easier and safer activity: participating vicariously in the Hollywood dream. By purchasing the right clothing and beauty products, they might not attain film stardom, but they could become the glamorous stars of their own lives.

HOW TO BE A STAR

The movie-struck girls, by all accounts, were a genuine source of concern for Hollywood. But at the same time, the film industry realized, they might also be quite profitable. If aspiring actresses were willing to substitute actual for vicarious participation—in other words, if they would try to emulate rather than try to become stars—they could become a tremendous source of revenue. If they channeled their yearnings for stardom into a passion for consumer products, they might become not a liability but an asset.

In this endeavor, the film industry depended heavily on the fan magazines. During the 1920s, *Photoplay, Motion Picture, Movie Weekly,*

Motion Picture Classic, Picture Play, and countless other fan publications filled their issues with beauty advice and fashion tips. Actresses and columnists counseled readers on proper dress, makeup, and etiquette. They also preached the most important beauty secret of all: to look like a star, one must shop like a star. Without the right clothing and beauty products, glamour was impossible.

Telling readers to emulate star styles was, of course, more than just a ploy to divert the energies of aspiring actresses. It was primarily part of a carefully engineered campaign to sell products by capitalizing on the widespread public interest in movie stars. Since the previous decade, national corporations had paid actors hefty sums to endorse a variety of products. The actor's photo and signature were then used in advertisements published in both fan and mainstream magazines. Between 1914 and 1920, Mary Pickford, Mary Fuller, Marion Davies, Constance Talmadge, Maurice Costello, and Francis Bushman, among others, lent their names to soft drinks, beauty creams, automobiles, and hair tonics.

It was not until the 1920s, however, that the relationship between corporations, fan magazines, and the movie industry really solidified. Middle-class prosperity, a burgeoning consumer culture, and the increased social importance of appearance and style had all intensified the public demand for consumer goods—cars, appliances, beauty aids, clothing, and luxury items. More than ever, the growing advertising industry invited the film industry to help sell these products, and the film industry eagerly accepted. Association with well-known consumer goods only enhanced Hollywood's visibility. It also sold movie tickets. If Americans saw Hollywood as the nation's leading fashion expert, they would "use the movies," as one fan magazine put it, to learn about the newest fads and trends.

By the mid-1920s, Hollywood had been firmly linked with glamour and consumption, and nowhere was this more apparent than in *Photoplay.* As articles on screen-writing faded from the magazine in the 1920s, features on fashion and beauty took their place. For those readers curious about the best ways to attain the movie star "look," *Photoplay* initiated a monthly column called "Friendly Advice," which offered tips on "clothes, charm and beauty." The magazine also featured beauty secrets from glamorous actresses. Norma Talmadge, for example, told readers that they should spend at least half an hour each day dressing, wear "soft, inconspicuous" lines and colors, and walk with grace and poise.[36]

According to *Photoplay*, looking as beautiful as a movie star was more than just a casual pastime. It was an important responsibility, perhaps one of the most important goals of a woman's life. "It is the duty of every girl to get the most out of herself," explained the magazine's in-house "beauty expert." "To make herself as attractive as possible. To accentuate a lovely curve, a beautiful line, a pretty feature. It is more than a duty—it is a rare privilege!" Marriages were often destroyed, actresses warned, when women failed to pay attention to their looks. "More happy homes are broken up by wives who look unattractive in the morning than through any other cause," claimed Norma Talmadge.[37]

The biggest source of beauty advice, however, came from *Photoplay's* advertisements, which often used movie stars or movie-related themes to promote consumer goods. Drawing an analogy between the screen and life, these ads tried to convince readers that they were stars in their own daily dramas. Like movie actresses, they were under constant scrutiny, facing dozens of critical judges each day at work and at home. "In this day and age, attention to your appearance is an absolute necessity if you expect to make the most out of life," said the manufacturers of a "nose adjuster," an elastic band worn around the face that allegedly changed the shape of one's nose. "Not only should you wish to appear as attractive as possible for your own self-satisfaction, but you will find the world in general judging you greatly, if not wholly, by your looks." In order to survive this struggle, Americans should work tirelessly to maintain their appearance, as did their favorite actors and actresses.[38]

The key to success on the screen—and in life—allegedly lay in the right beauty and hygiene products. As the makers of Woodbury's facial soap declared, dozens of film stars became beautiful and fresh-faced, radiant with "youth and beauty," thanks to the use of their product. Movie queens, claimed another ad, created their distinct looks through the use of Maybelline mascara. The Elizabeth Arden cosmetic company even marketed an inexpensive imitation of professional stage makeup. "Every star, every movie fan, every woman who ever dreamed to possess glamor, may share in the discovery of Screen and Stage Makeup," it announced. Users of the new product would, "like the people of stage and screen, discover their own beauty and live the days and nights of their private lives in rich fulfillment."[39]

Quirk encouraged readers to study the advertising as carefully as the magazine's articles. "Read the advertising!" read a full-page announcement printed in *Photoplay* each month. "It enables you to get more for your money by telling you what to buy. It's your guide to what's good to get." Quirk was so intent on linking his magazine, the movies, and consumer products that he frequently urged readers to think of name-brand products as "stars." Like the best actors and actresses, these goods continued to turn out quality performances in spite of their constant presence in the media spotlight.[40]

Quirk's campaign to promote consumer-product advertising had obvious financial benefits. As film historian Kathryn Fuller has noted, Quirk might have used the campaign to prove to potential advertisers his readers' interest in consumer culture, and thus to attract more advertising revenue. Encouraging the readers to spend time on the advertising may have also been a way to bring them back to the magazine's copy. In *Photoplay* during the 1920s, advertising and text supported each other. While ads offered a variety of products, articles instructed readers on the best ways to use them. Together, they sent readers a powerful message that fulfillment could be attained through consumption and fashion.[41]

When viewed in conjunction with the magazine's many warnings to the extra girl, this message took on even greater significance. Rather than actually try to become movie actresses, women could fulfill their longings by emulating movie stars. "Stay at your type-writers," *Photoplay* advised young women, but spend your earnings on clothing and cosmetics. Film studios also encouraged women to devote money and energy to imitating stars. In the late 1920s, studio publicists began the practice of sending "fashion updates" to national newspapers and magazines. Women were urged to buy—or, at the very least, create their own homemade copies of—the elegant dresses that graced the silver screen. The film industry also invited women to frequent the Cinema Shop, a chain of boutiques run by Macy's that specialized in movie-inspired gowns. In advertising manuals sent to theaters, studios asked exhibitors to create links or "tieups" between film fashions and the local Cinema Shop. MGM's manual for *Chained* (1934), for example, informed exhibitors that "in addition to the Adrian-designed gowns Joan Crawford features in the picture, she also appears in a riding habit, swim suit and slacks. This offers a possible tieup with the Cinema Shop. Joan Crawford is nationally known as one of the best dressed women of the screen and deserves the most important fashion tieup promotion." In 1932, the Cinema Shop sold a half-million copies of the dress worn by Crawford in the movie *Letty Lynton*.[42]

For fans, copying the stars' styles became a rewarding pastime. "Mary Pickford in *Little Lord Fauntleroy* so impressed me that I [bought] a pair of black velvet pants . . . like those Mary Pickford wore in that show," explained one woman in 1931. "I have a little two-piece sweater suit suggested by something I saw on Colleen Moore; Norma Talmadge was the inspiration for my dignified dinner dress . . . and I am wearing my hair with a view to getting the same entrancing effect that Greta Garbo gets with hers," a nineteen-year-old reported proudly. Another woman shared with fellow fans her secrets for success: "Fix hair like Carole Lombard. Speak distinctly and have the right pronunciation like Constance Bennett. Walk with shoulders back like Norma Shearer." By carefully selecting a favorite star and taking on some—but not all—of her styles and mannerisms, many women created a sense of identity and individuality. Though sometimes costly, imitating the stars often fostered excitement, fulfillment, and strong feelings of self-worth.[43]

By the early 1930s, the link between the movies and consumer products was successfully forged. Hollywood celebrated its recent triumph as a mass marketer in a film. In the opening scene of the 1933 movie *What Price Hollywood?* a young woman named Mary Evans, played by Constance Bennett, flips through the pages of a fan magazine. Turning to a feature article on "Hollywood star styles," she smiles and nods in approval—her dress is an identical copy of the outfit worn by a famous actress. Her lips, too, have been rouged with Kissable Lipstick, "the brand that Hollywood stars prefer," and her legs sheathed in Sheer Silk stockings, endorsed by "screen star Glinda Golden."

But in *What Price Hollywood?* Mary Evans does more than just look like a star. A waitress in Hollywood's famous Brown Derby restaurant, she uses her chic appearance to launch a successful film career. By 1933, however, most moviegoers had learned to take little stock in these "rags to riches" stories. Conditioned by two decades of fan magazine and studio publicity, many female fans knew that the chances of actually making it in the movies were one in a million. Rather than even think about going to Hollywood, they went to the drugstore, beauty parlor, or Cinema Shop. Or perhaps they went to the movies, where they could fantasize that they, like Mary Evans, had been plucked from anonymity and thrust into the spotlight.

THE HOLLYWOOD DREAM

Clearly, by the 1930s, fans' dreams of stardom had dimmed. But it had not always been that way. Only a decade earlier, tens of thousands of female fans had flooded Hollywood in pursuit of their acting aspirations. When their goals clashed with the interests of the film industry, their energies were diverted into a set of less ambitious pursuits: watching movies, reading fan magazines, shopping. The dream of working directly in the movies had been replaced by vicarious participation through consumption.

The effects on film fandom were significant. By the 1930s, imitating celebrity styles, purchasing star-endorsed products, and collecting actors' photos, autographs, and other Hollywood souvenirs had become important fan activities. The movies were no longer seen as a potential way to *earn* money, but an excuse to *spend* money on fan magazines, movie tickets, and a variety of products. The continued association of the movies with consumption also contributed to the further feminization of film fandom. As increasing numbers of women read fan magazines, copied Hollywood styles, and used the movies as a source of fashion advice, the association between women and fandom was strengthened and, as a result, many men discontinued their involvement. By the 1930s and 1940s, the most active and visible film fans were undeniably women.

Most of these fans had come to terms with the fact that they would never see their names in lights. They accepted that they would never attain stardom or take part directly in the movies. But that did not preclude other ways of exerting influence in Hollywood. Many fans actually learned to draw on their power as purchasers to leave their mark on the studio system. By threatening to boycott certain films or to withdraw their support for a particular star, fans tried to convince the studios to acknowledge their demands. The film industry would eventually be forced to appease and negotiate with the motion picture consumers it had worked so hard to create.

CHAPTER FOUR

THE INSIDE SCOOP

TO MOVIE FANS, the steady surge of movie star publicity was in many ways a dream come true. No longer would they have to write insistent letters to fan magazines, as they had in the early decades, asking about actors' homes, marriages, and habits. Personal information about popular actors could now be found everywhere, from *Photoplay* to the *Ladies' Home Journal* to cereal boxes and cookie tins. Fans were fascinated by this information, and filled scrapbooks with articles and clippings about their favorite actors. Many tried to outdo each other by uncovering more detailed and obscure movie-related facts.

To observers, fans' obsession with Hollywood trivia may have seemed frivolous, even childish. Who cared whether Clark Gable was divorcing or whether Ginger Rogers dyed her hair? But, to fans, this information was of the utmost importance. Since they wanted to confirm their idol's offscreen existence and know how he or she behaved away from the camera, fans were forced to turn to writers and journalists. Because they were never able to go behind the scenes, fans had to rely on the accounts and testimonies of those who could.

Many Americans in the 1930s were content to depend on Louella Parsons, Hedda Hopper, Sheilah Graham, Jimmy Fidler, and the several other journalists and gossip columnists who revealed the inner workings of the movie capital. They adored fan magazine writers and press agents for their articles and in-depth interviews. Others were not similarly satisfied. Many fans had become skeptical of Hollywood gossip and vowed to take Hedda, Louella, and their cohorts with a grain of salt. Some fans were so distrustful, in fact, that they tried to circumvent the columnists and uncover their own version of the truth. Hundreds of fans would camp out in front of celebrities' homes, follow actors around Hollywood, and try to sneak into film studios, all in an attempt to see for themselves what stars were really like.

During the 1920s and 1930s, fans came up with another way to learn the truth about Hollywood: the fan club. By joining an official fan club, fans were able to forge a direct link to their favorite actor, who provided them with autographed photos and information about his or her offscreen life. By the mid-1930s, fan clubs had become phenomenally popular, with memberships reaching into the millions. No longer dependent on untrustworthy gossip columns, newspapers, and movie magazines, many fans had become their own experts on their favorite star's private life.

By the time America entered the age of sound, fans' quest for authenticity had become more complicated than anyone had ever imagined. Not only did fans have to contend with the motion picture's capacity for deception and illusion, but they faced a slick Hollywood publicity machine that was often as misleading as the cinema itself. Not surprisingly, many fans found themselves in a constant state of uncertainty. What should they believe? Who had the inside scoop? How could they ever know what stars were really like? In their struggle to uncover the truth about the stars, movie fans were forced to confront one of the fundamental dilemmas facing Americans in the twentieth century. Living in a modern mass society, they had little choice but to depend on the media for news of the world around them. In lieu of direct experience, they had to turn to journalists, writers, and publicists for the information they could not uncover or validate for themselves.

A PASSION FOR TRIVIA

Although moviegoers in the first decade of the twentieth century were confused about the nature of the motion picture—whether it depicted, concealed, or distorted reality—they were clear on one thing. No matter how much they loved the movies, no matter how often they went to the theater, they could never really know what went on in a film studio. Unable to witness filmmaking firsthand, fans knew they would have to rely on experts to learn about the world behind the scenes.

One of the first movie experts was *Motion Picture Story Magazine,* the nation's first fan magazine. Each month beginning in 1911, the publication responded to hundreds of readers' questions about the moviemaking process. By 1915, it had even begun to address a subject formerly considered taboo: movie stars' offscreen lives. In the magazine's "Question and Answer" section, as well as its monthly columns and feature articles, *Motion Picture* revealed the latest news and gossip about the nation's most popular actors. "Edwin August has a charming bungalow in Hollywood. Marguerite Clayton and Josephine Rector are roommates at the Belvoir Hotel. Clara Kimball Young is a Democrat," it reported in a typical issue from 1914.[1]

Fans prized this information dearly. In letters written to actress Florence Lawrence between 1911 and 1916, fans admitted how much they depended on *Motion Picture* for information about their favorite stars. "I have just read about you . . . in the March copy of *Motion Picture* magazine, of which I have every number since it was issued in 1911," wrote one fan. Without the magazine, claimed another woman, she would have little chance of learning about Lawrence's latest activities. "I have read *Motion Picture* for a long time and try never to miss one. You know what a Florence Lawrence fan I am," she confessed.[2]

By the end of the decade, fans could read about their favorite actors not only in *Motion Picture* but in a variety of movie magazines—*Photoplay, Picture Play, Shadowland,* and *Motion Picture Classic,* among others. By the 1920s several prominent mainstream publications had also begun to feature regular articles on motion pictures. *Ladies' Home Journal, Collier's,* and the *Saturday Evening Post* frequently printed interviews with film stars; dozens of major newspapers, including the *Chicago Tribune* and the *New York Times,* ran daily film reviews and gossip columns. With facts about film-making, movie trivia, and snippets of information about popular actors, these publications worked diligently to bridge the gap between Hollywood and its audience. In particular, they tried to answer the questions that had consumed fans since the earliest days of the movies. What were movie stars really like? How did they behave when they were away from the camera?

In many cases, they assured their readers that actors were the same as they seemed in films. According to *Ladies' Home Journal,* Mary Pickford was as spunky, honest, and sincere as her film characters. Douglas Fairbanks, wrote another magazine, was as energetic and athletic as the young men he portrayed. "Doug knocks off work at 5 p.m., then starts his training schedule [by] wrestling, [then] running a mile in 6 minutes, followed by a dip in the pool," it claimed. Sometimes magazines suggested that actors were even more likable in person than in films. Rudolph Valentino, known to America as "The Sheik," was far more interesting than his image suggested, wrote *Collier's.* Not only was he a talented actor, but a gentle, compassionate, sensitive, and intelligent man with a college degree in horticulture. Aware of the public's infatuation with Holly-wood stars, magazines and newspapers sought to reassure moviego-ers that their favorite actors were really as wonderful as, if not much better than, they appeared on the screen.[3]

Before long, fans had become full-fledged information junkies. Knowing that printed facts and reports were the only way to confirm stars' offscreen existence, fans became voracious consumers of Hollywood trivia. Real movie fans, explained one reader of *Motion Picture,* had read so many articles and seen so many films that they "know every actor, actress, film company and director by name." "Through the movie magazines we hunt frantically for news and more news of this and that player," confessed one fan. "How does she wear her hair, and why? Is this his fifth wife, and why? Was she born in Kalamazoo, Michigan, of Italian descent, at three o'clock on a Thursday morning in September, and why?" An editorial cartoon in *Motion Picture Classic* satirized this obsession with movie star trivia. In the cartoon, a popular actor tries to beat back a crowd of screaming admirers. "What is your middle name?" shout the fans. "How long have you been in the movies? What is the make of your [automobile]? Which is your favorite flower?" This knowledge not only enabled fans to connect the movies to reality but often gave them a sense of intimacy with their idol.[4]

Encouraging this quest for information, as well as continued readership of their publications, many movie magazines sponsored quizzes and trivia contests. In 1925, *Photoplay* printed a 45-item intelligence test that probed fans' knowledge of actors and films. "How much do you know about motion pictures? Are you a real fan?" it asked. Readers who made less than ten mistakes were true movie experts, but those who made more than eleven were "only casually good fans." Movie magazines also printed games and puzzles based on Hollywood trivia. One magazine's monthly feature, "The Movie Fan's Crossword Puzzle," used clues such as "Every star has at least one," "New actor on the Universal lot," and "First name of Paramount actress." *Photoplay* even marketed a special encyclopedia on the stars. In an ad for its 250-page book titled *Stars of the Photoplay,* the magazine asked, "Do you know the name of Irene Rich's husband? . . . Why Will Rogers became a screen actor? What star weighs exactly one hundred pounds? How many times Alma Rubens has been married? How old is Marie Dressler? How Jack Oakie got his start? Gilbert Roland's nationality? Which fair-haired star was disowned by her father?" For 1.25 dollars, fans could have "the answers to these and hundreds of other questions—just the information that you and your friends want," *Photoplay* promised.[5]

By the 1930s, dispensing movie star trivia to curious fans had become an industry in itself. Each week, the publicity offices of the major film studios shipped out thousands of photos and press releases, including fabricated studio biographies of their most popular stars. Although some of this information found its way to national newspapers and general interest magazines, much of it was directed toward the fan publications, which now numbered more than a dozen. Fans could choose among *Film Fun, Screen Romances, Modern Romances, Movie Classic, Movie Mirror, Shadowplay, Screen Play, Screenbook, Screenland,* and *Silver Screen,* in addition to the old standards *Photoplay, Picture Play,* and *Motion Picture;* in 1934 these magazines reached an estimated one hundred million readers. One of the newer fan publications, a slick magazine called *New Movies,* shocked the publishing industry in 1930 by charging ten instead of the traditional twenty-five cents per copy. A price war ensued, and before long all the fan magazines, with the exception of *Photoplay,* peddled rumor, gossip, and Hollywood trivia for a dime.[6]

With so much competition, fan magazines consistently tried to outdo each other with more detailed articles about stars' private lives. As many film scholars have suggested, the increased sense of intimacy created by talking films—audiences may have felt closer to actors after hearing their voices—may have also encouraged magazines to divulge increasingly personal information about the stars. Emblazoned on bold and brightly decorated covers were enticements alerting fans to the treasures within: "The First True Story of Garbo's Childhood," "The Inside Story of Joan's Divorce," and "The Story Jean Harlow Never Told." "At last, Janet Gaynor breaks down and tells you all the things you've been wanting to know about her," advertised one publication. "*Modern Screen* outscoops itself!" proclaimed the magazine about its "exclusive story" on the marriage of Lupe Velez and Johnny Weismuller. In addition to their more sensational fare, movie magazines made sure to provide fans with their bread-and-butter staple: basic information about the most popular film stars. "Be up to date on the stars' lives with facts for your mental file," wrote *Modern Screen* in 1936. "Jean Harlow is 5 foot three, weighs 109 pounds, has gray blue eyes, and brownette [sic] hair. She loves to entertain and is an excellent cook. Her hobby is collecting phonograph records. Jean cannot play any musical instrument, but enjoys golf, swimming, tennis, and riding."[7]

Several movie magazine writers quickly earned a reputation for their in-depth reporting and passionate prose. Adela Rogers St. Johns, a reporter for the Hearst newspapers, became famous for her articles in *Photoplay* magazine. By the 1930s she had become so popular that she was hired by the Realsilk company to endorse their line of women's stockings. Ruth Waterbury, another *Photoplay* writer, was also well known; Adele Whitely Fletcher penned articles as well as edited *Motion Picture* magazine. Fans respected these writers for both their close association with film celebrities and their ability to explain in simple yet eloquent language what went on in the world "behind the scenes."[8]

But there was one female journalist who was more famous, more powerful, and more influential than any of these fan magazine writers.

By the 1930s, Louella Parsons had become America's most prominent and powerful Hollywood gossip columnist. To many actors and studio executives, she was a force to be reckoned with, a busybody who ruined careers with the stroke of her pen. But to her devoted readers, Parsons was a godsend, a talented and persistent reporter who could expose Hollywood like no one else. Fans pored over her daily columns, wrote her passionate fan mail, and even formed Louella Parsons fan clubs. Parsons became so popular that she was hired to host a radio show and made one film. In a fitting climax to their fascination with movie star trivia, fans turned Hollywood's most prominent fact-finder into a national celebrity.

THE QUEEN OF GOSSIP

On the surface, Louella Parsons was an unlikely candidate for stardom. Plain-faced and pudgy, she was hardly as glamorous as her Hollywood sister-celebrities. But then again, Louella Parsons did not need good looks to get noticed. All she needed was a typewriter. When Parsons wrote, people took notice.

It was not the quality of her writing that commanded attention. Her articles were filled with run-ons and cliches ("tempus sure does fugit" was a Parsons favorite); they were riddled with countless mistakes and malapropisms. In Parsons's column, Mary Pickford's new book *Why Not Try God?* became *Why Try God?;* a film called *The President Vanishes* was reported as *The Vanishing American.* Accuracy and creativity were hardly her forte. Instead, what contributed most to her success was her uncanny ability to sense new trends and her ceaseless efforts to thrust herself into the spotlight.[9]

Parsons's childhood in small-town Dixon, Illinois, hinted at the life she was to lead. In 1891, at the age of ten, she submitted a short story she had written to the local newspaper editor. Shortly afterward, she jumped from the rafters in a barn with a pair of scissors in each hand, hoping to injure herself. She was successful. As she lay in bed with a broken tooth and fractured elbow, she summoned the local editor and begged him to run her story, just in case she didn't live. Of course, she did. The sympathetic editor printed the piece, and Louella Parsons, through trickery, had launched her writing career.[10]

Newspapers, it seemed, had always been good to Parsons. After a few years of reporting for the *Dixon Star* after college—and a minor detour through marriage, divorce, and a job as a screenplay editor at the Essanay film studio—Parsons found herself once again in the newsroom, this time at the *Chicago Record Herald*. There, in 1915 she convinced the editor to run a daily column chronicling the lives and adventures of the most popular film actors. Like the fan magazines, "Seen on the Screen" combined film reviews with snippets of information about actors' vacations, marriages, and careers. "Kathleen Williams is still living. John Bunny is dead. Francis X. Bushman is married but he sees fit to deny it," she wrote in a typical column from 1915. In 1918, when the *Herald* was bought out by the Hearst corporation, Parsons lost her job. Hearst, she was told, had little use for her brand of reporting. Desperate, she moved to New York, where she eventually found a job as a columnist for the *New York Morning Telegraph*. But in 1924, Hearst came calling—this time for Parsons. Offering prestige and a high salary, Hearst commissioned her to serve as motion picture editor and columnist for his powerful New York newspaper, the *American*.[11]

By the mid-1920s, Louella Parsons was widely recognized among East Coast movie fans as one of the foremost experts on Hollywood gossip. "Alice Lake is in New York. There was a report made that she had kissed and made up with her husband, from whom she is seeking a divorce," she wrote in her "Flickerings from Filmland" column in 1925. "When Mary Pickford and Douglas Fairbanks sail for Europe in April it will be for a purpose other than for a holiday in Europe. Mary has taken into her little head that she wants to make her next picture in Europe." Compared to the scandals and infidelities reported in the tabloids of the 1940s and 1950s, including in Parsons's own column from those decades, her reports from the 1920s seem relatively tame. But for movie fans, they were groundbreaking. Although articles on movie stars appeared regularly in popular magazines, they appeared nowhere on a daily basis. Moreover, her reports were far more interesting and intimate than typical magazine fare; her column even rivaled fan magazines for detailed information about actors' private lives. With her meticulous chronicle of Hollywood happenings, Parsons brought the world behind the scenes to a wider audience than ever before. With the exception of Walter Winchell's more colorful (and more risqué) Broadway gossip column in the *New York Graphic,* there was nothing like it.[12]

The only problem with Parsons's column, however, was that it was written in New York. In 1926, after a year-long period of rest at a California resort—Parsons was suffering from tuberculosis, and Hearst financed her recuperation—Hearst urged Parsons to stay in Los Angeles and become the motion picture editor for his Universal News Service. The Hollywood writer was at last in Hollywood, and it showed in her columns, which became more intimate, detailed, and gossipy than ever. Setting up shop in an office across the street from the Hearst-owned *Los Angeles Examiner,* Parsons depended on an extensive network of informers—hairdressers, telephone operators, doormen—to keep her supplied with the latest celebrity news. In many cases, she relied on her own personal connection with stars for up-to-the-minute information. Feared by actors and film executives, Parsons was quickly welcomed into Hollywood society, where she was courted, toasted, and invited to exclusive parties. When a star, careless or inebriated, made an offhand comment, Parsons pounced. When Mary Pickford blurted out that she planned to divorce Douglas Fairbanks, the news reached Parsons's readers even before Fairbanks had been notified. As stars learned, a visit to Parsons's home could also lead to disaster. After extracting gossip from her celebrity guests, she often detained them in her home while she wrote her column, to prevent rival reporters from getting the scoop.

Not only did Parsons's new agreement with Hearst enable her to work out of Hollywood, it won her an international audience. By 1930, millions of men and women sat down to breakfast with Parsons each day; her column, now internationally syndicated, appeared in 372 newspapers throughout the world. Before long, Parsons found another way to spread gossip—over the airwaves. In 1931, she was invited by Sunkist Oranges to host a half-hour radio show featuring orchestral music, comedy, and interviews with Hollywood's most popular celebrities. Although the show earned fan letters and rave reviews, Sunkist mysteriously dropped the program after only four months. Undaunted, in 1934, she was back on the air, hosting one of the most famous programs in radio history, *Hollywood Hotel.*[13]

One of the first radio shows broadcasted from the West Coast, *Hollywood Hotel* transported millions of Americans each week to the

Orchid Room, a fictional lounge in the Hollywood Hotel where movie stars congregated after hours. Listeners were told that Parsons wandered from table to table, chatting with the guests as they dined on oysters and sipped champagne. For added authenticity, a swing orchestra played in the background; shouts of "There's Bette Davis!" and "My, doesn't Myrna Loy look gorgeous!" could be heard amidst clinking silverware and muffled conversation. Each episode centered around a featured celebrity: in one episode, Bebe Daniels discussed her new baby; in another, Joan Blondell dispensed beauty tips. In 1934, Claudette Colbert told star-struck listeners to "stay out of Hollywood" because the movie business was nothing but disappointment and hard work. "Don't I know what hard work means," replied Parsons, her voice revealing the strain of life as a columnist, radio host, and internationally renowned gossip expert.[14]

The popular program, which ran for three years, earned Parsons a following of devoted fans and an average of 800 fan letters each week. In 1937, it even became the subject of a movie, *Hollywood Hotel*, in which Parsons, naturally, portrayed herself. In the film, actor and singer Dick Powell plays a talented young man from a sleepy country town who struggles to make it big in Hollywood. Through luck and perseverance, he wins his big break—a chance to sing with the orchestra at the Hollywood Hotel—and is soon discovered by Parsons, who features him on her radio show. Although Powell's character eventually achieved movie stardom, Parsons did not. Reviewers panned her debut performance, calling it stiff and uninspired; one particularly harsh critic urged her to forget about show biz and "stick to her typewriter." Parsons may not have had the star quality necessary for screen success, but she did have the makings of another kind of celebrity. As one of the most famed and feared gossip columnists in America, Parsons had become as well known as the stars she interviewed.[15]

To many of her fans, her prominence was justly deserved. In their eyes, she was an extraordinarily talented writer and reporter with a knack for making Hollywood come to life. Throughout the 1930s, Parsons received hundreds of fan letters from young women who aspired to follow in her footsteps. "Some are so ambitious to break into the Hollywood writing game that they'll even work for [Parsons] without salary. One went so far as to offer to become a maid in the Parsons household provided she could study her syndicated writing technique," claimed one newspaper. Members of the Sigma Phi Epsilon fraternity of the University of Southern California were so enamored of her that they presented Parsons with an award for being the nation's "outstanding columnist." Many of these dedicated admirers joined together to form the Official Louella Parsons Fan Club, with branches throughout the country. The Chicago branch was so devoted that it trekked to Hollywood to visit her during one of her radio broadcasts.[16]

But many of Parsons's admirers loved her less for who she was than for what she knew. More than any fan magazine or columnist, Parsons was a walking repository of Hollywood facts. With her access to the world behind the scenes, she possessed what movie fans only dreamed of, firsthand information about Hollywood celebrities. In enthusiastic and inquisitive letters, fans showered her with pressing questions about their favorite stars. "I am a fan of Robert Montgomery," wrote one woman. "Will you please tell me the name of his wife, how old he is, what his favorite hobby is?" "How are Bebe Daniels and Ben Lyon getting along? Do the movie stars autograph their own photos? How can I correspond with Frances Dee?" asked another. Many letter-writers urged Parsons to delve even more deeply into the personal lives of the stars she interviewed. "The program with Sylvia Sidney was disappointing as the conversation was mostly of clothes," wrote one fan of *Hollywood Hotel*. "Although clothes are the utmost thought in every girl's life . . . the general public listening to your broadcast would rather like to know more about themselves [the movie stars]."[17]

But Louella Parsons, fans knew, was no ordinary columnist. Unlike most reporters, who were outsiders, Parsons was a genuine participant in the Hollywood scene. This not only lent credence to her reports, but gave the plump and plain columnist her own air of glamour, wealth, and mystery. Movie magazines frequently featured photographs of Parsons, bedecked in flowers and jewels, chatting at celebrity parties; the *Saturday Evening Post,* calling her "The First Lady of Hollywood," showed her dining with studio moguls Darryl Zanuck, Joseph Schenk, and Louis B. Mayer. To many fans, Parsons was as much a part of Hollywood as the most popular actresses. "I feel a little shaky in taking the freedom to write to you. It's almost like writing to the stars," explained one fan. "You are lucky to know such grand people; you must be grand yourself," wrote another. Some fans confessed that they felt as close to Parsons as they did to their screen idols. Actress Bebe Daniels, wrote one fan, "has been lovely to me, responding to my letters, and I feel like I know her even though I haven't met her in person. Being that you are so close to Bebe, it makes me feel like we are pals." Movie star magic, it seemed, rubbed off on those who surrounded them.[18]

Admired by fans, feared by Hollywood, and known throughout the world, by the mid-1930s Louella Parsons had become the undisputed queen of movie star gossip. No one, it seemed, could match her power and prominence. "I read your column every day for news about Norma Shearer as she is my favorite actress," wrote one admirer in 1934. "You are certainly doing your stuff when it comes to keeping movie stars before the public," wrote another. But not all Americans were eager to place their trust in the celebrity columnist. Accompanying Parsons's rise to prominence—and in general, the growth of Hollywood publicity and press coverage in the 1920s and 1930s—was a widespread undercurrent of skepticism and concern. Beneath the passion for gossip lay ambivalence, resentment, and fear.[19]

THE INFORMATION WAR

In the 1930s, Hollywood was the setting for a battle. Not a staged conflict on a studio set or a fight between two actors, but a real war with important consequences. The opponents were some of the most famous names in America—Louella Parsons, Hedda Hopper, Louis B. Mayer, Will Hays, *Photoplay* magazine—and the dispute concerned a serious matter—information. Whoever controlled news about Hollywood, they knew, controlled public opinion. And whoever controlled public opinion determined the fate of the film industry. Careers, reputations, profits—all depended on whether the right information, real or fictional, reached the public at the right time.

Fans were oblivious neither to the war nor their role in it. As some fans realized, the information they prized so dearly was part of a larger scheme to win their allegiance and earn their dollars. Although many fans trusted Hollywood news, others suspected that they were being deceived. Many fans developed a keen eye for fabricated stories; like bloodhounds, they sniffed out exaggerated hokum and phony claims. Some were so skeptical, in fact, that they went to Hollywood, armed with maps and binoculars, to learn their own firsthand truth about the stars. Hardly the gullible, uncritical spectators that they were often made out to be, many movie fans became active participants in Hollywood's ongoing battle over information.

Fans' suspicions of Hollywood news had deep roots. In the 1840s, P. T. Barnum introduced the concept of publicity ballyhoo and soon had many imitators: by the end of the century, side show barkers, theatrical press agents, and unscrupulous journalists had all made a business out of deceiving the public. Some of Barnum's most devoted disciples may have been the men who founded the film industry. In 1914, in one of the famous publicity campaigns of the early cinema, silent film vamp Theda Bara, the daughter of a Jewish tailor from Cincinnati, was described by studio press releases as a Middle Eastern princess whose name was an anagram of Arab Death. Publicity photos posed the actress in Egyptian costumes, standing in front of cardboard pyramids or atop mountains of sand.

Not surprisingly, fans quickly saw through the Bara ruse, forcing the studios to swap their exotic tales for more believable—but no less fabricated—accounts. Screen goddess Gloria Swanson, claimed press releases in the 1920s, lived in a lavish New York penthouse with a perfumed elevator and private movie theater. Rudolph Valentino, from a poor Italian peasant family, became a distinguished gentleman of refined breeding. Even though fans clamored for this information, which appeared in dozens of newspapers and magazines throughout the country, many suspected that it was not all it was cracked up to be. To confirm readers' suspicions, in 1921 *Photoplay* magazine, itself dependent on exaggerated studio press releases, warned readers of "bunk": it "is the mental perversion which causes the star, and the star's press agent, and the star's whole family to lie about everything that is the star's. If he buys a couple of pups, he has acquired a kennel; three suits are a wardrobe; one maid and a chauffeur become, in the public prints, a baronial retinue of servants." The *Saturday Evening Post* likened Hollywood publicity agents to fast-talking showmen from the days of Barnum; even Mary Pickford, in an article in *Collier's*, denounced the evils of "overactive press agenting." By the mid-1920s, magazines accused the studios of ballyhoo, studios charged the magazines with inaccuracy, and Louella Parsons argued that everyone in Hollywood, except she, had it wrong. The fight over gossip had begun, and fans were trapped in the middle.[20]

The mudslinging of the 1920s, however, seemed like a minor skirmish compared to the full-scale war of the following decade. The growing popularity of the movies had created an even greater public demand for news about Hollywood, and by the mid-1930s over 350 magazine and newspaper correspondents were stationed in the movie capital. Studios churned out a flood of sensationalistic stories for the journalists; they also intensified their regimen of publicity stunts. To win press attention, publicists falsely announced that stars were married or divorcing, had gone on elaborate shopping sprees, or were making extravagant donations to charities. Many journalists in the early 1930s, sensing that the public was growing dissatisfied with Hollywood hokum, tried to circumvent the studio publicity departments. Before long, reporters snapped candid photos of celebrities, hovered around their homes and dressing rooms, and probed them with personal questions. Outraged, the film industry quickly barred the "army of movie chatterers" from the studio lots and demanded that actors speak to no one but their press agents or official studio publicists.[21]

During this period of crackdown, the fan magazines were singled out for special treatment. Traditionally dependent on press releases and other studio publicity material for information, fan magazine writers in the early 1930s, like Hollywood news correspondents, tried increasingly to bypass the studios. *Motion Picture* and *Modern Screen,* among others, began revealing more personal and potentially scandalous information about the stars; even the traditionally more conservative *Photoplay* printed articles with titles like "Lupe [Velez] and Johnny [Weismuller] were Lovers" and "I Had to Leave John Gilbert." This minor rebellion did not go unnoticed by Will Hays, who had been hired by the film industry to protect Hollywood's public image; in 1934, Hays accused the fan magazines of "excessive sensationalism." Fearing that the Catholic Church would use the racy exposés in the fan magazines as ammunition in its fight for federal film censorship, Hays demanded that all fan magazine articles be censored by the studios. The studios, too, threatened to withdraw their advertising until the fan magazines showed greater restraint.

Not surprisingly, the fan magazines protested, and within a few weeks Hays retracted his demand. But he did exact from the magazine editors a pledge to "purge publications of sensationalism" and, with the help of studio publicity heads, he created an official "white list" of the 50 most respected fan magazine writers. Those on the list received "Hays cards" that allowed them into the studios; the 250 writers without cards were denied access. Although the approved writers were technically able to pursue their own ideas and story angles, they were carefully guided by the studios, which now edited and checked every article before publication. The MGM studio even gave fan magazine writers a monthly list of story suggestions about its stars. For Joan Crawford, recalled one reporter, writers had to "pick ideas like 'I'm Going Back to Dancing, Says Joan,' 'America's Girl Tells You How to Hold Your Man,' 'I Love The Great Outdoors,' and so on."[22]

In January 1939, however, one infamous *Photoplay* article slipped by the studios and caused a near-scandal. "Hollywood's Unmarried Husbands and Wives" revealed that several stars, including Clark Gable and Carole Lombard, Robert Taylor and Barbara Stanwyck, and Charlie Chaplin and Paulette Goddard, were living together but were not legally married. The issue sold out within hours after it hit the newsstands, and excerpts from the article were printed in newspapers throughout the country. Terrified of accusations of immorality, the studios urged the "unmarried husbands and wives" to marry as soon as possible and demanded a public apology from *Photoplay*, which they received the following month. ("The purpose of our story was to show that these relationships were so worthwhile that it was our hope that they could eventually culminate in happy marriages. We regret that the purpose of the story was misinterpreted," the magazine explained in February 1939.) Following the controversy, the film industry policed the fan magazines so carefully that they almost never contradicted the studios again.[23]

The studios' most formidable opponent in the 1930s, however, was clearly Louella Parsons. Although the studios often used her to their advantage—a carefully planted tip with Parsons could mean priceless publicity for a star—at the core they feared and despised her. Their wrath was justified: reputations could be tarnished, careers ruined, and profits destroyed by a single unflattering mention in her column. At the same time that MGM head Louis B. Mayer flattered

Parsons with gifts and praise, he encouraged former B-movie actress and aspiring journalist Hedda Hopper to try to dethrone Parsons with a column of her own. By 1942, Hopper's syndicated column had a circulation of six million, and the two gossip queens were locked in a well-publicized feud, competing viciously for publicity, readers, and the latest and most titillating Hollywood news.[24]

Everywhere fans looked lay the unmistakable signs of battle. In monthly articles and editorials, fan magazines accused their competitors of exaggeration and fabrication. Writers and journalists, including syndicated Hollywood columnists Sidney Skolsky, Sheilah Graham, Jimmy Fidler, and Walter Winchell, sometimes spent more time denouncing each other than reporting the facts. And attacking Parsons was a pastime shared by all. In 1935, a scathing article in *New Theater* claimed that the "chief function of Louella Parsons" was "to ballyhoo Marion Davies," an actress who was William Randolph Hearst's mistress. According to the *Saturday Evening Post*, Parsons was a terrible writer, unscrupulous journalist, and power-hungry opportunist who would do anything short of murder to advance her career.[25]

The biggest exposé of the information war, however, came from one of its primary participants. Aware that it faced an increasingly media-savvy audience, in 1933 the MGM studio released *Bombshell*, a hilarious satire of its own publicity methods. In the film, a press agent named Space Hanlon, played by Lee Tracy, harasses, torments, and otherwise destroys the private life of the movie star he is assigned to publicize. Hoping to get the name of Lola Burns, played by Jean Harlow, into the paper, Space deports her lover, a French marquis, and hires a crazed fan to stalk her. One of Space's biggest challenges comes when Lola announces that she wants to adopt a child. "You can't adopt a baby. The fans don't want to see the It girl surrounded by an aura of motherhood. I dubbed you the Hollywood Bombshell and that's the way they like you!" he argues. On the afternoon that representatives from the orphanage visit Lola's home, Space creates such a scene that they flee in terror, declaring the innocent and heartbroken actress an unfit mother. The spectacle, of course, makes the news the following day.

By joking with the audience about its own unscrupulous tactics, MGM tried to assure moviegoers that they were insiders, experts on rather than victims of Hollywood publicity. If the conniving press agents hurt anyone, *Bombshell* suggested, it was stars, not fans. But not all moviegoers saw things the way MGM did. Although some fans gladly consumed the gossip columns and press reports, others resented the attempts at deception. Skeptical and dissatisfied, these fans concocted strategies to beat Hollywood at its own game. In their ongoing search for authenticity, fans battled an elaborate publicity machine that was as potentially confusing and misleading as the cinema itself.

BALLYHOO

By the late 1930s, the untrustworthiness of Hollywood news—and in general, the constructed nature of film stardom—was no secret. Although some fans at the beginning of the decade may have held on to their illusions about Hollywood (*Modern Screen* reported that some fans were genuinely disappointed at *Bombshell's* "debunking"), by the end it was difficult to remain wholly idealistic. Fans knew that the film industry depended on the press, that columnists relied on sensationalism, and that much that was published was untruthful. Some fans seemed content to accept this reality. "Picture people are more or less 'dream people' to most every fan, and we prefer to keep our illusions about them, even if interviewers are forced to resort to the fictional in some cases so as not to disappoint us," explained one fan in 1935. One fan begged *Photoplay* to avoid the "too-ugly details" of stars' private lives: "Must we stand idly by and watch the glamor of the movies murdered slowly and surely by thoughtless columnists?" he asked.[26]

But others were less willing to accept the fabrication and ballyhoo. In letters to magazines, fan club journals, and fellow moviegoers, many other fans expressed their frustration with Hollywood publicity. Studio publicists, alleged one fan, insulted the public with their trumped-up stories and "deliberate falsification." "Perhaps we picture audiences are not the most intelligent in the world, but we are not altogether stupid," he wrote. Newspapers and magazines, too, said fans, filled their pages with "bunk," "hokum," and "propaganda." Even movie stars were not to be trusted. "I think divorce for publicity is a sign of weakmindedness," one woman claimed. "Gloria Swanson, John Gilbert, and some others positively disgust me."[27]

It was not that fans minded publicity for its own sake. Indeed, most fans accepted that films needed to be advertised and that actors needed public exposure. "At this age and generation," admitted one fan, "advertising plays a strong role in everything, including the motion picture." What fans did resent, however, were the studios' blatant attempts to sway public opinion. Fans wanted to choose for themselves, without pressure or influence, which actors deserved to be stars. Gloria Swanson, accused one fan, had a "overzealous press agent" who "through the newspaper tried to convince people they liked her when they didn't." One fan club president in the mid-1930s longed for the days when "stars attained their heights of popularity and box office by sheer hard work, consistent histrionic achievement, [and] smart showmanship." "Very little artificial high-pressure was used to catapult them to stardom. Now a newcomer reaches Hollywood, undergoes a very brief training course in screen technique, and is assigned to a co-starring part in a picture. Supported by an avalanche of publicity, frequently of questionable value, and with much advertising, the nonentity becomes a name," he explained.[28]

But what most offended fans were the lies. Committed to uncovering the truth about the stars, many fans despised the fibs that columnists and press agents tried to pass off on the public. Movie magazines, lamented one fan, churned out nothing but "exaggerated rumors, detrimental gossip and unconfirmed stories." A real fan magazine would report the truth, he explained, but "movie magazines are obviously not edited by and for movie fans." Nine times out of ten, wrote another disgruntled fan, newspaper stories about Hollywood could not be trusted. Even though they weren't true, "movie titles in newspapers catch the eye and sell well, so [newspapers] take every opportunity to put such headlines as 'Famous star elopes with married director,' and 'Movie actress sues for divorce,'" she explained. "Movie fans are fed up with the bunk regularly served them," complained another. "You can kid Hollywood, but you can't fool movie fans."[29]

Dependent on the press for news about stars, yet aware of the possibility of deception, fans were faced with a dilemma that had few easy solutions. One option that many fans chose was to play along with the game—to read and believe Hollywood news even though they knew it was false. Another alternative was to become cynical about *all* movie star gossip. By the end of the 1930s, some fans had become so jaded that they saw every report as publicity ballyhoo. When newspapers accurately wrote that Clara Bow had lost thousands of dollars gambling in a Nevada casino, some moviegoers attributed the report to publicity-seeking press agents. Many fans, however, chose a middle path. Rather than give up Hollywood news altogether, they became selective, placing their faith in a few trusted magazines and reporters. "Some movie magazines seem to get a great deal of pleasure out of printing ridiculous stories about the stars. But *Modern Screen's* articles are always interesting, never offensive, and the reader knows they must have truthful foundations," wrote one fan in 1936. One *Photoplay* reader praised the magazine's unwillingness to overdramatize Hollywood news. "Somehow [*Photoplay*] seems to ring true and human, without being sensational," she explained. A Louella Parsons devotee assured the columnist that she would rely on no other. "Don't worry about Walter Winchell, and give us all the news you want," she wrote. "We're for you, Louella Parsons, and we'll be listening to you next Wednesday."[30]

For many fans, intuition and common sense enabled them to distinguish the true from the false. "I'd like to find out if Katharine Hepburn is as strange and variable and gaga as the press would have us believe. Personally, I don't believe it. I think it's an act," claimed one admirer. But Ruby Keeler, he believed, was really as charming as the press depicted her. "In other words, just as I seriously doubt the Hepburn publicity, I believe almost 100 percent the Keeler publicity. I believe she is sweet and natural and that she honestly adores her husband." Only the most gullible fans, explained one moviegoer to Louella Parsons, would believe everything they heard. "Say I am laughing over that publicity story I heard over the radio last week about Anna Sten's mother throwing buckets of cold water on her to make her beautiful. These days some of the studio publicity being pulled off is a *scream*," she wrote. "To my mind, Garbo's last publicity act, the one about being in love with her new director and treating [her ex-lover John] Gilbert like the dust under her feet, is the best yet. And yet the American public goes on eating up this bosh," wrote a cynical fan in 1934.[31]

Some movie fans, like E. M. Orowitz, refused to be satisfied with the inaccurate stories and press reports. In 1935, he founded the EMO Movie Fan Club, an organization that tried to bypass the media and uncover its own truth about the stars. The club, which by 1936 had over 40,000 members, sponsored a special Research and Information Division that routinely dispatched fans to Hollywood on fact-finding missions. In an editorial in the club's monthly journal, *The Movie Fan,* Orowitz criticized the studios and the press for their feeble attempts at deception:

> Tell the movie fans the truth. They are entitled to that. If millions of them are equipped with facts instead of exaggerated rumors, they will be prepared to refute detrimental gossip and unconfirmed stories. No one can be stopped from delving deeply in research to obtain this official information.
>
> We have spent thousands of dollars in this work. We have official copies of birth certificates, marriage licenses, divorce decrees, diplomas, etc. We use this information in answering thousands of movie questions each week.

"We contend that movie fans whose shekels make the wheels of the industry go around are entitled to more consideration," he concluded. "Some day Hollywood will discover that these movie fans know more about pictures than the experts who create them." In 1936, the organization scored one of its greatest triumphs when it proved that George Raft was only five foot five, instead of five foot nine, as a studio press release reported.[32]

For some fans, birth certificates and written records were not enough. They would not be satisfied until they could view the stars with their own eyes—until they could see for themselves how tall the stars were, what they wore, and whether they were as handsome as they seemed. As early as 1910, fans clamored to see their favorite actors in person. During their war bond tour in 1917, Mary Pickford, Douglas Fairbanks, and Charlie Chaplin were met by throngs of admirers at each stop. Sometimes fans risked life and limb to see their idols. In 1920, a mad rush to see Pickford and Fairbanks honeymooning in London injured dozens of admirers; at Hollywood premieres during the 1920s and 1930s, thousands of fans pushed, shoved, and fought each other to catch a glimpse of the stars. The payoff, however, was worth the risk, said many fans. By seeing their favorite star in the flesh—and if they were lucky, shaking her hand or speaking with him—fans could achieve a sensation of intimacy with their idol. Perhaps even more important, they could answer a question that consumed millions of moviegoers throughout the nation: did stars exist in real life, and were they the same on the screen as off? As one woman explained in 1936, "I can see the pictures and judge them as actors and actresses myself. But their real characters—that is a different story. What I wish I could know is: off the screen, what are they like?"[33]

In many cases, fans reported, the stars' real and reel selves were identical. "When I met Roy Rogers in person, I found that he is one movie actor who is exactly the same in real life as he is on the screen," wrote one admirer. Gloria Jean, claimed one fan, looked just like she did in her movies: "Her large eyes are very blue, fringed with dark lashes, and the impish twinkle in them so often seen in Gloria's movies is even more apparent in real life." Sometimes stars seemed even more remarkable in person than in films. As one Irene Dunne fan told *Modern Screen,* "I have had the pleasure of meeting her and the outstanding characteristic about her, that even seemed to make one forget her rare beauty and loveliness, was her innate kindness of heart and good fellowship." Fans were thrilled to discover that they had not been deceived—their idols were really as wonderful as they appeared. Some, however, may have been in for a surprise. On a tour of the RKO Studio, one Ginger Rogers fan was shocked to see the glamorous actress chewing gum on the set. "For me, Wrigley struck down an idol," she explained. "It hadn't occurred to me that movie stars chewed gum, wheezed with head colds, or used the john."[34]

For some fans, film premieres and studio-sponsored public appearances were too brief and too staged to provide a candid, in-depth look at a star's offscreen personality. Determined to see what their favorite actors were really like, some dedicated fans tried to catch stars off guard. "The answer to every movie fan's dream is to see their idol in the flesh," explained one fan club member. "The solution, with plenty of luck added, can be found in nightclubs and resort cafes where they dine." By the 1930s, fans had become notorious for the lengths they went to see celebrities in person, behavior that sometimes verged on stalking.[35]

The first step, of course, required going to Hollywood, which was fast becoming a tourist destination for movie-struck sightseers.

Once in the movie capital, fans used their knowledge of Hollywood geography—fan magazines frequently printed the names and addresses of popular celebrity hangouts—or relied on persistence and street smarts. One fan, Herbert Strock, boasted to *Modern Screen* magazine that he had devised "ingenious methods to get at the stars." "Learning that Miss [Jean] Harlow was having lunch in a popular Hollywood restaurant, I gathered together a group of autograph collectors and induced them to stand in front of the eating place," he explained. Strock was particularly proud of his ability to spot and follow celebrities' vehicles: he had spent so much time star-watching that he had memorized "the license numbers, makes and types of automobiles owned by the various stars." Fans also used the "star tours" that had been established in Hollywood during the 1920s. For a price, local entrepreneurs would drive fans around the city, pointing out studios, celebrity nightclubs and, of course, actors' homes. By the 1930s, ferrying tourists around Hollywood had become a minor industry, with fly-by-night companies like Movieland Tours offering "thrill packed hours in the glamorous Hollywood of your dreams." "You will see the homes of the great film stars and other fascinating never-to-be-forgotten sights," it promised.[36]

Although a few fans actually saw their idols—Bing Crosby, Myrna Loy, and Claudette Colbert, among others, were particularly receptive to fan visits—most were not so fortunate. According to the *Washington Herald,* 11 out of 12 movie-crazy fans who visited Hollywood were unable to meet their favorite stars in person. In 1936, the Hollywood Chamber of Commerce dealt with over 300 of these fans each month. While some fans admitted defeat and went back to their homes, others refused to give up. "Sometimes if a hero worshipper is very determined (and insists he will keep on coming back until he meets his favorite) an effort is made to reach the star," reported the *Herald.* When one admirer of John Boles refused to leave Hollywood, the Travelers' Aid Society at last arranged a meeting with the actor. Satisfied, she went home the following day. Other fans resorted to more drastic measures. In 1932, two Jean Harlow fans, knowing that the actress was ill, tried to enter her home disguised as nurses. Two years later, another fan, John Stoneburg, followed Harlow around the studio until he was arrested by the Los Angeles police. Jeanette MacDonald's fans pursued her in groups: when the actress married

Gene Raymond in 1937, over 1,500 fans, who had somehow learned the location of the wedding, camped out on the church lawn.[37]

For the lucky and persistent fans who were able to see the stars in person, the thrill was tremendous. "Should anyone ever ask me if I believe in miracles," wrote one fan after seeing Deanna Durbin in Hollywood, "you may be sure I shall answer most emphatically yes, because my wish came true. I met Deanna." Meeting Billie Dove, admitted one fan in 1939, was "the one thing exciting and thrilling that has happened to me." For a few moments, fans could see their beloved idols in person. Without relying on the press, they could experience firsthand the reality behind the screen.[38]

Although many fans continued to rely on fact-finding missions or sightseeing visits to Hollywood, others found a more effective way to connect with their favorite celebrities. By joining an official fan club, fans were able to forge a direct, personal link to their idol, who updated them on his or her latest activities, wrote them letters, and even met them in person. Some of the most skeptical movie fans, fan club members saw their activities as a way to combat the media and the Hollywood publicity machine. No longer dependent on columnists, press agents, or fan magazines, club members could become their own experts on the offscreen life of their favorite star.

WITH A GRAIN OF SALT

To believe or not to believe—that was the question for movie fans in the 1930s. Throughout the decade, millions of fans struggled to reconcile their passion for Hollywood news with the possibility of deception. Some fans trusted Hollywood gossip in spite of its reputation for exaggeration. Others were much more skeptical of the media's ability to deliver the truth. Part of this cynicism resulted from Hollywood's information war, the conflicting, sensationalistic, and often highly contested celebrity journalism that flooded newsstands during the 1930s. A greater part of fans' skepticism, however, might be traced to a growing national awareness of the politics of publicity and image creation. After more than two decades in a modern society, one dominated by the constant presence of the mass media, many Americans had grown unable to trust fully all that they read and heard. "I never believe anything that has not been proven in court," said one *Photoplay* reader who denounced the "yellow journals" and "scandal-mongers" that reported on movie stars. "If some extra clouts his wife on the bean, you can be sure that the papers will have it, WELL KNOWN ACTOR ARRESTED FOR WIFE BEATING," explained another fan in 1932. "Newspapers are always ready to pounce upon some petty fault or transgression, magnify it, and spread it all over the front page." Like many Americans, he had learned to take all news "with a grain of salt."[39]

Rather than dampen fans' enthusiasm, however, the potential distortions of Hollywood journalism actually spurred them to greater activism. Uncomfortable with the possibility of deception and willing to expend great energy in pursuit of the truth, the media-savvy fans of the 1930s vigorously and actively challenged the press. They pointed out journalists' mistakes, complained about inaccuracies, and exposed exaggeration. In a world of white lies, half-truths, and ballyhoo, fans frequently took their quest for authenticity into their own hands.

CHAPTER FIVE

THE MOVIE STAR FAN CLUB

IN AUGUST 1934, HUNDREDS OF DELEGATES from around the nation assembled in the Knickerbocker Hotel in Chicago for an important meeting. Around a large table in the hotel's Silver Room, the delegates meticulously planned the future of their organization. What were their goals and objectives? they asked. Toward what should they aim? By the end of the discussion they had reached a conclusion: in the year ahead lay growth. "Plans for increased activities and further development make the coming year look like a big one," read the official postconference report. As they left the convention, the delegates vowed to work diligently in the months ahead and to meet again the following August.[1]

Had the delegates been heads of corporations, the convention and resolution would have been typical. Had they been advertising executives or government officials, the meeting would have been routine. But the participants were movie fans, and the conference, the Second Annual National Convention of Movie Fan Clubs, the brainchild of a nationwide federation called the Movie Club Guild. The hundreds of fans who attended the event promised to expand their clubs, host a variety of activities in the coming year, and publicize the many virtues of film fandom.

To many observers, the idea of a fan club convention might have seemed somewhat unusual if not astonishing. Most Americans saw fan clubs as juvenile and trivial—in the words of one critic, they were "inane little clots of adulation" centered around mindless hero-worship. Yet as the activities of the second annual national convention suggest, the reality was much different. More than mere cheerleaders or admiration societies, movie fan clubs in the 1930s and 1940s were often serious and highly organized. They were ambitious, hard working, and diligent. Many club members saw themselves not only as movie fans but as the watchdogs of mass culture, vigilantes against Hollywood's corruption and deception.[2]

The men and women who joined fan clubs loved the movies. They admired the beauty and talent of their favorite stars and the creative vision of skillful directors. But there was one facet of Hollywood that they often did not respect. Some of the most skeptical of all movie fans, fan club members distrusted the studio executives, publicists, and journalists who made the movie capital their home. These fans worked not only to celebrate actors but to protect them from an industry in which glamour prevailed over genuineness, rumor over truth, and profit over everything.

A major part of this campaign involved what came to be known as "boosting." Believing in strength in numbers, club members banded together and wrote hundreds of letters to studios demanding better roles and greater publicity for their idol. Dissatisfied with the inside deals and publicity stunts that turned unworthy actors into celebrities, fan clubs envisioned a more democratic process of star-making, in which an actor's talent and integrity, not to mention the force of public opinion, actually mattered.

In spite of their apparent generosity, however, fans demanded a price for their efforts: the continued cooperation and support of their honored star. Most official fan clubs maintained relationships with their idols, who provided them with autographed photos, updates about their latest activities, and occasionally even met them in person. For many fans, this relationship with the actors, and the personal information that they provided, was one of the biggest rewards of the fan club experience. No longer dependent on gossip columns and magazines, fan clubs managed to become their own experts on the private life of their favorite celebrity.

Fan clubs, of course, were not only about activism and hard work. Amidst the letter writing campaigns and meetings, fan club members socialized and shared dreams with one another. They discussed the movies, confessed secrets, and forged friendships that would last for years. But beneath the camaraderie and enthusiasm for the cinema lay serious concerns and complaints. Clipping photos from magazines one hour and writing an angry letter in another, planning a club party for Sunday and a protest for Monday, fan clubs in the 1930s and 1940s combined their work and play, praise and complaint, into a single labor of love.

THE HISTORY OF THE FAN CLUB

The history of the movie star fan club is almost as old as the movie star. Not long after the creation of the motion picture star system in 1910, enthusiastic moviegoers began forming organizations in honor of popular actors. Although *Motion Picture Story,* the nation's first fan magazine, advised the fledgling clubs to "promote a higher standard in the moving picture" through serious study and discussion of the latest films, most fans had another purpose in mind. Like the Rah Rah Girls, an early group devoted to collecting star photos, or the Pansy Correspondence Club that joined together to write fan letters, the typical club was formed to praise, celebrate, and forge contact with its favorite stars.[3]

Many of these early groups were casual. One group, founded in 1912 in Winnipeg, Canada, met every Thursday night to sip refreshments, chat about its favorite stars, and clip photos from fan magazines. Another club, in Appleton, Wisconsin, "didn't do anything novel," its leader confessed. "We all sat around the table . . . and spoke of the different pictures we were anxious to see, and of the framed portraits of our favorites on the walls." One of the members of the Bill Hart Tribe, named in honor of cowboy star William S. Hart, admitted in 1919 that the group spent all its time "going to movies and buying movie books."[4]

As motion pictures gained greater popularity, and as more and more Americans became movie fans, many clubs began to trade their easy informality for greater seriousness and professionalism. Contrary to what is often assumed, film studios rarely if ever initiated fan clubs for their stars. Although there are a few famous cases of studio-sponsored fan clubs—in the early 1930s, the MGM studio helped organize a series of "Platinum Blonde Clubs" to promote Jean Harlow—the vast majority of fan organizations were started by the fans themselves. By the mid-1920s, many fan clubs issued membership cards, elected officers, and even screened potential members before admitting them. At weekly meetings, groups planned a full slate of activities: preparing for club parties, petitioning theater managers to show their star's films, even holding a fund-raising drive for a local charity. Although informal groups continued to exist—like the ten-member Movie Star Trading Club or one neighborhood's Kit Kat Club that held meetings on the sidewalk—they were increasingly overshadowed by the larger, more elaborate clubs that attracted hundreds, even thousands of members.[5]

The Norma Talmadge Fan Club, founded in Cleveland in 1924, was a typical example of this new breed of ambitious and meticulously organized fan club. Founder and president Constance Riquer spent hours each day planning fan activities, working on the monthly club journal, and corresponding with club members who lived too far away to attend group meetings. When one of Talmadge's films was playing in Columbus, Riquer planned a group excursion to the city, where club members plastered posters for the upcoming film in windows and theaters. When *Picture Play* magazine interviewed Riquer in 1925, she and her 500 fellow members were busy writing letters to several well-known actors, inviting them to become honorary members of the Talmadge club. "Do not start [fan club] activities with the idea that you can carry on in your spare time," *Picture Play* warned its readers. "Be prepared to give to the undertaking *all* your time and energy, and some money."[6]

Even though they were diligent and dedicated, most of these clubs had another side—spontaneous, light-hearted, even silly. In 1922, the Bug Club, a group that honored actors Monte Blue, Lillian Gish, Harold Lloyd, and Colleen Moore, held a dance to which each member brought an escort dressed as a movie celebrity. Members wore "bug rings," "cheap plastic rings with a bug made of sealing wax on it," and greeted each other with a secret sign. The Pickbanks Movie Fan

Club, named after Mary Pickford and Douglas Fairbanks, performed scenes from their favorite films, complete with elaborate sets and costumes, for a neighborhood audience. The Movie Fans Friendship Club of Staunton, Illinois, sent gifts and greetings to members who were sick. Many groups tried to outdo each other with more witty and creative titles for their club journals: the Billie Dove Club published "Dove Tales," the Joan Crawford Club "The Crawford Chatter," and Gloria Stuart's fans "The Gloria-ous News."[7]

Whether they gave hours each day or only a few minutes to club activity, whether they were informal or serious, movie fans recognized that the mere act of joining a club was a sign of devotion. Unlike casual fans, who wrote an occasional letter to an actor or sometimes perused movie magazines, the fan club member made a commitment, both to the group and to the honored star. Even the least involved club member was expected to pay dues, help with the club journal, and, if the fan lived near club headquarters, to attend meetings. Fans were also encouraged to help with annual membership drives by urging friends to join the group. As Constance Riquer put it, joining a club symbolized that a fan had passed beyond the stage of mere infatuation or "burning adoration." Being a club member meant that a fan not only worshiped a star but agreed to work on his or her behalf.[8]

By the 1930s, millions of dedicated fans had banded together in clubs ranging from small neighborhood groups to the Shirley Temple Fan Club, whose 384 branches contained over 3,800,000 members. Each week these fans spent thousands of dollars on membership fees, traveled hundreds of miles to attend meetings and conventions, and devoted countless hours to organizing and planning. In the early 1930s, *Photoplay* magazine received so many letters expressing interest in fan clubs that it initiated "The Fan Club Corner," a monthly column of the latest activities and accomplishments in the fan club world. "Movie fan clubs are growing in number and popularity," it reported in 1935. "Groups of movie-minded people in every locality are busy organizing clubs to sponsor their favorite screen stars."

> The Bing Crosby Fan Club is starting its fourth year. Congratulations! Bing sent a congratulatory program for the club's birthday celebration, attended by the members.

"The Chronicle" is the new publication of the Ginger Rogers Club. The last issue of their club news contains the names of the sixty-seven active members and much news of the happenings of the club. Marion Hesse is president.

Members of the Gloria Stuart Fan Club are extremely happy over their new membership cards. These were furnished to the club by Miss Stuart herself and are personally autographed. A birthday party in honor of Miss Stuart was held by members of the Chicago branch.[9]

For some dedicated admirers, fan club activity became a passion if not an obsession. "I am working every night on the club work and often give up personal pleasures to promote the club, and I find more interesting pleasure in the club work than in other outdoor pleasures or shows," confessed the president of the Buster Collier Fan Club. Another club president confessed that she could not wait to finish high school so that she could devote herself fully to fan activity. "Well that's over," she said after she finally graduated. "Now I can give *all* my time to the fan club." As fans repeatedly admitted, participating in fan clubs required dedication, commitment, and hard work. But the effort was worth it, they explained, for it was all to the glory of their favorite stars.[10]

SINCERITY AND AUTHENTICITY

For many fan club members, their honored star was more than just a talented and attractive actor or actress. Although fans often raved about their star's dramatic ability and spoke passionately about her face or his physique, what drew them most to their idol, they claimed, were the inner qualities of warmth, sincerity, and compassion. Of course, most fans had never met their idol in person, but that did not prevent them from drawing conclusions about personal characteristics. To many fans, the way an actress presented herself on screen—her sweet smile, sincere expressions, or gentle voice—accurately revealed her true persona. "You are very kind and gentle," wrote an admirer to Jennifer Jones. "One can tell just by looking at you."[11]

Fans showered stars with praise. They called them "sweet," "distinctive," and "generous." Guy Madison, one fan wrote, embodied "all the ideals of young manhood"; Jennifer Jones was "the perfect model of American womanhood." But none of these could compare with the highest compliment that a fan could give a star—that of being sincere. It took a rare and remarkable individual, they believed, to remain genuine and unaffected in the face of stardom. Fans repeatedly told their idols how their simplicity and honesty contrasted with the artificiality of other celebrities. "You're so different from the other stars, with your down to earth naturalness," a woman told Johnny Sands. "You're different from any actor I have ever seen—so human and natural," raved a fan to Joseph Cotten. "The screen needs people like you—people that are real," one woman explained to Dorothy McGuire.[12]

Critical of the notorious celebrity lifestyle—wild parties, alcohol, and divorces—many fans praised their idols for having resisted Hollywood's corrupt values. "She is the sweetest, most considerate, most generous, daintiest, most genteel woman I have ever met," wrote one fan about Billie Dove. "She has none of the wild qualities of some of the other Hollywood stars. She does not drink, smoke, nor curse. While a certain amount of publicity is necessary for one in her position, she does not seek the glamorous, scandalous kind, as some of them do." Unlike other actresses, Esther Williams, said one fan, "is a perfect example of all that is good and pure. Her natural, neat and clean appearance is a grand example for women of all ages." Because fans tended to see their idols as role models if not friends, they wanted to believe that stars possessed qualities they would desire in a confidante or companion. Often quite morally conservative, fans praised such values as "wholesomeness," "humility," and "selflessness" in a star, while condemning evidence of "fast living" or sexual impropriety.[13]

Many fans believed so deeply in their stars' honesty and virtues, in fact, that they sponsored charitable activities in their honor. "Because we recognize his basic goodness and his sympathy for the unfortunate and his interest in them, we members consider the prime purpose of our fan club to honor our star by doing as much good as we possibly can in his name," explained the president of the Roy Rogers Fan Club. Inspired by the kindness of their honored star, the Alan Ladd Fan Club collected funds to buy a radio for an amputees' ward. One of the most ambitious and respected fan clubs of the 1930s and 1940s, the Ramon Novarro Service League sponsored a Ramon Novarro Bed at a home for destitute men, donated food and clothing to charities, and even supported an animal welfare branch that sheltered stray cats and dogs.[14]

Because their stars were so extraordinary, fans believed that they should be praised, publicized, and shared with the rest of the world. Sincere and down to earth, their stars countered the negative influence of the slick sophisticates and glamour girls who too often rose to fame. At the same time, because they were so genuine and innocent, they were particularly vulnerable to the abuses of malicious reporters and money-hungry studio executives. Fans needed not only to promote their stars but to protect them from the abuses of the Hollywood system.

These two imperatives met in an activity that came to be known in the fan club world as "boosting." Boosting meant doing everything in one's power to publicize a star—writing letters to fan magazines, urging theaters to play their star's films, and convincing friends of the actor's excellence. It also involved defending the star from mismanagement. Believing that studios exploited actors and sometimes ruined their careers, fans wrote hundreds of letters to film executives demanding that their star receive better and more prominent roles. Believing that the media promoted glamour rather than substance, they pressured magazines to run articles on their actor's great talent and virtue. For many fan clubs, boosting was not just the focus of group activity but a serious matter involving honor, integrity, and pride.

BOOSTING

Since the earliest days of the motion picture, fans have always been inquisitive about what went on behind the scenes. In response to a flood of questions from readers, fan magazines ran hundreds of articles that attempted to unravel the mysteries of movie-making—how screenplays were written, movies filmed, actors trained. Many early films, too, catered to the curiosities of eager fans. A series of movies, including *A Vitagraph Romance* (1912) and *Mabel's Dramatic Career* (1913), and two Charlie Chaplin films, *A Film Johnnie* (1914) and *His New Job* (1915), dramatized the joys and pitfalls of filmmaking for all the world to see.

Inundated with information about the inner workings of the studio system, many fans soon considered themselves full-fledged movie experts. Fans could proudly explain how stunts were performed, costumes made, and sets built. They knew that actors needed studios for contracts and studios needed stars to draw audiences. They learned that studios depended heavily on the press for publicity and advertising. They also had the inside scoop on a topic that fascinated audiences throughout the country—how actors were transformed into stars.

As moviegoers generally agreed, it took talent and charm to make a star. No actor could hope to succeed without a requisite amount of beauty, charisma, and dramatic ability. Even though publicity agents tried to conceal an actor's lack of talent with glamorous photos and media campaigns, the publicity-made star could not shine for long. When one movie critic claimed that actress Colleen Moore had more publicity than ability, fans rebelled. "Is Colleen Moore a publicity-made actress? Well I should say not!" responded one fan. "Anyone with common sense can see that she isn't. Colleen has won stardom by her many marvelous portrayals. I think she has rightfully earned her place among the leading actresses."[15]

But publicity, fans realized, was not always deceptive. Without a healthy dose of positive press, even the most skilled and deserving actor would never gain the following needed for stardom. Prominent roles were crucial, too—without important and visible parts in films, actors and actresses might never have a chance to display their talents. As fan magazines frequently reported, countless stars had moved out of the spotlight when they were miscast, underpublicized, or misrepresented by the media. Popular actor Francis X. Bushman, for example, was ruined when magazines in 1918 ran scandalous reports about his home life. Florence Turner's popularity fatally declined when her studio refused to grant her leading parts.

Fearing that their favorite actors would meet a similar fate, many early film fans used their knowledge of Hollywood to assist their idols with their precarious careers. In 1914, one of Florence Lawrence's fans wrote a string of letters to studio executives demanding more prominent roles for the actress. She also offered to help Monte Katterjohn, Lawrence's biographer and press agent, with magazine and newspaper publicity. "Now I want Mr. Katterjohn to know that we people 'out front' are only too eager to do our share to help put our darling where she belongs—20 miles higher than Mary Pickford in the clouds," she wrote to Lawrence. Another devoted admirer, passionate about fashionable actress Gloria Swanson, told *Picture Play* magazine that he had been her "unofficial press agent" for years. When his friends claimed that Swanson was "nothing but a clothes horse," he staunchly defended her. "I knew that she could act. I had faith in her. For years I have boosted her and told people to wake up and see her possibilities," he explained.[16]

By the 1920s, promoting or boosting a star was absolutely essential for any serious movie fan. As one fan explained in 1925, dedicated admirers did more than just collect autographs or photos. It was only when one agreed to help a star, she claimed, that one became a *true* movie fan. It was from this rage for boosting that many fan clubs were formed. Realizing that boosting worked better when done in groups—studios might ignore a single letter of complaint but could not overlook hundreds—fans joined together to support, publicize, and defend their star from any insult or injustice.

Boosting, as it turned out, was a perfect club activity. Simple and inexpensive—most campaigns required only pens, paper, stamps, and sometimes theater tickets—it could be conducted year-round. Moreover, it was appropriate at nearly any stage in an actor's career. Stars at their peak, fans reasoned, needed as much publicity as one whose career was just beginning. The Alan Ladd club admitted to "bombarding the magazines, studio and broadcasting stations with letters" while the actor's career was flourishing in the mid-1940s. The Esther Williams club printed the addresses of several fan magazines in its monthly journal and encouraged members to "write regularly and let the editors know you want more pictures and articles on Esther. When writing, suggest that they have Esther [as] cover girl." Some clubs even boosted stars who were no longer living. The Wallace Reid Memorial Club, created shortly after the actor's death in 1923, organized to raise funds for a memorial and pressure Reid's former studio to reissue his films.[17]

One of the most appropriate times for boosting, however, was when an actor's career was in transition; in particular, when he faced a chance at promotion. In 1937, when producer David O. Selznick announced that he was casting the role of Scarlett O'Hara for the upcoming production of *Gone with the Wind*, dozens of fan clubs sensed opportunity knocking. Before long, Selznick was barraged with letters, many of them from fan clubs, advocating different actresses for the part. The Joan Crawford club mailed ten letters each day on behalf of their star, while the Paulette Goddard club sent a petition signed by over 100 members. Organizations honoring Katharine Hepburn, Bette Davis, and Norma Shearer also submitted hundreds of urgent letters and pleas. (The actress who finally won the part, Vivien Leigh, was perhaps the only candidate without an organized fan club at the time.) In their enthusiasm to boost their star, clubs often criticized potential rivals. One Boston club, after having discussed the issue at a weekly meeting, unanimously decided that Clark Gable was "hopelessly inadequate" for the part of Rhett Butler. "He is too crude a personality and would be utterly incapable of portraying the character acceptably," the group concluded.[18]

Hollywood newcomers also needed boosting to attract the attention of the studios and the press. After Guy Madison appeared in a bit part in a Selznick film, fans across the nation formed clubs to boost the handsome young actor to stardom. Pressured by hundreds of letters, Selznick gave the young actor a more prominent role in his next film. The president of one branch of the Guy Madison Fan Club revealed his tactics: "I used to get my 25 odd members to write letters to *Modern Screen* magazine each month and Guy got so high that they had to feature him. After that everyone knew who he was and what he looked like and they started sending fan mail to Selznick and to other magazines." Once Madison achieved fame, however, many fans believed that there was no longer a need for the club. "He is so popular that he doesn't need a fan club anymore," one member explained. "A fan club's for some crumb who wants to get up and needs a following. Our job is really finished because we got Guy there."[19]

It was character actors who required the most support, according to the EMO fan club, a national organization devoted to several different stars. Because they were neither glamorous nor scandalous, these actors were overlooked by the press and faced few chances at stardom. "One of the most pitiful situations in Hollywood concerns the character actor. Audiences know their faces but not their names because they have received comparatively little publicity or exploitation," the newsletter explained in 1936.

> We propose to right this wrong. After you enjoy a picture and like the work of a character player, please write a letter to your theater manager. Tell the manager you enjoyed the actor. These expressions will be relayed to Hollywood where casting directors will get a better understanding of movie fans' likes and dislikes.
>
> Movie fans can do a lot of things to help where aid is necessary. Assistance in giving screen character players a break has been missed by fan magazines. But those publications are obviously not edited by and for movie fans.

"Let's not forget them because the gossipers and others pay no attention to them," it concluded. "Movie fans are human, kind, and above all, a powerful influence."[20]

But no situation sparked more aggressive boosting than when studios seemed to ignore, mishandle, or otherwise jeopardize the career of their honored celebrity. Members of the Jeanette MacDonald fan club wrote "An Open Letter to Metro-Goldwyn-Mayer" when they felt that directors and studio executives were, through carelessness, damaging MacDonald's career. Although they praised MacDonald's performance in the 1938 film *Sweethearts,* they criticized the studio for portraying her in unattractive poses and urged MGM to appoint an official who would ensure that all film images of MacDonald were flattering.[21]

Fan clubs also mobilized when they sensed that their star's popularity was on the decline. When Rory Calhoun was unable to find work following his debut role in *The Red House* (1947), fan clubs sent over 2,000 letters a week to studios demanding that he be cast in an upcoming film. The successful campaign, and the role Calhoun eventually received, propelled the actor to new heights of success. When Gene Autry was in the Army, his club "kept his name alive by their postcard patrol. It waged most effective contact with the fan magazines," reported one club journal. In some cases, struggling actors directly appealed to fans for assistance. Worried about small turnouts on his public appearance tour, actor Jimmy Wakely sent out letters to his fan clubs. As a result, hundreds of fans were waiting to welcome him at every stop.[22]

Fan clubs were deeply offended when their stars were snubbed or publicly insulted. When a magazine proclaimed in 1948 that June Allyson was one of the worst-dressed women in Hollywood, her club responded with a 90-foot long letter of protest signed by 19,000 members. After Gloria Swanson was nominated but failed to win the Oscar for Best Actress in 1951, her fan club sent angry letters to the Academy criticizing their misjudgment and accusing them of corruption. In a letter to Swanson, club members explained, "We are all pretty disgusted at the way the awards went and feel there were many 'behind the scenes' matters that influenced the outcome. [We] have nothing but disgust for them."[23]

Sometimes fans were so infuriated that they sent letters directly to actors, urging them to resist exploitation by the studios. Afraid that their stars would be miscast, fans insisted that they reject roles that were demeaning or threatened their screen image. "Please don't let them make a vamp out of you as you will be ruined," one fan told Jennifer Jones. "We like you as the sweet type." "Do not let them give you parts which do not do full justice to your extraordinary talents," insisted another. Admirers repeatedly begged Ingrid Bergman not to change her simple and natural style, nor to allow herself to be slandered by the press. "Do not become glamorized!" wrote one fan. "Do not allow yourself to be stereotyped by magazines." One fan, disappointed with a recent performance, urged Guy Madison to stand up for better roles: "Just recently saw your latest release and must tell you that I was deeply disappointed," he wrote. "The plot was weak and at times silly. I sat through a feature of truly inferior value. You can do better than that, Guy. Don't let those money hungry studio bosses hand you a script that makes a monkey out of you."[24]

Fans also offered stars suggestions and advice on their acting. Knowing that just one poor performance could earn them the unflattering distinction of being box-office poison, fans urged their idols to exercise great control and caution. One fan, who had recently watched Greta Garbo in the film *Love,* warned her that "the scenes with the child were very touching, although I did not find you convincing here as in your scenes with Mr. Gilbert." "As a singer may I make a suggestion?" wrote one fan to Gloria Swanson. "Do work like the Dickens on your breathing. You simply must have your breath control." Another Swanson fan, who had recently seen *The Trespasser* (1929), sent in a full list of complaints:

> I was disappointed in your acting only twice. The first scene in which Marion asked Jack to send his father away seemed a little overdrawn. It didn't sound sincere and the contrast with the rest of the picture was disappointing. I have two other slight criticisms to make: a tendency to raise your left hand and clutch it in mid air. It is expressive but please don't do it too often. Also please don't burst into song for no apparent reason.

Because they felt great intimacy with their idols, because they perceived them as friends rather than strangers, fans thought they had a right to advise them. Believing themselves personally responsible for their idols' successes or failures, fans often felt obligated to help perfect their acting techniques.[25]

To some observers, all this advice-giving and letter-writing may have seemed frivolous, overzealous, even self-righteous. One critic called it "commercial and calculating," while another characterized it as capricious and vengeful. Fan clubs, of course, believed otherwise. In their eyes, boosting promoted talent, integrity, and substance over the superficiality of the Hollywood system. It forced studios and the press to remain responsive to audience demands. It helped actors turn out consistently stellar performances. And it enabled fans to thank their idols for countless hours of joy and entertainment. As one fan wrote to Billie Dove, boosting enabled her to express "gratitude for the beautiful hours you have given to me, for the inspiration your charm has caused me to feel."[26]

But fan clubs were not entirely altruistic. For all their campaigning and promoting, they demanded a price: the continued support and attention of their honored star. When stars failed to uphold their end of the bargain, when they ignored, overlooked, or otherwise disappointed their clubs, fans rebelled with harsh words and angry letters. Sometimes they even disbanded clubs, transferring their attention to

1. In response to pressure from curious fans, in March 1910, IMP studio head Carl Laemmle revealed the name of his new leading actress—Florence Lawrence. The movie star system was born. (Academy of Motion Picture Arts and Sciences)

2. "Mary Pickford is pretty. . . . But her ornamental attributes, including her curls, are only the garnishings of something far more durable—a magnetic personality," wrote one fan in 1923. (Photofest, reprinted with permission)

3. In a famous ad campaign from the early 1920s, Mary Pickford lent her name and image to Pompeian Beauty Products. For ten cents, Pompeian issued customers a color portrait depicting Pickford's "rare beauty and charm," along with five product samples. (Author's personal collection)

4. Douglas Fairbanks displayed his famous vigor and personality in *The Thief of Baghdad* (1924). (Author's personal collection)

5. Clara Bow, known to movie fans as the It girl. In the late 1920s, the rise of It, and of the movie star as an icon of glamour and sexuality, was contemporaneous with the decline in popularity of Mary Pickford, Douglas Fairbanks, and their brand of wholesome personality. (Photofest, reprinted with permission)

6. Gloria Swanson signs autographs at a 1934 Hollywood premiere, while actor Herbert Marshall appears bored. During the 1920s and 1930s, thousands of fans pushed, shoved, and fought each other to catch a glimpse of the stars. By seeing their favorite star in the flesh and, if they were lucky, shaking the star's hand or speaking with him or her, fans hoped to achieve a sensation of intimacy with their idol. (Photofest, reprinted with permission)

7. Louella Parsons played herself in the 1937 film *Hollywood Hotel*. Reviewers panned her performance, calling it stiff and uninspired; one critic urged her to "stick to her typewriter." (Photofest, reprinted with permission)

8. Unlike most reporters, Louella Parsons was a genuine participant in the Hollywood scene. Movie magazines frequently featured photographs of Parsons, bedecked in flowers and jewelry, chatting at celebrity parties, as here, in 1942 with film stars Errol Flynn and Joan Crawford. (Photofest, reprinted with permission)

9. Clark Gable in *Gone with the Wind* (1939). Pressured by hundreds of fan letters, producer David O. Selznick agreed to cast Gable as Rhett Butler even though it meant sharing the film's profits with MGM. (Photofest, reprinted with permission)

MPGP-7874

10. Before: Joan Crawford, Hollywood's quintessential flapper, in *Sally, Irene and Mary* (1925). (Photofest, reprinted with permission)

11. (right) After: Crawford, recast as a working girl, in *Grand Hotel* (1932). (Photofest, reprinted with permission)

12. To support Greta Garbo's screen image, the MGM publicity department sent out a series of photos and articles that portrayed the actress as a seductive, brooding temptress. (Photofest, reprinted with permission)

13. Rudolph Valentino in the film that made him famous, *The Sheik* (1921), with costar Agnes Ayres. At Valentino's funeral six years later, thousands of men and women massed in Manhattan streets around the funeral parlor to catch a glimpse of the actor lying in state. (Author's personal collection)

14. To convince audiences that Clark Gable was as rugged in person as he appeared on the screen, MGM released a series of publicity photos that depicted the actor as an avid outdoorsman. (Photofest, reprinted with permission)

15. Frank Sinatra mobbed by fans before a New York concert. The fan frenzy over Frank Sinatra, reported the *New Republic,* was "a terrifying phenomenon of mass hysteria that is seen only two or three times in a century." (Photofest, reprinted with permission)

16. (following page) Jeanette MacDonald in *Sweethearts* (1938). Fans complained that MacDonald had been portrayed in "unattractive poses" in the film and urged MGM to appoint an official to ensure that all future images of the actress were flattering. (Photofest, reprinted with permission)

another, more cooperative celebrity. After all, fans reasoned, the star who was too Hollywood, who became too arrogant to fraternize with admirers, did not deserve a club. That actor had lost sight of the most fundamental principle of stardom: that fans could destroy a star as easily as they could make one.

A DIRECT CONNECTION TO THE STARS

Although thousands of fan clubs formed between 1910 and the 1950s, not all of them were official. Unlike many informal clubs, which existed unbeknownst to their idols, the official club had organized with the approval of its honored star. Would-be club presidents typically wrote to their idol, requesting permission before admitting members to the group. When Georgina Murray decided to form a club for Gloria Swanson, for example, she sent a letter informing the actress of her plans. Weeks later, she received Swanson's enthusiastic blessings: "Of course you may start a fan club. I will send you a photo soon and I wish you the best of luck in the new club." The Official Gloria Swanson Fan Club, called The First Lady, was under way.[27]

With permission came a host of benefits. A mark of legitimacy, official status meant that a club was serious rather than frivolous, that it existed to help to honor a star, rather than to steal money from gullible fans as did a widely publicized ring of illegitimate fan clubs in the 1930s. It also meant that a club promoted the accepted truth about a star, rather than unfounded rumors. So important was official authorization that *Movieland* magazine, which ran a monthly column on fan clubs, refused to print news from any club that could not furnish proof of celebrity endorsement.[28]

But there was another important reason why fan clubs so eagerly sought permission. Although the agreement was never written or formal, a star entered a kind of unspoken contract by endorsing an official fan club. In return for support and boosting, the star agreed to maintain contact with the organization—to send autographed photos, correspond with members, and keep the group posted on his or her latest activities. For many fans, this personal contact with the star made their diligence and letter-writing worthwhile. Rather than depend on the mass media for news and information about the stars, fans could see, firsthand, what their idols were really like. As the president of the Deanna Durbin Devotees admitted in 1941, the group was formed not only to boost the actress, but "to provide a closer contact with the star than is possible through ordinary channels of newspaper and magazine publicity."[29]

Perhaps the greatest thrill for many fans was meeting their honored star in person. Stars often went out of their way to visit their fan clubs; others arranged to meet with members during public appearance tours. Actress and singer Jeanette MacDonald, who went on national concert tours, invited fan club members to meet her backstage and even fired a Philadelphia theater manager who refused to let her meet with her fans. Popular young Deanna Durbin, who was honored by one of the largest and most publicized fan clubs of the 1940s, chose to meet her fans on the sets of her films.[30]

Fan club members were excited—and perhaps a bit relieved—when they discovered that their idols seemed the same in person as in the movies. "When I met Roy Rogers in person, I found that he is one movie actor who is exactly the same in real life as he is on the screen," wrote club president Jean Meade. Others may have been more dismayed than pleased. According to one of Gloria Swanson's friends, when the actress went to visit a fan club in New York, she was appalled that the members, sitting in chairs, did not rise to greet her. "After viewing the group, she told them loudly that they should stand up. Didn't they know that when an older person enters a room they should respect that person? She told them that she was older than anybody in that room and was entitled to the respect due older people. And with that she exited the room and the gathering."[31]

Whether exciting or shocking, the experience of personally meeting a star was rare. A few lucky club presidents may have seen their stars on a regular basis, but the majority of fans counted one, perhaps two encounters in a lifetime. In lieu of direct personal contact, most clubs maintained their relationship with their star through correspondence, in particular, through the monthly letters that stars frequently sent to their organizations. Warm and personal, these letters often gave fans the sensation that they were dear and treasured friends, chatting with their star over a cup of tea. "Hi everybody! Are you having wonderful vacations? I certainly am!" Esther Williams wrote to her fan club. "My work at the studio is completed, including interviews and publicity of all types and now I can settle down and enjoy the waiting for my baby. It's the most wonderful time for me. Thank you, too, for all your nice letters to me and if we don't always get the answers right back just be patient. My mom and I do most of the fan mail ourselves and sometimes we're a little snowed under."[32]

Fan clubs cherished these letters and printed them prominently in their monthly club journals. With their simple, friendly tone, the notes conveyed not only warmth and sincerity, but something else that was equally prized in the fan club world: personal information. Learning the details of an actor's private life had always been an important goal of movie fans. Not only did it enable them to feel close to their star, in possession of the kind of detailed, familiar knowledge that one would share with a friend, but it allowed them to confirm the star's real life existence. By reading about their idol's offscreen experiences, fans reassured themselves that there was a human behind the image. Underneath the makeup and bright lights, there was a living, breathing person who seemed as honest and genuine as the worshiping fans.

In a perfect world, fans explained, they would be able to interact freely with stars. Fan magazines, gossip columns, and other intermediaries would be unnecessary; if a fan wanted to know about his or her star's personal affairs, he or she could simply ask. But such ideal circumstances hardly existed. Fans were forced to rely on the press for information, and many, like avid moviegoer E. M. Orowitz, founder of the EMO Movie Club, deeply resented this dependence.[33]

Of particular concern to Orowitz were the fabricated biographies that film studios wrote about their stars. "The official biography issued on a player usually is not based on facts. The most flagrant falsification is in the matter of ages of screen players. We still cannot understand why Edith Fellowes is heralded as ten years old when she is really thirteen. We cannot understand why experts reveal that Rockliffe Fellowes, former screen star, is her father. Edith Fellowes' father is a carpenter and her mother hails from Canada. If movie fans want accurate and official biographies of screen players, our research department will be glad to supply it," he offered.[34]

The official fan clubs' direct links to their honored stars often enabled them to uncover the detailed firsthand tidbits their fans so dearly prized. Every few months, Jeanette MacDonald's club sent her a questionnaire with their most pressing inquiries about her favorite foods, colors, and hobbies. The answers, as well as other snippets of information, were regularly printed in the club's journal. Joan Crawford's fan club devoted an entire section of its monthly publication to Crawford trivia. In a typical issue, fans learned that Crawford's favorite foods were salads, cereal, and rhubarb, that she wore a size four shoe, and that she took four showers a day.[35]

Though often trivial, this information was important to fans. It was a symbol of proximity to know these personal details and a sign of their skill: through their serious efforts and perseverance, they had managed to circumvent the media and to become their own experts on their star. Clubs often contrasted their superior knowledge with the inaccurate reports of newspapers and magazines. "Deanna has no intention of selling her new home, as was reported in a current magazine," claimed the Deanna Durbin Devotees in 1942. Gloria Swanson's fans felt they knew the actress so well that they could refute the claims of the nation's most famous gossip columnist. "There was no truth to the Louella Parsons' item I read; you are well and busy as always," wrote one admirer. "So many of her articles seem to be erroneous rather than authentic." Esther Williams's club vowed to combat the unfounded rumors about their idol by publicizing their version of the truth. "There are many kicks in life, and a newsman can add better or worse to them," it explained. "They will continue trying to toss many more lives of public figures around and the only way to beat the game is to fight fire with fire."[36]

For all this personal information, attention, and contact with their star, fans were deeply grateful. As fan club president Marion Oppenheim raved about her idol, Bette Davis, "The first and most important requisite of a club is that the [star] take an active interest in it and Bette certainly does. There are few stars busier, yet she always finds time to write a letter to the members for each issue of our club journals. She sends out a large, personally autographed photo of herself to each member upon joining the club." "Miss Crawford takes a keen interest in all our activities. Not only does she send personally autographed pictures to all of our new members, but she writes a long letter to the members for each edition of our club publication," boasted club president Marian Dommer. Ingrid Bergman, fans claimed, always treated her admirers with respect. "She remembered our names and commented on our sweaters. When we walked on the avenue with her, it was arm in arm. So close to her did we feel that her problems were our problems and ours hers. It is a feeling of comradeship that we feel for Ingrid, not that awed feeling one has for the great," wrote one devoted fan club member.[37]

But many of Bergman's fans did not feel that way for long. When the actress, in 1949, began a well-publicized extramarital affair with director Roberto Rossellini, many of her fans withdrew their support. According to Claire Rochelle, who handled much of Bergman's mail, many fans wrote angry letters claiming that they had crossed her off their list of favorites and refused to attend her films. To them, Bergman had committed one of the worst offenses that a star could inflict on her admirers: she shattered their dreams. In the eyes of many, she had broken her contract with her fans by contradicting her proper, conservative screen image.[38]

In some cases, fans' love for their favorite star was truly unconditional. Some fans believed so deeply in their idol's fundamental goodness that they shunned reports to the contrary. After Wallace Reid died in 1923 from a widely publicized drug overdose, for example, admirers formed the Wallace Reid Memorial Fan Club to commemorate his "clean and wholesome" personality. When Errol Flynn was on trial for rape, over 10,000 letters a week poured into the Warner Brothers studio from admirers who refused to believe the charges. "The story behind the headlines is quite different than what the public is dished out. So let us be tolerant in our judgments. Remember the pleasure he has given by his ability and artistry," pleaded one Flynn fan. Because many fans perceived their idols as personal role models, they refused to believe them capable of any crime or injustice. In their desire to turn stars from mere performers into heroes and model citizens endowed with talent, grace, and impeccable morals, fans were willing to overlook if not directly challenge any evidence to the contrary.[39]

But in many cases, fans were not so forgiving and demanded that their idols fulfill their expectations. Those who did deserved respect; those who did not, they claimed, were unworthy of fans. Most commonly, fan clubs were angered when a star was late with correspondence, failed to send autographed photos, or otherwise ignored them. Such behavior was not only careless, fans reasoned, but indicated something far worse: that he thought himself too rich, too "important," too "Hollywood" to associate with his admirers. With angry letters and complaints, fans sought to bring these inflated idols back down to earth. One Greta Garbo fan complained bitterly about her idol's arrogant and "discourteous" behavior: "If you weren't my favorite, I wouldn't be . . . decent enough to go see your films after you refused to send me one of your photographs," she wrote. "You should think this over and treat your fans with a little more courtesy. It's your fans that made you. What have you given them? Not even a photograph." In the late 1940s, another fan made a similar complaint to Guy Madison:

> Well I received a surprise today. I wrote you one of the nicest letters I had ever written anyone, telling you how much I thought of you and all I asked for was a picture personally autographed. But I reached into the mailbox and pulled out a cheap postcard. Guy, do you know how important fans are? Don't you think you could show us that you appreciate us by sending us personally autographed pictures?
>
> Take Betty Hutton for example. I collect movie star pictures as a hobby. I wrote her and she sent me a large picture personally autographed to me. Now Guy she's a popular star and her fans think a lot of her.
>
> No kidding, Guy, I was really hurt when I saw the postcard because I always thought so much of you.

"If this letter is not answered," wrote another fan, "I will know you are not the Guy Madison you're put up to be."[40]

Fans were often shattered when stars refused to comply with their wishes. Many fans were disappointed that their idols did not share their enthusiasm for fan activity. Others felt insulted personally—they had been rejected by their heroes. As a result, many fans lashed out against their star, hoping to win his or her affection and cooperation. When this failed, as it frequently did, fans often became so upset that they threatened to disband their club. Terminating the Guy Madison club was inevitable because "Guy really doesn't have any interest in the club," lamented one member. Some dedicated fans tried to justify their star's lack of attention ("Guy is really busy with his new film now") and hoped that he might become more interested in the future. Other fans were so disgusted that they turned their attention to another celebrity, or even gave up fan activity altogether. In the mid-1930s, 150 members of the Jane Withers fan club found themselves unexpectedly barred from their idol's studio, Twentieth Century Fox. "They were in despair until Warner Brothers' Studio heard the story and hurried down to capture the delegation and entertain them on their own lot," recalled one observer. "The Jane Withers Fan Club promptly offered to rechristen themselves in appropriate honor of some Warner Brothers' star."[41]

As countless fans learned, movie fandom, although often rewarding, had its share of disappointments. When fans succeeded, when they won the cooperation of their star, or convinced a studio to listen to their demands, they felt tremendous pride. But when a studio or star ignored them, they were offended, angry, even cynical. Sometimes, one fan remarked, participating in a fan club was like being on a roller coaster, with peaks and valleys of excitement and dejection. But fans never took the ride alone. Whether triumphant or defeated, in a fan club, there were always friends to share the thrills or cushion the blow.

WARM AND LASTING FRIENDSHIPS

"Wouldn't you like to join a fan club?" wrote *Movieland* magazine in 1947. The rewards, it asserted, were many. Club members received letters and gifts from their star. They earned the pride that came with successful and responsible boosting. And they learned firsthand information about the star, something few moviegoers could boast. "It's great fun to be in the know about your favorite star. And even more fun to be on the receiving end of those personally autographed photos," it raved. But for all these benefits there was a price to pay. A professional, well-organized fan club attended all of its star's films and many of his or her personal appearances. It sent petitions to studios and letters to fan magazines. It printed a neat, informative, typewritten club journal. It contributed to charities such as the Red Cross and the Cancer Drive, and held regular chapter meetings. "You know what a chapter is—it's a group of members from the same town working together to boost their particular Van or Frankie." Lest prospective members feel overwhelmed by this list of responsibilities, *Movieland* reminded them that fan clubs were not only about work: "It sounds grim, but remember, there's plenty of play and friendship interspersed with the boosting!"[42]

Amidst the frenzy of fan activity, it was easy for many groups to forget what lay behind the boosting and campaigning: deep and lasting friendships. Whether corresponding by mail or socializing during weekly meetings, fans formed bonds that lasted years, decades, even lifetimes. In some fan clubs, these relationships were so intense that they even threatened to rival enthusiasm for their honored star.

In the Jeanette MacDonald International Fan Club, fans' friendships, like their commitment to MacDonald, were intense and long-lived. Founded in 1937, by the mid-1940s the group had become one of the largest and most respected fan clubs in the world, with over 1,800 members, hundreds of branches, and a typewritten quarterly journal called the *Golden Comet*. As the *Golden Comet* and many other club journals illustrate, fans adored and respected their friends as much as their star. Sometimes fans even treated fellow club members like stars, proudly celebrating their achievements and talents. *Golden Comet*, for example, often printed reports of members' activities as prominently as updates on MacDonald, meticulously chronicling their vacations, marriages, and career achievements. In some cases, clubs featured more detailed descriptions of individual members, like *Golden Comet*'s series, "Portrait of a Fan." Long-time member Betty Corpe, explained a typical portrait in 1942, had brown eyes and hair, was five-foot-four, and was 22 years old. She worked as a chocolate packer, enjoyed outdoor sports, and spent much of her free time admiring and developing "her most prized possession": her movie star photo collection.[43]

These descriptions, sincere, humble, often awkwardly written, shatter many stereotypes of fans. Hardly the giddy gangs of teenage girls that they were often made out to be, many fan organizations, like the MacDonald group, attracted a much broader membership. Although thousands of adolescents did participate in fan clubs, they were joined, in greater numbers, by mature women. According to *Motion Picture Herald*, the typical fan club member was a woman between age 16 and 45. The average club president, too, was not a high school student but "a girl in her twenties, often a married girl," claimed a magazine in 1947. *Golden Comet,* like many other club journals, reflected this predominantly adult, female membership. In each issue, wives, mothers, and young working women aired their latest news and concerns. As a typical 1943 issue of the *Golden Comet* announced, member Elizabeth Smith had just found a job as secretary to a county school superintendent, and Florence Witte had been hired by the government to do photographic work. Olive Genz hoped to spend Christmas with her husband, who was stationed in Virginia, while Billie Kretschmar struggled to manage her household in the midst of wartime rationing.[44]

But the fan club was not an exclusively female domain. Many adult men actively participated in fan clubs; some organizations were even headed by men. Jay Gordon began his career as a fan club president in 1938, when he sent a letter to *Life* magazine, thanking them for printing a photograph of actress Deanna Durbin. "Thanks a million for the liveliest picture ever printed in *Life.* I'm framing it and redecorating my room around that portrait," he confessed. In response, hundreds of Durbin fans contacted Gordon, urging him to start a club. In many cases, the loyalty and devotion of male fans surpassed that of their female counterparts. Whenever Joan Crawford made a personal appearance at a movie theater, department store, or Hollywood premiere in the 1930s, her loyal fan Isidore Freeman accompanied her. Freeman's dedication, the subject of a story in the *New Yorker,* won him not only an engraved watch from Crawford but eventually a job as a publicist at the MGM studio. Charles "Chaw" Mank, a songwriter and musician known in the fan club world as the "demon film fan of Staunton, Illinois," belonged to over 250 fan clubs.[45]

Fans built strong friendships around their shared interests, and they took nearly every opportunity to meet and socialize, hosting countless teas, dances, fund-raising drives, and parties. One particularly popular activity was the theater party, in which club members went as a group to see their star's latest film. Many clubs held special anniversary events and birthday parties for their honored star; they also sponsored auctions to earn money for club outings. Weekly meetings, too, were an excuse for relaxation and celebration. At a typical meeting in the early 1940s, the New York Chapter of the Jeanette MacDonald club combined business with pleasure. After reading the minutes of the last meeting and making plans for future club outings, the group sat down to an elegant meal prepared by one of the members. For dessert, the group had ice cream cakes in the shape of MacDonald and her costar and husband, Gene Raymond. The club closed the evening by singing selections from MacDonald's films.[46]

When fans lived too far away to see each other in person, friendships were maintained through letters. Most clubs encouraged correspondence and regularly published members' addresses in club journals. Sometimes clubs printed short descriptions of members who were interested in meeting other fans through the mail. This practice not only created many pen pals but "resulted in lasting friendships," as one club president proudly explained. Movie fan Betty Rosser met one of her best friends through her admiration for Mary Pickford. For years she corresponded with fellow fan Jenabel Gretter, "with Mary as our common bond." "[Jenabel] writes excellent letters," wrote Rosser in her memoir:

> She has told me of the different occasions in which she has seen Mary. She sends me clippings [of Mary] from papers. Her hobby is a remarkable collection of photos of Mary. When I was in the hospital with the birth of my son in 1934 she sent it for me to see. When I was in California last summer I looked her up. It was fun to meet her but a little embarrassing as we know each other so well through letters. We talked Mary for hours.[47]

During the 1940s, Jane Smoot of Austin, Texas, regularly wrote to several other Jeanette MacDonald fans across the country. Her ongoing correspondence with Mary Dunphy, whom she met through *Golden Comet,* reveals the kind of friendship and intimacy that fan friends often shared. Although Mary and Jane often wrote about their admiration for MacDonald and eagerly described their experiences meeting the actress in person, they also shared the details of their everyday lives: problems with friends, health and job concerns, holidays and weekend outings.

Although close, Jane and Mary's relationship was not without rivalry. Like many fans, Jane and Mary subtly competed over their memorabilia collections—who had the most records, the best photos, the largest and most elaborate scrapbooks. A collection of newspaper clippings, photographs, concert programs, and letters, scrapbooks played an important role in movie fan culture. Not only did they serve as a repository of memories, chronicling a fan's interest in a particular star, but they also symbolized commitment and dedication. In the fan club world, the larger and more elaborate one's scrapbook, the greater one's devotion to a star.[48]

Jane Smoot pasted hundreds of photos and clippings of MacDonald, as well as her personal correspondence with fellow fans, into seven large scrapbooks. A longstanding MacDonald fan, Jane had assembled her books over the course of several years. Mary, however, had only been keeping scrapbooks for a year and admitted that hers were probably not as large as Jane's. But Mary did boast about the quality of her collection, claiming that one of her scrapbooks was so meticulously and beautifully assembled that MacDonald herself had asked to see it. In her correspondence with Jane, Mary also bragged about her MacDonald memorabilia collection, including numerous autographed photos and several letters from MacDonald and her husband, Gene Raymond.[49]

Like many other fan organizations, the Jeanette MacDonald club perceived itself as a community or "fan family," as they sometimes called it, with an obligation to support and encourage its members. *Golden Comet* regularly listed members' birthdays and encouraged fans to mail gifts and cards to each other. The club also sent flowers and good wishes to members who were sick or injured. When a long-time MacDonald fan lost the use of his legs in an accident, the group started a Therapy Fund to support him. Even MacDonald sent her condolences to members grieving the loss of a relative or spouse.[50]

Long after MacDonald's death in 1965, the club endures. Many original or early members joined by hundreds of newcomers work to keep MacDonald's name alive, pressuring television stations and movie theaters to run her films. Sustained by friendships and unfailing loyalty, the Jeanette MacDonald fan club flourishes well after their star and her grand, glamorous musicals have long since disappeared from the spotlight.

A DEMOCRACY OF ENTERTAINMENT

Idealistic yet jaded, hopeful yet cynical, movie fan clubs in the classical Hollywood era were a study in contradiction. Hollywood's most loyal customers, they attacked studios for their poor judgments and inattention to audience demands. Voracious readers of fan magazines, they distrusted the press. Devoted admirers of internationally renowned celebrities, they insisted that stars grant them attention. To the outside observer, these fans must have appeared remarkably confused or hopelessly hypocritical.

Yet in reality, there was a logic to fans' seemingly paradoxical behavior. Though they loved the movies and stars, they were often dissatisfied with the impersonal, commercial nature of the mass media and worked to develop a direct, intimate, participatory relationship with the movies. Not content with reading about stars or seeing them from a distance, they wanted to interact with their idols. Skeptical of media reports, they hoped to uncover their own version of the truth. Fan club members tried to create a kind of audience-friendly democracy of entertainment in which their demands and interests would be acknowledged and public opinion, rather than Hollywood politics, would turn actors into stars.

Although fans' efforts were not always successful—studios often ignored their suggestions, and fan magazines continued to churn out inaccurate reports—what is important, ultimately, is that they tried. The very fact that fans formed clubs, and that these clubs served as flourishing social organizations and aggressive lobbying groups, contradicts many widely held assumptions about film fandom. Far from passive spectators and naive dreamers, fan clubs in the 1930s and 1940s were intensely aware of the publicity-generating, profit-making ambitions of the studio system and actively worked to change the way films and stars were created and publicized. Fan clubs were not frivolous and temporary, but serious, lasting organizations through which fans met, worked together, and formed meaningful friendships. Idealistic yet active and savvy, these men and women stood with one foot in the world of glamour and make-believe, and the other firmly planted in reality.

CHAPTER SIX

THE VIEW FROM HOLLYWOOD

THROUGHOUT MOVIE HISTORY, fans have always perceived themselves as more than just spectators. Individually and in groups, they tried to participate in the movies—to befriend actors, influence production and casting decisions, and boost their favorite actors to greater heights of success. Convinced that they had a role to play in the Hollywood studio system, they continually attempted to inform filmmakers of their likes, dislikes, and demands.

As many fans learned, communicating with Hollywood was easy. One effective method was through theater attendance. Nothing sent a stronger message to the studios, fans realized, than soaring or falling box office returns. Another popular mode of communication was fan mail. In thousands of letters to the studios each month, fans poured out their thoughts, complaints, and suggestions. During the 1930s and 1940s, for example, fans advised producer David O. Selznick on nearly every possible aspect of filmmaking. They urged him to adapt popular novels for the screen, improve stars' costumes, and use more dramatic filming techniques. They begged him for greater accuracy in historical films, and more lavish and exciting epics. Perhaps more than anything, they barraged him with casting suggestions. "Please give us more Ingrid Bergman," asked one fan. "Don't ever let [Jennifer Jones] make another film with that silly Charles Boyer," wrote another.[1]

Like many other film executives, Selznick took fans seriously, and often responded to their wishes. In the 1940s, for example, Guy Madison's fan clubs sent Selznick so many letters that the producer cast him in a prominent role. Rory Calhoun, too, became a similar beneficiary of fan mail. "It was the loyalty of Rory's fans, their faith and their letters . . . that is largely responsible for this tall young actor being on top," proclaimed *Movieland* magazine.[2]

Fans were thrilled with these victories. At last their favorite actor would receive a share of the spotlight. His or her talent, good looks, and personality would now be visible for all the world to see. What many fans did not fully realize, however, was that their letters and feedback in many ways *created* their idol's personality. Rather than simply help publicize their star or win him or her better roles, fans actually determined what qualities the star would possess.

During Hollywood's studio era—roughly 1920 to 1950—stars were not born but created. As soon as an actress signed a studio contract, she was immediately transformed. Dressmakers and makeup artists gave her a flawless appearance, studio executives bestowed a new name, and publicists endowed her with a set of fabricated personality traits. This new image, marketed to the public through press releases and films, was often highly successful. Molded into a gangster by Warner Brothers, James Cagney was a hit. As a stunning blonde bombshell, Jean Harlow thrilled millions. But not all of the studios' efforts were equally well received. Initially publicized as a seductive vamp, Bette Davis won little praise. Before she was transformed into a fashionable clothes horse, Gloria Swanson went unrecognized. Actors often went through several image changes until studios found one that worked.

It was during the studios' search for an appropriate personality that fan letters became most crucial. Studios relied on fans, through notes and comments, to inform them whether they approved or disapproved of an actor's persona. If fans seemed less than enthusiastic about a star, publicists manipulated the image. But if fans appeared truly captivated, the studio knew it had a hit. In the words of film historian

Alexander Walker, "the [actor] was exposed to the public as if on a spit, and his or her personality was rotated until a physical feature or character trait got a significant response." Using fan mail and audience feedback as a barometer, studios like Metro-Goldwyn-Mayer shaped hundreds of actors into glamorous, captivating celebrities.[3]

FAN MAIL

Depending on who you asked in Hollywood, fans were either pests or saints. To the men and women who ran the fan mail departments in the major studios—who sent response letters and photographs to the thousands of fans who wrote each week—fans may have seemed like a nuisance. Employees in fan mail departments often made lists of the absurd requests they received: one such list, compiled in 1939, reported that fans asked actors for cigarette butts, shoes, chewed pieces of gum, a "blade of grass from star's lawn," and locks of hair. Fans were also less than popular with the Hollywood police department. Devoted admirers were known for their attempts to sneak into studios by hiding in cars, scaling fences, or masquerading as film extras.[4]

But to stars, fans were less an annoyance than an important constituency, the lifeblood of their livelihood. When faced with declining popularity or with studios that refused to grant them leading roles, many stars turned to the fan clubs that boosted them in exchange for letters and autographed photos. During the 1930s, Joan Crawford was known for her particularly intense relationship with her fans. Hoping to keep them loyal, she sent out monthly correspondence, answered their questions, and frequently arranged for fan visits. "Those fans put me where I am," she once explained. "If it wasn't for them, I'd be back in Kansas City." Stars also knew that snubbing fans could lead to negative publicity. When Jean Harlow refused to speak on the phone with a group of admirers from Arkansas, an organization of theater owners penned a resolution condemning Harlow and her negative attitude toward the fans "who have made her what she is today." The resolution was wired to film distributors, magazines, and newspapers throughout the country, forcing Harlow to make an embarrassing and well-publicized apology.[5]

For film studios, too, fans were absolutely crucial—overbearing, costly, and sometimes troublesome, but nonetheless crucial. It was fans, they knew, who went most often to the movies and brought in much of the revenue to finance the film industry. It was fans who went to the movies five, six, or seven times a week, and who often took friends and family members with them. Many studios noticed that fan clubs, which grew and flourished during the 1920s, pressured local theaters to run films. They also saw that fans were temperamental and threatened to withdraw their support when actors did not reply to fan mail. Fearing the wrath of fans who were jilted by stars, studios in the 1920s created fan mail departments to send speedy and cordial responses to letter-writers throughout the country. Some studios gave their actors the option of using the fan mail department (many stars chose instead to have their mail handled by a personal secretary), while others like MGM, which meticulously controlled its stars' publicity, insisted that all fan correspondence be handled by the studio.[6]

The fan mail enterprise was important—and expensive. In 1928, Hollywood studios received over 32,250,000 fan letters and spent nearly two million dollars on postage, photographs, and salaries for the fan mail departments. But alienating fans would have been far more costly. Determined to appease fans—and to keep them coming back to the box office—studios sent out thousands of letters each month, filled with the warmest greetings and friendliest wishes from the stars. "Dear Movie Friend, Your very kind note is in front of me, and I hasten to answer you to tell you how much I appreciate it. Thank you, indeed," went a typical response from actor Clive Brook. "My Dear Fan Friend, I have your letter, and it pleased me very much. When the day starts out all wrong, you can't imagine how my fan mail cheers me up and makes things look bright again," began a letter from Esther Ralston. Movie magazines, too, tried to assure readers that their fan letters were much appreciated. "All the stars are vitally interested in fan mail," claimed *Photoplay* magazine in 1928. "Every letter . . . is perused by Clara [Bow]. She takes a youngster's pride in her mail, especially in the invitations she receives." "I have received so many beautiful letters from people I have never known," gushed Lillian Gish to readers of *Picture Play*. "And I cannot tell you how much they have meant to me." "I think my fan mail is a truer gauge of what the public wants of me . . . than any press criticism. After all, the public who write the fan letters are the final judges," explained Richard Barthelmess.[7]

Many fans may have envisaged their letters lovingly and carefully perused by their idols, who gleaned them for praise, advice, and constructive criticism. The reality, however, was much less poetic. Most stars rarely saw the bulk of their fan mail: as soon as a letter reached the studios, it was bundled and sent to the fan mail departments. Moreover, the cordial, seemingly personal responses that most fans received were not penned by celebrities but by studio-employed writers. Even the signatures on the letters were faked. "Members of the [fan mail] department became expert at imitating all signatures," recalled former MGM story editor Samuel Marx. "When Garbo refused to supply hers for this purpose, it was copied from her contract. [When] Norma Shearer was in the Swiss Alps . . . letters and photographs went forth to her fans in enormous volume, supposedly signed by her." Most fans did not realize that the comments, opinions, and confessions in their letters often never reached their intended recipients.[8]

But fans' efforts were not entirely in vain. Although most fan mail was not received and handled in the way most fans believed, it was neither thrown out by the studios nor written off as the mindless babbling of frivolous admirers. Most studios in the classical Hollywood era found fan mail a valuable indicator of public opinion. Some studio heads, like David O. Selznick, scrupulously investigated the content of fan letters for what fans had to say about particular actors or films. In 1936, Selznick read dozens of letters from fans complaining about his latest film, *The Garden of Allah*. According to one moviegoer, the film was marred by a "fatal break in unity that could not possibly happen." One letter pointed out the mistake of having a "rosary around the priest's neck during the marriage ceremony." To Jack Greenfest the entire film was a bore: "In short, as an interesting screen story, you have nothing to sell to the public," he wrote.[9]

Not surprisingly, fans were most vocal on the subject of stars. Each month letters poured into the Selznick studio filled with casting suggestions. A nun tried to convince Selznick that Joan Fontaine's "graceful movements, exquisite expression and extremely sincere acting would fit wonderfully in a religious picture." "When is Jennifer Jones going to play opposite a man her own age?" asked another fan.

"I would like to see Shirley Temple in any different role, other than the usual sweet character parts she has been playing," wrote another. Several fans complained to Selznick about the dearth of black film actors and urged him to help bring racial diversity to Hollywood. "If you should really like to do something different and worthwhile, why not take a colored girl as your latest discovery?," wrote one fan: "There is nothing that would make the colored people feel more that this is their America and there is no racial strife as far as the motion picture industry is concerned. *Just One Negro to the Many of Our Race.*" "I would have been an actress if the field for Negroes were wide enough," explained another fan in 1937. "Mr. Selznick I am counting on your considerate nature."[10]

Selznick's fan mail department compiled a list of these comments that was presented to the producer on a regular basis. Although Selznick undoubtedly overlooked or ignored most of the suggestions, he could not help but notice a few. In the mid-1940s, Guy Madison's fans sent in so many letters that Selznick was practically forced to give the actor more prominent roles. When casting for *Gone with the Wind,* Selznick also relied heavily on fan mail. During 1937 and 1938 he received thousands of suggestions that were recorded, tabulated, and carefully analyzed. As Selznick learned, fans clamored to see Clark Gable as Rhett Butler but were less enthusiastic about the possibility of Bette Davis as Scarlett O'Hara. "Surely you have prettier actresses than her," wrote one fan in 1937. "Even my own pictures as you can see are prettier than Betty Davis."[11]

In most cases, however, studios were less interested in the content of fan letters than in their quantity. Considered second in accuracy to box office returns, fan mail was often used to gauge an actor's drawing power—the more letters received, the greater the popularity, or so most studio executives believed. Mailbags full of fan letters were often taken as the ultimate sign of stardom: when Clara Bow, in the late 1920s, received over 30,000 pieces of fan mail in one month, the Paramount studio knew it had a celebrity on its hands. In 1933, Warner Brothers satirized the importance of fan mail in a hilarious comedy called *Lady Killer.* Desperate to be elevated from bit player to star, aspiring actor Dan Quigley, played by James Cagney, pens hundreds of phony fan letters and sends them to his studio. Quigley's friend mails the letters from several different Southern

California towns, ensuring a variety of postmarks. Impressed by the volume of mail, the studio immediately grants him leading roles, and before long the actor is a star.[12]

Although *Lady Killer* spoofed the studio's eagerness to read popularity from fan mail, the reality was not much different. When bombarded with enough fan letters, studios could be convinced to do just about anything—to raise actors' salaries, grant them more prominent parts, or even groom inexperienced newcomers for stardom. When MGM hired Greta Garbo in the mid-1920s, it feared that the foreign actress would fail to make an impression on American audiences. Public reaction to her films, however, convinced the studio otherwise. After the release of Garbo's second film, *The Temptress* (1926), MGM was swamped with fan mail. "That was the ultimate sign," explained Samuel Marx. The studio immediately rushed Garbo into leading roles in *Flesh and the Devil* (1927), *Love* (1927), and *A Woman of Affairs* (1928) costarring romantic hero John Gilbert. Her fan mail skyrocketed. There was no question that MGM had a bona fide celebrity on its hands, and Garbo's prominence and salary increased accordingly.[13]

Like most film executives, David Selznick meticulously monitored the volume of fan mail received by his studio. He commissioned his secretaries to compile monthly "fan mail reports" that tabulated the number of letters received by each of his stars. Shirley Temple, who collected more than 3,000 letters each month, "is still first on the list by a wide margin," he commented after reading a 1943 fan mail report. "Jennifer [Jones] has passed Ingrid [Bergman] and has taken number two position for the first time." In many cases, the monthly reports notified Selznick of rising stars and warned him of potential box office failures. As he wrote to Daniel O'Shea, general manager of Selznick Productions in 1942,

> The most startling item [about the fan mail report], and one that completely contradicts what we have thought about Dorothy McGuire is the fabulous amount of mail she is receiving—practically 1000 letters. Apparently she is a real star and we ourselves haven't appreciated her.
>
> The most encouraging item is Joe Cotten's tremendously growing fan mail indicating that we were right in thinking of him as having romantic appeal. A thousand fan letters in a single month

is astonishing, considering that he has had scarcely any romantic roles up to now.

"The most depressing item," he concluded, "is that Vivien [Leigh] has sunk to 96 letters." Terrified by what he saw as Leigh's declining popularity, Selznick urged his publicists to take speedy action and "get this matter settled." "The decrease in Vivien's mail is an indication of the frightening extent to which she has undoubtedly lost following. We ought to be ashamed of ourselves for the shabby way we have handled [her], which I think is our worst failure in our entire operation to date," he explained. Despite attempts to publicize the actress and cast her in future productions, Leigh left the studio, forcing Selznick to focus his attention on his other stars: Jennifer Jones, Joan Fontaine, and Gregory Peck.[14]

For most major film companies in Hollywood's studio era, fan mail provided a unique and important opportunity to win the support of audiences throughout the nation. If studios responded to fan letters swiftly and courteously, they earned the loyalty of thousands of fans. If they took fans' suggestions seriously, they assured themselves greater audience satisfaction and box office revenue. Perhaps most important, fan letters enabled studios to transform their actors into captivating personalities. With the help of fan mail, studios shaped their new recruits into intriguing, glamorous celebrities, who drew fans and dollars to the box office time and time again.

INVENTING STARS

Throughout the twentieth century the film industry operated on a single crucial principle: stars sell. Because fans were so fascinated by actors' private lives and personalities, studios knew that they had to glamorize their players in order to successfully sell them. Depicting actors as they really were—as troubled souls, alcoholics, and adulterers, or, at the very least, average men and women—would certainly fail to attract audiences. As a result, studios granted each of their stars a new personality, one that often stayed with them throughout their careers. It is hard to imagine James Cagney as anything but a tough-talking rogue, Humphrey Bogart, a hard-boiled cynic, and Greta Garbo, a mysterious temptress. These personalities were so frequently and artfully presented that they seemed almost natural. Yet in reality they were largely fabricated. During Hollywood's golden age, film studios became masters of illusion, creating artificial identities and distorted images for a personality-hungry public.

The process of personality creation started as soon as an actor was contracted by a studio; in some cases, even before he was hired. Studio executives such as Jack Warner of Warner Brothers and Louis B. Mayer and Irving Thalberg at MGM would decide they needed a particular type—a romantic hero, a gangster, a comedian—for an upcoming film. Scouts would search Broadway theaters, casting agencies, and the studio's own pool of extras. Eventually, after interviews and screen tests, an appropriate candidate would be chosen, cast in a part, and shipped off to the publicity department. There, writers penned a studio biography, a semifictional version of his life that paralleled the role he was to play. Sometimes the studio biography was relatively accurate. But in most cases publicists had to drastically alter the truth. In the 1930s, actor Wallace Beery, bitter and disagreeable, was portrayed by the MGM publicity department as warm and lovable, like the characters he played. "Wallace Beery, in private life or on the screen, is much the same in at least one notable characteristic. He is as gentle as a St. Bernard," read the official studio biography.[15]

To convince the public that Greta Garbo was as mysterious and passionate as the women she played in films, MGM released a series of fabricated stories about her personal life. Garbo's short-lived romance with costar John Gilbert became, according to the publicity department, the love affair of the century. Press releases sensationalized the torrid romance; some went as far as to claim, quite inaccurately, that the two were married and living together. Another myth put out by the MGM publicists was Garbo's famed secrecy and seclusion. Although Garbo was by nature a private person, she was never as reclusive as the publicists claimed. With epithets like "The Enigmatic Swede," "The Swedish Sphinx," and "The Mysterious Stranger," the studio persuaded moviegoers that the actress was in life a seductive, brooding temptress.[16]

The most vexing problem for studios was the player who did not yet have a strong screen image. For example, when MGM hired 16-year-old Lana Turner, the studio knew it had talent on its hands but was unsure how to use it. In its search for an appropriate image, MGM cast Turner in a variety of different roles—a schoolgirl in the Andy

Hardy series, a frisky teenager in *Rich Man, Poor Girl* (1938), and a gangster's moll in *Calling Dr. Kildare* (1939). Her physical appearance, too, was manipulated: her hair went from brunette to red to light brown, her wardrobe was constantly refined, and her makeup altered. Yet nothing seemed to work. Critics paid little attention to her and, judging from her fan mail, she seemed to have only a handful of admirers. What her fans said, however, gave the studio a crucial insight. "Miss Turner, we are students of Alhambra High," read a typical letter. "We have a sort of club. We want a picture of you in a glamorous pose. You know what we mean . . ."[17]

Inspired by fans' comments, the studio cast Turner as an alluring, conniving showgirl in *Ziegfeld Girl* (1941). The decision was wise. Cast and publicized as a knockout blonde, Turner seemed to have real star quality. From that point on, studio press releases advertised her as a "hard core pinup girl," in the words of one publicist; fan magazines paid homage to her "oomphterrific" looks, and starring roles in *Honky Tonk* (1941), *Johnny Eager* (1942), *Slightly Dangerous* (1943), and *The Postman Always Rings Twice* (1946) reinforced the image of glamour and sensuality. After several false starts, MGM had at last found Turner a marketable personality.[18]

During Hollywood's studio era, Metro-Goldwyn-Mayer, generally regarded as the most prestigious film company of the period, became a master of personality creation. With ruthless publicists, expert makeup artists, and a constant eye on glamour, the studio quickly earned a reputation for its powers of transformation. Almost overnight, unknown, nondescript actors were transformed into brilliant, captivating celebrities. But even MGM could not avoid making mistakes. In its search for marketable personalities, the studio often stumbled, miscasting actors and inappropriately publicizing them. It was in these moments, as we will see, that movie fans saved MGM from its miscalculations. Through letters, feedback, and constant pressure, fans steered the studio toward successful star images.

A MODERN-DAY CINDERELLA

In the spring of 1924, three events took place that would have a lasting impact on the American film industry. A Broadway musical, *The*

Passing Show of 1924, opened in New York. An unemployed stage actor moved to Hollywood to find work as a film extra. And nearby, in Culver City, plans were made for the creation of the Metro-Goldwyn-Mayer studio, which would begin production the following month. Though seemingly unrelated, these incidents would soon be linked in a historic tale of glamour and stardom. From them grew two of the world's most popular film celebrities and a system of image manipulation that would set the standard for the film industry for years to come.

A merger of the Loew's theater chain, the Samuel Goldwyn film studio, and the film production company of Louis B. Mayer, MGM started with several advantages. It had the equipment and location for film production, expert directors and producers, and movie theaters across the nation. What it needed, more than anything, were scripts, ideas, and, in particular, stars. Hoping to find fresh talent for upcoming productions, studio head Mayer dispatched talent scouts throughout the world. Agents combed acting schools, Mayer looked in Europe, and his assistant, Harry Rapf, searched in New York.

Rapf's journey proved successful. Intrigued by one of the dancers in a Broadway musical, *The Passing Show of 1924,* Rapf summoned her for a screen test. What he saw was promising: energetic and candid, 19-year-old Lucille LeSueur had a captivating screen presence. After some prodding and cajoling—"I want to be a dancer," she insisted—LeSueur affixed her name to a five-year contract and boarded a train for California.

When she stepped off the train, she was greeted by Larry Barbier, who worked in the MGM publicity department. Before long, Barbier took her to his boss, publicity director Pete Smith, who was given the responsibility of typing the actress: laying the foundations for her screen personality. Knowing little about LeSueur except that she had been a prize-winning dancer, Smith decided that she should be publicized as an athlete. LeSueur and fellow recruit Dorothy Sebastian, neither of whom were particularly athletic, were taken to the University of Southern California track, where they were photographed running the 50-yard dash and leaping over hurdles. Other shots showed the actresses playing volleyball or throwing a football.[19]

As eye-catching as the images may have been, they had little market value. MGM had no intention of casting LeSueur in any athletic roles—in fact, it had few ideas about how to cast her at all.

During her first year at MGM, she floated through a number of random parts, including a lady in waiting in *Old Clothes* and a homeless girl in *The One Thing*. Sensing that his protégé was drifting, in 1925 Rapf decided to anchor LeSueur to a stronger, more stable screen personality. She needed a striking image, Rapf reasoned, and a unique, distinctive set of traits. Perhaps more than anything, she needed a new name.

LeSueur, Rapf thought, sounded too much like sewer. It sounded too foreign; it was hard to spell and even more difficult to pronounce. Eager to find a name that would be popular with moviegoers, Rapf decided to consult the fans themselves, who would start Lucille LeSueur on her path toward stardom. In conjunction with the fan magazine *Movie Weekly*, MGM offered 500 dollars to the reader who came up with the best new name. Still tied to her athletic image, Rapf fibbed to *Movie Weekly* readers, "second only to her career is her interest in athletics, and she devotes much of her spare time to swimming and tennis." He also distorted her impoverished background. "Tiring of the social life of a debutante, she left home to become an actress," Rapf explained. Hundreds of fans sent in suggestions—Joan Arden, Ann Morgan, and Joan Grey, among others—but the grand prize went to a name now immortal: Joan Crawford. With a new name and plenty of free publicity from the contest, Lucille/Joan embarked on a new film project, *Sally, Irene and Mary* (1925), with renewed vigor.[20]

But as Crawford, Rapf, and the MGM publicists eventually realized, a new name did not necessarily mean a new *personality*. Still searching for an appropriate image, the studio cast her in a series of "breezy little comedies," as one reviewer put it; never a star in her own right, she typically played the romantic interest of the films' male leads. Then, in 1928, Crawford received a much-needed opportunity: a leading role in *Our Dancing Daughters,* a story of a society girl who becomes a dancing, drinking flapper. The film was a success. Audiences throughout the country loved Crawford as the rebellious Diana and sent mountains of fan mail telling her so. A publicity photo from the period showed Crawford gleefully clutching a bundle of letters; behind her, fan mail spilled out of a mail truck. Crawford was so touched by the outpouring of affection that she tried to respond personally to each letter. "Reviews and fan letters were pouring in. The studio gave me bundles of them every day and I read every word. I answered every letter personally, addressed and stamped the envelopes and took them to the post office myself," she later explained. Before long, however, the studio stepped in. In an internal studio memo from 1929, MGM executive M. E. Greenwood wrote to the publicity department urging them to "take charge of [Crawford's] mail until further notice. I would suggest we reply to all the intelligent letters and keep a record of the cost." From that point on, the studio read, tabulated, and responded to the thousands of letters that arrived each month—letters from young women claiming that they wanted to be "just like Joan Crawford," from others who praised her charm and talent, and from others asking permission to establish Joan Crawford fan clubs.[21]

By 1929, MGM had come to two important conclusions about the career of Joan Crawford. Swayed by the fan mail and rave reviews, studio executives made an important decision: she was to become an official MGM star. Her salary was doubled to 1,500 dollars a week, her contract was rewritten to include paid vacations, and her publicity stories and press releases were increased enormously. The studio also arrived at a judgment on her screen personality. Given the overwhelming fan response to her role in *Our Dancing Daughters*, MGM decided that Crawford should continue to play fast-living socialites. Press releases and fan magazines trumpeted her as the quintessential jazz baby, and *Our Modern Maidens* (1929) enabled her to reprise her flapper role. F. Scott Fitzgerald paid the ultimate compliment to the MGM publicity and casting departments when he wrote the often-repeated lines, "Joan Crawford is doubtless the best example of the flapper, the girl you see at smart night clubs, gowned to the apex of sophistication . . . dancing deliciously, laughing a great deal, with wide, hurt eyes. Young things with a talent for living."[22]

But as MGM soon realized, the climate was changing not only in Hollywood but throughout the nation. With the depression, Americans were no longer interested in seeing rich young women in fast cars and lavish gowns. The working woman was fast becoming the ideal Hollywood heroine, and fans clamored for stories about shopgirls, waitresses, and chorus girls who struggled and triumphed over adversity. In other words, the popularity of Joan Crawford's flapper image was seriously endangered, a fact that put MGM in an awkward position. Drastically changing Crawford's personality would risk upsetting her fans but, on the other hand, the same society girl roles would eventually grow stale. To complicate matters, Crawford herself was demanding more challenging projects. "I had wearied of the [flapper] part—to me it had become totally passé," she recalled. Thus in 1930, MGM slowly put Crawford through yet another personality change. She would no longer play a vain, headstrong flapper reveling in her privilege but one who has been humbled. In *Montana Moon* (1930), she played a wealthy New York woman who marries a cowboy and is forced to adjust to a rugged life out West; in *Dance, Fools, Dance* (1931), she was a young society girl, impoverished by the stock market crash, who takes up work as a newspaper reporter. The energy that Crawford's characters once spent celebrating their prosperity was now channeled into a struggle for survival.

Reviewers praised Crawford's work, and audiences encouraged the direction that her image was taking. Upon hearing a rumor that their idol was to play another Dancing Daughter role, fans rose up in protest. "Although I realize that she was splendid in that type and far surpassed anybody else in those roles, I don't think she ought to be kept in the old part continually," wrote one fan. Confident of the success of the new Crawford personality, MGM cast her in a series of working-girl roles: between 1931 and 1935, she depicted a chorus girl, secretary, factory worker, and maid. In *Laughing Sinners* (1931), she played a cabaret dancer who finds hope in her new life as a Salvation Army worker; in *Possessed,* from the same year, she was a young woman working in a paper-box factory who marries her way into New York society. Crawford earned brilliant reviews for her portrayal in *Grand Hotel* (1932) of Flaemmchen, an unscrupulous stenographer willing to do anything for money.[23]

As fan magazine articles and studio press releases were quick to note, Crawford's own background was in many ways similar to the characters she portrayed. Once hesitant about revealing her origins, MGM saw an opportunity to publicize (if not overdramatize) her impoverished childhood and real-life struggles for success. "Joan Crawford is a modern day Cinderella," read her official studio biography. As a child, she "spent her days drudging as a general helper and waitress at boarding schools, for which she received the bare necessities of existence. She often cried herself to sleep in the true Cinderella tradition." It was only after years of hard work, faith, and sacrifice, claimed MGM, that she eventually became a "Hollywood princess." Her well-publicized marriage to Douglas Fairbanks, Jr., the child of movie royalty (the son of Douglas Fairbanks and stepson of Mary Pickford), further reinforced the rags-to-riches image. "Her life is a sermon for any woman," praised one reader of *Photoplay* magazine. "She was a clumsy awkward girl, but she wouldn't stay that way. She had no one to help her, but her own perseverance and persistence has made her the lovely, poised, graceful, cultured woman that she is."[24]

As a working girl turned Cinderella both on and off the screen, Joan Crawford was a hit. In fan letters, thousands of women asked for the secrets of her success and called her the star with whom they identified most. Crawford was also barraged with mail from over a half-dozen flourishing Joan Crawford fan clubs, which begged for the details of her luxurious lifestyle. In response, they received long letters, regular updates on her activities, and mimeographed menus from her elaborate dinner parties. "The Crawford fans couldn't get enough," wrote biographer Bob Thomas. "They eagerly accepted every piece of information about Joan and passed it on." Fans also clamored to see her in person. When Crawford and Fairbanks were in London, the MGM publicity department arranged for her to give a speech to an audience of 3,000 working women. "But the girls started clamoring 'Our Joan! Our Joan!' and all she could manage was a faint 'Bless You,'" according to Thomas. MGM needed no further encouragement; it had found a winning personality for Joan Crawford, one that it was ready to exploit in film after film.[25]

But the studio made a fatal misjudgment when it loaned Crawford in 1932 to United Artists for *Rain*. Based on the W. Somerset Maugham story of a prostitute who seduces a missionary in the South Seas, the film had been made in 1927 under the title *Sadie Thompson*, starring Gloria Swanson. Believing that a successful performance would prove Crawford's serious dramatic ability, both MGM and United Artists had high hopes for the project. But the results were deeply disappointing. Fans sent her hundreds of letters complaining about her performance and the cheapness of her role. Although Crawford had played gold diggers and young women willing to sleep their way to the top in *Laughing Sinners*, *Possessed*, *Grand Hotel*, and *Letty Lynton* (1932), fans were somehow unwilling to see Joan

Crawford as a bitter hardened prostitute. "They would accept me as Letty Lynton who was just as vulgar, but she had style. Cheapness and vulgarity they would not accept," she wrote in her 1962 autobiography. Perhaps more than anything, they protested her lipstick. For the film, Crawford painted on bright, bold lips "because that's the kind of woman I thought Sadie was," she explained. She later regretted the decision. In an interview with the *Saturday Evening Post*, Crawford apologized to her fans for her exaggerated makeup and promised greater restraint in the future. "You ought to read the bushels of letters razzing me for going too far in lipstick. I was astonished at the attack, but I saw that my objecting friends . . . were right," she confessed.[26]

Following the failure of *Rain*, fans were restless. "When will she return to peppy, lovable roles again?" asked *Photoplay* in August 1932. Thankfully, they did not have to wait long. Sensing that Crawford's career was slipping, MGM rushed her back into the established formula. In *Dancing Lady* (1933) she played a poor young dancer desperate to become a Broadway star. After learning the art of stylish dress and sophisticated speech from a wealthy lover, the dancer eventually wins the leading part in a show, not to mention the love of a tough-talking theatrical producer played by Clark Gable. As the studio had hoped, the film was a triumph—it was so popular, in fact, that for years it was used as the yardstick by which MGM measured the success of its other productions. Audiences and reviewers praised the plot, the musical numbers, and Crawford's return to her true working-girl personality, which prevailed again in her next three films: *Sadie McKee* (1934), *Chained* (1934), and *Forsaking All Others* (1935). Fans also applauded the chemistry between Crawford and Gable, MGM's latest screen sensation.[27]

For audiences in the 1930s, Clark Gable—handsome, self-confident, aggressive—was the perfect match for Crawford's energy and sexuality. Rough yet romantic, cynical yet sensual, Gable typified the street-smart, proletarian screen hero so popular during the depression years. Throughout the decade, fans celebrated the rugged King of Hollywood; "there is no one man on the screen whose personality so intrigues the audience," wrote *Photoplay*. What fans may not have realized, however, was that Gable's celebrated personality, like that of Crawford, Greta Garbo, and the entire stable of MGM stars, was in many ways an illusion. The Gable mystique had been fabricated deep within the studio, a product of imaginative publicists, creative casting directors, and the continued input of fans.[28]

THE KING OF HOLLYWOOD

In 1924, as Lucille LeSueur was dancing on Broadway and the MGM studio was celebrating its inauguration, a struggling actor and his wife-to-be moved to Hollywood. Like many young hopefuls, William Clark Gable had a little stage experience (he had performed in small theaters in Portland, Oregon) but lacked the fame and talent to win a screen test. Desperate for work but unwilling to give up his quest for stardom, he took jobs as a film extra, tried to befriend actors and directors, and hounded the studios daily. But Clark Gable's fate seemed not to be in the movies. Discouraged by the failure of his Hollywood career, he returned to the theater, where he won a few starring roles on the New York stage and a reputation, in certain circles, as a dashing matinee idol.

But in 1930, Gable returned to Hollywood, this time with the odds in his favor. Five years in successful theater productions had given him valuable experience. The rise of the talking film had created a demand for trained actors. And a fellow stage performer, Lionel Barrymore, was urging Gable to take a screen test at the MGM studio. Gable's first screen test, however, proved a disaster. Production head Irving Thalberg complained about his gawky appearance, protruding ears, and uneven teeth. After playing bit parts at the Pathe and Warner Brothers studios, Gable returned to MGM for another try. "Don't smile," Barrymore told him. The strategy worked. Gable was hired to play a supporting role in *The Easiest Way* (1931), a part that started him on his path toward stardom.[29]

The film was hardly memorable. The story of a poor young model who becomes her boss's mistress, *The Easiest Way* was "disappointing" and "invariably tedious," wrote the *New York Times*. Gable's part, as the young woman's brother-in-law, was also unexceptional. The public reaction, however, was not. At a preview of the film in suburban Glendale, California, moviegoers cheered Gable so vocally that the studio could not help but take notice. "At the preview at the Alexander Theater, Gable electrified the audience," explained MGM story editor Samuel Marx. "Everything that was wrong about his appearance suddenly seemed right. Thalberg stood in the patio when the picture was over, asking men and women leaving the theater how they liked [Gable]. Then he drew the studio executives to a corner of the parking lot and said, 'We've got ourselves a new star.'" The next morning, Thalberg signed Gable to a contract and rushed him into a series of films.[30]

Audiences adored Clark Gable, that much was clear. What was less obvious to MGM, however, was why they liked him. Was it his handsome looks? His raspy voice and rapid-fire delivery? Unsure about how to market Gable, the studio tried him in a variety of roles: as a crusading newspaperman in *The Secret Six,* an adulterous politician in *Possessed,* a Salvation Army captain in *Laughing Sinners,* and a bootlegger and killer in *Dance, Fools, Dance* (all 1931). Fan letters informed MGM which parts had been successes and which were mistakes. "Clark Gable may be a knockout as gangster, but it stops right there. Mr. Gable was not at all suited for his part as a Salvation Army worker in *Laughing Sinners,*" wrote one fan. Complained another, "As a hard-boiled gangster he is swell, but when they try to make him a gentleman, he just isn't there." Taking its cue from fan comments, MGM cast Gable in one of the meanest roles of his career, as the gangster Ace Wilfong in *A Free Soul* (1931). It was a brilliant decision. Audiences loved his tough talk, brazen confidence, and shameless brutality; as the seedy lover of leading lady Norma Shearer, he slaps her, insults her, and throws her to the ground. Before long, the studio was swamped with thousands of fan letters that praised Gable's performance and demanded to see him in more films. It was then that the Gable formula became clear: the studio would market Gable as an aggressive romantic hero, an "adroit opponent in the duel of sex," in the words of *Photoplay.* After *A Free Soul,* Gable was issued a new contract and a higher salary. Thalberg frantically searched for scripts that would showcase the Gable machismo, while publicity director Howard Strickling launched a massive campaign to convince audiences that Gable was as rugged in person as he appeared on the screen.[31]

Strickling's task was challenging, although perhaps not as difficult as it might have been. In real life, Gable was something of a womanizer, and as a teenager, he had been a manual laborer to support himself. In Strickling's hands, however, the rougher elements of Gable's background were magnified to extreme proportions. "Rubber factory worker, oil driller—and now a screen star," began Gable's studio biography. To complement the image, the actor, who had never hunted or fished in his life, was portrayed in press releases as an avid outdoorsman, passionate about sports. Publicity photos showed the actor surrounded by fishing equipment, astride a horse, or leaning against a fireplace while cleaning a gun. "Clark Gable is a race horse enthusiast," explained the official studio press kit for *Chained* (1934). In conjunction with the film, MGM encouraged exhibitors to sponsor a Clark Gable Handicap, "a series of race horse events in many cities. Clark Gable trophies, contributed by theaters, would be the awards to winners."[32]

For the most part, Gable was eager to be molded by the MGM publicity machine. To support his new screen image, he cast out his fancy New York actor wardrobe and bought sports clothes. He went regularly to a gym and even tried his hand at hunting and fishing. For a while, Gable was the darling of the MGM publicity department—that is, until he slipped and revealed to reporters how much he was a pawn of the studio, and how much it controlled his image. "I just work here," he told a reporter in 1932. "They have an investment in me. They've spent money on me. It's my business to work, not to think." Terrified that Gable's frank comments would ruin his mystique, Strickling demanded that publicists accompany the actor to all interviews. Under the watch of the press agents, Gable made no more careless mistakes. In a typical conversation with a writer from *Screenland,* he said that his greatest joy in life was to "get outdoors and take up sports"; in an interview with *Modern Screen,* he claimed that in real life he was "Gable the roughneck and [not] Gable the gentleman." For its sheer inventiveness and fabrication, the Gable publicity campaign is recognized by many writers as one of the true masterpieces of image manipulation in Hollywood's studio era.[33]

Now that the Gable image was securely in place, MGM exploited it in film after film. In *Red Dust* (1932), Gable played a cynical rubber plantation owner who slaps, insults, and eventually romances tawdry Jean Harlow; in *Dancing Lady* (1933), *It Happened One Night* (1934), *Chained* (1934), and *Manhattan Melodrama* (1934), he also played rogues, aggressive, domineering, and inconsiderate, but irresistibly charming and handsome. Once again, audience feedback, box office returns, and fan mail confirmed Gable's success. According to MGM's tabulations, Gable's monthly fan mail surpassed that of top stars Wallace Beery and Joan Crawford. Gable had also become a powerful national icon and trend-setter. When he appeared in *It Happened One Night* without an undershirt, thousands of men copied him, sending the undergarment industry into a panic. He had become so popular and such a symbol of rugged masculinity that he even inspired a new phrase. When their boyfriends seemed too tough or overconfident, women often asked, "Who do you think you are, Clark Gable?"[34]

With such an overwhelming response, MGM saw little reason to change the Gable image. In its official press kit for *After Office Hours* (1935), the publicity department urged exhibitors to publicize Gable as "the not always noble lover":

> Sell him that way. Sell him as the fast worker who knew what he wanted and took it. Gable was anything but sweet and charming in *It Happened One Night*. He was rough and tough and damned independent . . . and the gal liked it. And how the audiences liked it. Here you have the same kind of a Gable, independent, resourceful, always charming, but never soft. Gable is rough, but he's swell—just the type that women—all women—like. Sell him that way.

The more films Gable made—*China Seas* (1935), *Mutiny on the Bounty* (1936), *San Francisco* (1936)—the greater his stardom, it seemed, and the more extreme and enthusiastic the antics of his fans. Whenever he appeared in public, he was literally attacked by admirers who crowded around him and yanked at his clothes. "When Gable was sent on a cross-country personal appearance tour, the crowds were the largest and most unruly since FDR announced he was shutting down the nation's banks for a day in 1933," recalled one observer. In 1937, one female fan from England was so infatuated that she claimed that Gable had fathered her child. The ensuing court case hardly damaged Gable's image (the actor had not been in England, and the woman seemed clearly unstable); instead, it became another testimony to the power and popularity of the Gable persona.[35]

In 1937, as far as many moviegoers were concerned, Clark Gable truly was the King of Hollywood, until *Parnell*. The story of the famous late-nineteenth-century Irish Nationalist leader, the film was not only a colossal box office failure but a definite setback in Gable's career. In cards filled out by preview audiences as well as thousands of letters, moviegoers complained about Gable's "stiff, sober" role as the serious, idealistic Parnell. "Clark's mug does not fit the character. It is too coarse. Not enough idealism manifested in his features," wrote one member of a preview audience in Santa Ana, California. "The leading people [Gable and Myrna Loy] are always fine but this is not their kind of picture," explained another. "Clark Gable, where have you gone?" asked one fan. "When I saw you in *Parnell* you were so strained. Come back in roles that let you be your cheerful dashing self. We want the Clark of *It Happened One Night* and *San Francisco*." Although they may have been satisfied with Gable's physical appearance—an "avalanche of protests from movie fans" convinced director John Stahl that Gable should have only sideburns in the film, rather than a beard—fans were upset, even horrified at their idol's new image.[36]

In the wake of *Parnell,* many fans abandoned Gable. Having seen their idol weak, serious, and uncharacteristically dignified, it was difficult to believe any longer in the Gable mystique. Many moviegoers saw the failure of the film as an excuse to vent longstanding complaints. "I'm quite fed up with Clark Gable," explained one woman. "He always seemed so conceited in his roles and characters. Hence I'm not on his FAN list, you note." Yet other fans stuck by their idol and pledged to help Gable restore his image. In 1937, hearing that David O. Selznick was casting for the role of Rhett Butler in *Gone with the Wind,* hundreds of fans sent letters on Gable's behalf. "Above all," explained movie fan Beth Young, "Clark Gable must be Rhett Butler."

> He is the only person for the role. I could see him from the moment he entered the story until the very end. Please don't disappoint millions of others just like me. I positively will not so much as make an effort to see the picture if he is not cast in that role. I would rather wait five years for him, if MGM has so many pictures scheduled for him that they cannot spare Mr. Gable.[37]

In her strong support for Gable, Beth Young was not alone. In 1938, Selznick received 495 fan letters demanding Gable for Butler; the next closest contender was John Mack Brown, with only 160 letters. Selznick, overwhelmed by the outpouring of support, agreed to cast Gable, even though it meant distributing the picture through MGM, which would halve his profits. "The public wanted Gable, and I was determined that the public should have Gable," Selznick admitted in a private letter to Ed Sullivan, Hollywood columnist for the *New York Daily News*. It was a decision that changed film history. As the aggressive, cynical Rhett, Gable won rave reviews, an Academy Award nomination, and the praise and congratulations of thousands of admirers worldwide.[38]

Following the triumph of *Gone with the Wind*, fans also congratulated themselves. It was they who had shaped a crucial casting decision. It was they who had made a vital contribution to one of the most phenomenally popular films in American history. To an extent, they were right; their letters and comments did significantly sway Selznick. But their influence, in many ways, extended far beyond what they imagined. Their desire to see a rugged screen hero, translated into fan letters, audience comments, and box office receipts, actually created Clark Gable, the cool, cocky, charming persona that continues to win followers to this day.

CREATING PERSONALITIES

Given fans' concern with truth and authenticity, one wonders whether fans knew the effect of their feedback on the creation of star images and, more generally, whether they were aware of the constructed nature of actors' personalities. Didn't fans notice the differences between the Crawford personality of 1927 and that of 1935? Didn't they see the contradictions between the carefree, headstrong flapper and the serious, struggling working girl? Didn't they realize that her persona was being actively manipulated by the studio?

Fans in the 1930s had become increasingly aware of the ability of the press and Hollywood to mislead and deceive. This did not necessarily mean, however, that they suspected stars' personalities were fabricated. Although they knew that gossip columns were often false, they may not have thought that celebrities themselves were created by film studios. Like the fan club members who called their idols genuine and sincere—and other stars phony and superficial—

they believed that their favorite actors had escaped Hollywood's unscrupulous system of image creation. Many Joan Crawford fans, for example, loved her so much that they could not believe her personality was artificial. They could not imagine that their idol was anything less than she claimed to be, or that she would willingly deceive the fans who adored her.

How did these fans reconcile their belief in Crawford with the inconsistencies in her personality? What did they make of the fact that she had once been called a fast-living socialite, then a modern-day Cinderella? It is possible that some fans did not follow Crawford that closely. Those who fell in love with the actress in 1934, for example, may have never been aware of her *Dancing Daughter* days. But many fans who had monitored Crawford's career found a convenient way to explain her transition. Rather than attribute the shift to the studio and publicity heads, they traced it to genuine changes in Crawford's life. Because Joan Crawford had matured, because she had married Douglas Fairbanks, Jr., because she worked diligently to learn sophistication and glamour, she had outgrown the Dancing Daughter roles and had become a serious actress, they said. "Rising from a lower status to her present heights is in truth a modern fairy tale that holds the working girl of today totally entranced," explained one fan in 1931. "Every interview she gives out, every picture that she plays in, every photograph she has made is of vital interest because of the remarkable change that has been wrought in her since her early pictures." Fan magazines, too, attested to the authenticity of the personality change. "Joan has become a woman—a woman of importance, a woman of poise with a clear thinking mind," wrote *Photoplay* in 1931. "She has changed utterly, completely. Today Joan Crawford Fairbanks is no more Lucille LeSueur than Will Rogers is Mahatma Gandhi." In other words, many fans admired their idols so much that it sometimes blinded them to the truth. Because they wanted to believe in their favorite stars, they temporarily suspended their suspicions of the Hollywood publicity system and instead tried to justify or rationalize the changes in stars' personalities.[39]

As a result, fans tended to be naive about the function of their comments to studios. They believed that their fan letters were merely boosting stars, not shaping their personal qualities. In reality, though, fans had more control over Hollywood than they realized. In direct response to fans' suggestions, studios manipulated and altered stars' images, often sparing no expense in the process. They bought actors new wardrobes, issued new press releases, refilmed scenes, and meticulously monitored fan correspondence, all in an attempt to retain fans' loyalties and box office dollars. More than just a creation of Hollywood, the memorable celebrity personalities of the 1930s and 1940s were produced jointly by stars, studios, and thousands of active movie fans.

CHAPTER SEVEN

THE FANDOM MENACE

IN 1947, ELLEN ROUFS CAME UP WITH AN IDEA that thrilled film fans throughout the nation. As president of the International Fan Club League, an umbrella organization that coordinated the activities of over 500 different movie star fan clubs, she decided to revive the idea of the national fan club convention, a meeting that had been held annually in the 1930s. In June, she proposed that over 250,000 fan club members meet in Hollywood, learn about each other's activities, go on studio tours, and meet their favorite stars. According to *Movieland* magazine, it promised "to be the biggest thing that ever happened to fan clubs."[1]

But when news of the proposed convention reached the studios and the press, Roufs's hopes began to dim. Rather than generating enthusiasm, her announcement sparked a tremendous outpouring of antifan sentiment. The Motion Picture Producers Association, the film industry's governing body, quickly protested the convention. Shortly afterward, the *New York Times,* supporting Hollywood's decision, urged the clubs to keep their "half-neurotic, half-idiotic hero worship" at home. Seeking a more long-term solution, *Today's Woman* suggested that Americans strengthen their religious commitments to curb the spiritual hunger that apparently motivated these "ravenous fans."[2]

In spite of the opposition, Roufs had her way. Unfazed, she pushed forward with the convention, which eventually took place in late 1947, minus the studio tours. But the widespread criticism of movie fans persisted long after the convention had passed. Prompted by public alarm over the apparent increasing popularity of film fandom, newspapers issued a series of articles that criticized fans, who were said to be gullible, "drooling," and victims of "social and emotional poverty." One writer remarked that fans "eat up the baloney"—the lies and gossip printed in fan magazines. "These fans accept the whole Hollywood myth," explained another.[3]

Although extreme, the outcry surrounding the 1947 convention was far from an isolated outburst. Instead, it was the culmination of over 40 years of discussion and debate on film fandom and, more generally, on the nature of film spectatorship. Throughout film history, fans have been accused of a variety of sins. They have been called hysterical and uncontrollable, naive and unintelligent. They were so infatuated, critics claimed, that they spent hours dreaming about the stars. Perhaps more than anything, they seemed to confuse fantasy and reality. Fans were so obsessed with the movies, said critics, that they could not tell where the cinema ended and real life began.

This attack on film fandom had deep roots, dating back to the earliest days of the motion picture, in particular, to an early theory of film spectatorship. During the decade following 1910, psychologists, writers, and social scientists, all concerned with the impact of the motion picture on society, issued a shocking statement: the movies were like a drug. With their intense close-ups, larger-than-life images, and emotional appeal, they incited viewers to abandon all rational thought. Under the spell of the cinema, spectators entered a powerful realm of make-believe, a hypnotic fantasy world that seemed as vivid and real as life itself.

Thankfully, said critics, the spell wore off. After a night at the movies, most adults had the sense to leave the dream world behind. But some moviegoers did not. Movie fans, it seemed, remained stuck in the cinematic fantasy long after the show had ended. They wrote passionate letters to actors and daydreamed about Hollywood. They spent hours discussing films and even imitated what they saw on the screen; they reenacted scenes from films and copied stars' styles and mannerisms. In children, such behavior was understandable, but in adults, it was inexcusable. Men and women should know, after all, that "it's only a movie."

Throughout the 1920s, psychologists and other experts worked diligently to publicize these insights on film spectatorship. In pamphlets, books, and articles, they repeated, again and again, the difference between normal and abnormal attitudes toward the cinema. Mature viewers remained cool and distant from the movies; the immature became intensely involved. Mature spectators saw the movies as trivial entertainment; to fans, they were as important as life itself. But the strongest evidence against movie fans may have come from the fans themselves. During the 1920s, a series of well-publicized events convinced many Americans of the immaturity, gullibility, and even pathology of the average film enthusiast. At Rudolph Valentino's funeral in 1926, fans screamed, swooned, and wept hysterically. At movie premieres, they created near-mob scenes as they pushed and shoved to see the stars. Overtaken by their love for film celebrities, fans seemed to have lost all sense of reality.

In the wake of the spectacles of the 1920s, movie fans no longer seemed just a nuisance. To many Americans, they had become a pressing national crisis. As more and more moviegoers became fans during the 1930s, the attacks flew fast and furious. Popular magazines analyzed the psychology of film fans and discussed their pathological tendencies. Novelists satirized their antics and pathetic naiveté. Even Hollywood used films to lampoon its most loyal devotees. No longer limited to scholars and social reformers, the war against movie fans had been taken up by a broad and diverse range of opponents.

Although many fans tried to defend themselves, others retreated. Fearing the accusations, many denied being true film fans. "I never write letters to movie stars, but this time I made an exception," wrote one woman to Gloria Swanson. "I am not a movie-struck child," claimed another. As more and more adults shunned association with film fandom, it was children and adolescents who became its most eager participants. Not afraid to be called juvenile, they screamed and swooned before stars, only strengthening the association between fandom, immaturity, and the misperception of reality.[4]

Ironically, fans were probably more concerned with reality than the average spectator. They read movie magazines, wrote fan letters, and learned everything they could about the movies in an attempt to learn about the reality behind the screen. Fans formed clubs, sent suggestions to studios, and tried to befriend their favorite celebrities in the hopes of having a direct, real-life relationship with the men and women who made the films. If fans were obsessed with anything, it was reality and authenticity.

But to the writers, scholars, and reformers who attacked them, film fans seemed hopelessly deluded. Immature and naive, they appeared to succumb wholeheartedly to Hollywood's temptations. Rather than think for themselves, they imitated what they saw on the screen; rather than follow traditional codes of moral and sexual behavior, they embraced Hollywood's glamour, gaudiness, and sensuality with incredible affinity. More than just gullible spectators, to many critics, fans were living symbols of the profound social changes that had swept American society: the liberalization of sexual ethics, the rise of an entertainment-oriented consumer culture, and the growth of a powerful mass media. Between 1910 and 1950, critics not only fought a war against film fandom but against the modern, mass-mediated consumer society in which Hollywood played an increasingly central role.

THE CELLULOID DRUG

Although their opinions and objectives often clashed, filmmakers, spectators, and cultural critics in the first two decades of the twentieth century agreed on one thing. Powered by electricity, imprinted on celluloid, projected in dimensions larger than life, the cinema was unlike anything anyone had ever seen. But it was not only the technology that was revolutionary. The way the movies entertained audiences—by stirring intense emotions of excitement, passion, and fear—was unprecedented, even shocking. Some viewers were so moved by the movies that they screamed and shouted in the theater. Others wept at tragedies and laughed uncontrollably during comedies. More than the theater, music, dance, or art, the movies possessed an almost magical capability to engage viewers, intensely and emotionally, with their entertainment.

While moviegoers were thrilled by the cinema's ability to provoke passion and mimic reality, social reformers were terrified. They were concerned not only by the images of sex and violence in films, which they claimed would corrupt children, but by what the movies seemed to represent. Inexpensive, popular among immigrant and working-class audiences, and sometimes frankly sexual in content, the movies symbolized some of the most profound (and to reformers, deeply disturbing) changes taking place in American society. The influx of millions of immigrants into rapidly growing urban centers, greater social and sexual freedom for women, and the decline of restrictive Victorian morals, among other changes, seriously threatened the power of the middle-class Protestant elite, which sought drastic measures to curb what looked like impending social breakdown.

In the spirit of the Progressive movement, which advocated legislation as a means to social reform, religious and social welfare organizations in the first decade of the century called for strict government regulation of the movies. Social reformers attempted, unsuccessfully, to bar children from nickelodeons; they instituted a short-lived movie rating system in Chicago and even tried, in 1908, to shut down movie theaters altogether. When these efforts to curb film attendance failed, they began clamoring for state and federal film censorship. Activists issued books and pamphlets that vilified the movies; the film industry responded with a flurry of anticensorship propaganda, and by 1915, a battle was under way.

Both pro- and anticensorship forces predicted that the war would be short. In the eyes of the film industry, Americans would quickly see the folly of censorship. It violated free speech, cost taxpayers thousands of dollars, and stripped the public of control over their entertainment. Reformers thought otherwise. They claimed that no self-respecting American could ignore the crisis that would ensue if movies were left uncensored: the children, for example, who would imitate the crimes depicted on the screen, or the innocent young women who might be corrupted by detailed scenes of passion and romance. In the end, however, both sides were wrong. The censorship war did not last for several months, a year, or even a decade: it stretched out for over 20 years, until it at last died down in the early 1930s.

Most accounts paint the film industry as the ultimate victor. Federal censorship was never enacted, the movies became phenomenally popular, and film attendance skyrocketed. With adept public relations skills and a careful program of self-censorship, culminating in the creation of the 1934 Production Code Administration—a regulatory board, operated by the film industry, which carefully controlled the sexual and moral content of films—Hollywood triumphed over its opponents to become one of the most important and influential forces in American society. But the reformers' efforts were not entirely in vain. Not only did they force the film industry to become more cautious in its portrayals of crime and romance, but they publicized a set of arguments that would forever shape popular thinking about motion pictures.

The movies were dangerous. This the reformers deeply believed. But no matter how frequently and fervently they repeated it, they knew that their success would be limited unless they showed exactly how and why the movies constituted such a threat. To prove to lawmakers and the American public the dangers of motion pictures, early censorship activists set out to theorize, calculate, and classify the harmful effects of the cinema on its viewers. They consulted psychologists and philosophers. They talked to moviegoers, observed their behavior, and sometimes even went to the cinema themselves. By 1920, they had reached a tentative conclusion: the movies were like a drug. Like a sedative or strong drink, they heightened emotions, reduced inhibitions, and altered the senses.

The danger started the moment audiences looked up at the screen. Sitting in a darkened theater, watching bright moving images projected larger than life, viewers entered a kind of trance that made them particularly receptive to suggestion. "We are all suggestible," argued one psychologist. "But when we sit in a darkened moving picture house, we are one hundred percent more so. The mind becomes uncritical [and] reasoning, logic, and judgment practically cease functioning." Writer P. W. Wilson put it more poetically. "An automobile takes you up in one place and sets you down in another, but does not change your mind. An elevator only raises or depresses your physical anatomy. But in the movie, you sit in a dim religious light . . . and your imagination, so rendered as impassively sensitive as a film itself, has impressed upon it scenes that do often lie too deep for tears," he explained in 1921. "No fiction, no drama has ever reached an audience in a mood so credulous, so impressionable."[5]

But it was not only the atmosphere that drugged audiences. The images and stories on the screen, claimed reformers, created a vivid illusion of reality that left many spectators completely spellbound. In the eyes of some viewers, wrote Harvard psychologist Hugo Munsterberg in 1916, the movies may have seemed even *more* real than reality. Rather than depict actions as they might unfold in the real world, the movies sped up, dramatized, and simplified events, giving viewers an "intensified feeling of life." In addition, he argued, the movies mimicked "mental action." With its swift, sometimes illogical movements between images and scenes, the camera duplicated the human psyche. Close-up shots, with their intense focus on a particular person or object, "do what in our mind our attention is doing." Cut-back scenes, which recall earlier events, are "really an objectivation of our memory function."[6]

Although Munsterberg did not advocate censorship, his insights into the psychological effects of motion pictures were quickly taken up by social reformers. No other form of entertainment operated at such a deep psychological level, they claimed. No other kind of amusement created such intense emotions or invited viewers, so convincingly and seductively, to mistake fantasy for reality. According to the news magazine *Current Opinion* in 1921, one man, "now serving sixty years," believed that he could commit crimes and elude the police, just like the characters in movies. Another woman, deeply upset by a tragic film, committed suicide. Some viewers were so taken in by the cinematic illusion that they claimed to "receive touch or temperature or smell or sound impressions" from the images on the screen. "It would be a great mistake to underestimate the power of this seduction," warned one psychologist. "Think of the drug habit, of alcohol, of the Saturnalia and other orgies of antiquity, all of which perform the same mental function."[7]

Like "a poisonous flow of gas," wrote censorship advocates, the movies quietly but fatally intoxicated their viewers. Powerful, enticing, and addictive, they placed viewers in a "primitive, instinctive" state that caused them to "drink in everything the eyes see without question." How could Americans sit idly by while the cinema tainted millions of moviegoers? reformers asked. Worse yet, how could they sanction the slow but sure corruption of innocent children? If the movies could drug adults, what might they do to impressionable youth?[8]

MENTAL "DEFECTIVES"

In the eyes of the reformers and censorship activists, the movies were harmful to all who saw them, but they were undeniably most threatening to children. Although all moviegoers entered a state of heightened suggestibility during films, mature adults might resist falling completely into the trance. Because they possessed experience and intelligence, they might remind themselves, in moments of passion or suspense, that "it's only a movie." Or perhaps they might enter deeply into the cinematic fantasy while watching a film but return to reality at the end of the show.

Children, however, lacked the mental and emotional skills necessary to make such a transition, claimed the activists. Immature and inexperienced, they fell deeply—and perhaps permanently—under the cinema's spell. "One of the characteristics which mark the difference between children and adults is in their reaction [to the movies]," explained psychologist Samuel Heckman in 1920. "The imagination is less modified, is less controlled in relation to realities." Unable to distinguish between fact and fiction, missing "the fact and experience of the world to counteract the cinema," they took the movies to be real. "The movies are, after all, a make-believe world in which the characters are not real, mere shadows on the screen. Evidence, however, [suggests] that to many young people . . . the world of the movies is not less real than life itself; the emotions and responses of the young to the fevered life of the screen are much the same as to those in actual life," explained another writer.[9]

In some cases, children fell so deeply into the illusion that they became infatuated with actors, dreamed about becoming a cowboy or movie star, or even imitated the actions in films, often with disastrous consequences. "Scarcely a day passes by that the public press does not contain accounts of children committing crimes and the excuse is often offered that they were attempting to reproduce something which they had witnessed in a motion picture," reported the New York State Motion Picture Commission. In 1920, two boys accused of murder cited the movies as their motivation; the following year, two Michigan teenagers confessed to an attempt to wreck a passenger train because they "wanted to see in real life a railroad wreck like those they had seen on the screen."[10]

Throughout the censorship war, reformers would return to the negative influence of motion pictures on children. The Women's Christian Temperance Union, a major censorship advocate, issued pamphlets with lurid tales of young movie fans turned robbers and murderers. Sixteen educators and reformers interviewed by *Parents' Magazine* agreed that the movies had damaging effects: "It does not necessarily require scientific analysis . . . to know that the strain is too severe for ten-year-old children of our civilization," explained one social worker. As psychologists and reformers presented it, the fight for film censorship seemed exclusively like a crusade to save the nation's children from corruption.[11]

The concern with youth may not have been as authentic as it seemed. By centering the argument for censorship around children, reformers were able to disguise their true motives: to control, even turn back, the forces of modernity rapidly transforming the nation. It was much easier to blame the movies for the tremendous social changes from 1910 through the 1920s—changing sexual ethics, greater independence for women, a new emphasis on consumption, glamour, and personality—than to address the true economic and demographic causes. It was much simpler to attack films and film fandom than to decry the social and economic forces that brought increasing numbers of women into the workforce, or that attracted immigrants to the growing cities, or that gave birth to a thriving consumer culture. To social reformers, the movies became a convenient scapegoat for all that was new, wrong, and potentially threatening about modern American life.

Not surprisingly, the movie fan, one of the most obvious symbols of the new, movie-made culture, became a natural target of attack. Not only were fans vulgar and uncouth, said critics, but they suffered from deep mental and emotional problems. Turning to the theory that mature moviegoers resisted the movies and that juveniles succumbed to them, many scholars decided that adult movie fans, with their intense enthusiasm for the cinema, were remarkably childlike. Naive and gullible, they fell in love with stars and daydreamed about

Hollywood. Immature and uncontrolled, they allowed themselves to be taken in fully by the cinema's illusion of reality. In their many articles on the movies and youth, social critics claimed that fans were no better than children.

In some cases, argued psychologists, the fan's immature behavior stemmed from genuine mental defects. According to censorship advocate Dr. A. T. Poffenberger, who wrote extensively on the cinema and youth, many adult movie fans were actually "morons" with the mental age of an 11-year-old. Thinking that the movies depicted reality, fans believed and frequently imitated what they watched, including "murder, burglary, violence, and crime." More threatening than young movie fans, "they constitute a real danger, since their physical age, which may be from fifteen years up, places them in a position to act upon suggestions more readily than the child," Poffenberger explained.[12]

These "undeveloped" viewers, scholars implied, were genuinely unable to distinguish between the movies and reality. Through no fault of their own, they lacked the mental tools necessary to resist being drugged by the cinema. But not all movie fans were psychologically retarded. Many, according to critics, were fully functioning adults with normal mental capabilities. They had normal families, a normal appearance, and normal jobs. But in one way they were not average: they had deep character flaws that prevented them from behaving maturely. Some fans were simply gullible, and like children, trusted everything they saw and heard. Many moviegoers, wrote psychologist Louis Bisch, "are just as likely to be beguiled into believing what they see in a movie as they are into believing what actually occurs before their eyes in real life." Other fans were so troubled or unfulfilled that they consciously *chose* to be taken in by the movies. To avoid or escape reality, they willingly succumbed to the cinema's narcotic effects.[13]

These fans, suggested psychologist George Humphrey, were less to be pitied than despised. In a 1924 article on the movies and youth, he suggested that adult fans, like some children, were "mentally lazy." Rather than behave responsibly, they sought refuge in the unreal world of the screen. "Where the movie habit has developed into a passion, it should be regarded as a symptom, perhaps of mental sloth, perhaps of sheer weariness, perhaps of some underlying trouble," he wrote. In many cases, the symptom actually became part of the problem. By going too frequently to the movies, "the movie fan gets out of the habit of thinking with facts and into the habit of thinking pleasantly. This develops a type of person who is necessarily out of touch with his surroundings, essentially unhappy, for whom the world must be out of joint because it cannot be made over to his impossible wishes." In other words, said critics, fans lingered so long in the cinematic fantasy that they lost touch with the reality around them.[14]

THE CULT OF VALENTINO

On August 25, 1926, Peggy Scott's life changed forever. Her idol, Rudolph Valentino, the dashing hero of *The Sheik, The Four Horsemen of the Apocalypse,* and other phenomenally popular films of the 1920s, died of a perforated ulcer in a New York hospital. Heartbroken and depressed, Scott, a young woman working in London, found solace in a fatal bottle of poison. "I am only a little butterfly made for sunshine and I cannot stand loneliness and shadow," she wrote in a suicide note. "With his death, my last bit of courage has flown."[15]

The announcement of Peggy Scott's suicide on August 28 was only one of the many shocking reports to make the news that week. Only a few days earlier, newspapers and newsreels had reported the presence of a terrifying, unruly mob, screaming and rioting on the streets of New York. In front of the funeral home where Valentino rested, an estimated 50,000 to 75,000 men and women pushed, shoved, and fought one another to catch a glimpse of the actor lying in state. Windows were broken, property damaged, and onlookers trampled, all the result, said papers, of the uncontrollable hysteria of movie fans.

By 1926, the image of the aggressive, violent film fan was not entirely new. In 1921, the London honeymoon of Douglas Fairbanks and Mary Pickford had created similar riots, as frenzied admirers screamed, swarmed around them, and tore at their hair and clothes. When the couple drove down the street in a convertible, onlookers nearly pulled Pickford out of the car; while attending a garden party, the actress was almost crushed by a crowd of curious fans. The "mob madness," wrote Alexander Woolcott, "took on the nature of an epidemic." At movie premieres, a popular method of studio publicity in the 1920s and 1930s, fans seemed similarly possessed. On the opening night of *Madame Sans Gene* in 1925, over 10,000 fans mobbed a Los Angeles theater to catch a glimpse of Gloria Swanson. In some cases, premieres erupted into near-riots as eager admirers, seeking handshakes or autographs, descended en masse upon their favorite stars.[16]

But the Valentino riot created a spectacle like no one had ever seen. The street in front of the funeral home, remarked observers, looked like a battlefield. Fans pressed against the windows, hoping to get a glimpse of the coffin; in the process, the glass shattered, and several onlookers were injured. When the funeral parlor at last opened its doors to the public, the crowd surged. "The mass pushed forward, a foot at a time, even shoving the horses along the sidewalk, so great was the pressure from behind," said the *New York Times*. "When the throng got too close to the doors . . . the police charged, breaking it up, pushing it back to the corners." By the end of the day, over 100 men and women were seriously hurt; several were taken to the hospital with bruises and broken limbs. "The rioting was without precedent in New York, both in the numbers concerned and in the behavior of the crowd, which in larger part consisted of women and girls," claimed the *Times*. "Many of these suffered discomfort for hours for whatever satisfaction it gave them to be hustled by the coffin and to gaze for an instant."[17]

The *Times* probably exaggerated. Although newsreel footage does show many women in the crowd, men also showed up in great numbers. In addition to the female admirers, recalled one observer, more than a few "young men and boys, 'sheiks' and collegians, were also in evidence." But newspapers could not resist temptation. The stereotypical image of women swooning over a handsome matinee idol was far more sensational—and sold more copies—than the more accurate picture of an aggressive, bewildered, mixed-sex mob. As a result, press coverage of the Valentino funeral, which focused heavily on the "hysterical behavior" of female fans, only further cemented the connection between fandom and pathology. Like children, women could not resist the cinema's temptations. To irrational and emotional females, it seemed, Valentino was as vivid and intimate as a real-life lover.[18]

Critics were appalled at the spectacle. "I am greatly disappointed at the way men and women acted when they were allowed to see Valentino's body," said the late actor's manager, Charles Ullman.

"They showed the most gross irreverence. I am sorry they were allowed to see him at all." Shocked by the forthright display of female sexuality, others commented disgustedly on the "middle-aged matrons" and "hysterical women who prostrated themselves before his tomb." But the greatest offense, according to the New York Times, was the tremendous attention given to Valentino in the first place. Although former Harvard president Charles Eliot died the same day, few Americans took notice. Even the near-death of revered writer Rudyard Kipling a few years earlier had not stirred the kind of mass mania provoked by the movie star. The Times observed: "The immense interest shown in the outcome of Valentino's illness is a striking sign of what moving pictures have done to create a new mental attitude in vast multitudes of people. They come to regard a favorite screen actor as one whom they have known intimately. He is a household name in millions of homes where a mere writer of books could never hope to enter."[19]

The Times's attack was hardly surprising. As society's traditional elites knew well, America by the late 1920s was rapidly becoming "Hollywood-ized." The movies seemed to impress the public more deeply than literature or religion. Stars often commanded more attention and respect than political leaders. Understandably, the extreme conduct of the Valentino fans—and their seemingly all-consuming obsession with motion pictures—sparked considerable disdain among educators, social reformers, and intellectuals. It also brought, for the first time, criticism of fans by the film industry and by fans themselves.

Both Hollywood and many movie fans were thoroughly embarrassed by the Valentino affair. Terrified of association with fanaticism and violence, the film industry insisted that the rioters were not true movie fans, but unscrupulous, conniving publicity seekers. Men and women "seized upon his sickness to publicize themselves. [They] shrieked and fainted at his bier for the sake of reporters only," wrote Moving Picture World in an article entitled "Valentino, The Martyr." Many Valentino fans made a similar complaint. In a letter to Picture Play magazine, one woman criticized the onlookers at the funeral, particularly "those who are carrying to extremes the methods in which they are advertising their mourning for him." "One of the things that Valentino most disliked was sentimentality and gush," explained another fan. The histrionics in the New York streets simply weren't "fair to Rudy."[20]

The year 1926 marked a watershed in the history of film fandom. In the wake of the Valentino incident, fans became the subject of more widespread public attention and condemnation than ever before. In the 1930s, popular magazines and newspapers spent pages discussing, analyzing, and criticizing film fans. Novelists teased and lampooned them. Even Hollywood created films that chastised overeager enthusiasts. Once limited primarily to social reformers, censorship advocates, and other opponents of the cinema, the attack on film fandom was joined by some of the motion picture industry's most enthusiastic supporters.

A MODERN MENACE

A few reasonable observers may have seen the Valentino incident for what it really was. Although many of the men and women in the crowd were true Valentino fans, many, perhaps even the majority, were not. Most of the rioters probably had never belonged to Valentino's fan clubs. Many never followed his career, and some may have never seen his films. In many ways, the Valentino riot was less a product of movie fan culture than of American celebrity culture. Fascinated and titillated by the possibility of seeing a famous figure in person, aggressive curiosity seekers descended on the Valentino funeral with remarkable ferocity.

But many Americans did not see it that way. In their eyes, the spectacle became a testimony to the immaturity and pathology of movie fans—not just those who were aggressive and violent, but *all* fans. Within each fan club member or autograph seeker, they feared, lurked the possibility of hysteria. The millions of men and women who participated in movie fan culture might be as illogical and uncontrollable as the rioters. Shocked by the Valentino incident and by the increasing popularity of fan clubs and magazines in the 1930s, critics launched yet another attack on the growing fandom menace. However, they did not have to start from scratch. Rather than reinvent the arguments wholesale, the new critics of fandom drew on many of the assumptions and theories pioneered by the psychologists and reformers who had been active in the censorship debate. Fans succumbed to the cinema's illusions and believed the movies real: that much had already been discussed and confirmed. What remained to be investigated was precisely *why* fans confused fantasy and reality. Was it lack of education or naiveté? Was it mental deficiency or spiritual and emotional emptiness?

According to scholar Margaret Thorp, who spent several years in the mid-1930s researching stardom and fandom, it was gullibility, above all, that caused fans to conflate fact and fiction. Fans were simply so immature and trusting that they placed their faith in everything they saw on the screen. "So seriously do the fans take advice, so conscientiously do they copy their models that publicity men can no longer indulge in flights of fancy about baths in goat's milk and honey . . . or exquisitely imaginative reducing diets. Every beauty hint must now be checked by an expert lest the fan sicken in her enthusiastic imitation—and sue," she explained. Carl Cotter, writing for the *Coast* magazine in 1939, agreed. Not only did fans "pattern their hairstyles, their clothes, their cookery, and their behavior after those of their favorite actors . . . [but] also base their most profound thinking on the words of those same authorities." Echoing the accusations of the psychologists and censorship activists, Cotter suggested that fans were unable to resist suggestion.[21]

Cotter also leveled an accusation against movie fans that would continue throughout the century. Because fan magazine articles were simply and plainly written—hardly highbrow prose—their readers must be simple-minded, Cotter reasoned. Uneducated and naive, they voraciously consumed the "hack writing" printed in *Photoplay*, *Modern Screen*, and *Motion Picture*. To one critic, fans were "filmorons" who desperately craved the "idiotic slop" in fan magazines; according to *Variety*, they were mindless "gum-chewing gals" who devoted hours each day to the "fan mag guff." One prominent scholar, according to Thorp, made an extensive study of the letters written by fans to the editors of movie magazines. The scholar concluded that "each letter writer has at her command, for the expression of the whole gamut of rapture and disgust, just one hundred and fifty words."[22]

Perhaps even more tragic than fans' lack of education and intelligence, said critics, was the great faith that they put in film celebrities. Unable to see through the publicity stunts, fans seemed to believe that stars were the same in person as in films, that they were as warm and intimate as they appeared on the screen. This misperception often had ridiculous if not disastrous consequences. Some fans fell so deeply in love with stars that they became obsessed. Others concocted elaborate schemes and fantasies built around their false assumptions. One fan, explained the *Washington Herald* in 1936, spent her last dollars to go to Hollywood and propose marriage to George Raft. Screen swashbuckler Errol Flynn received invitations from fans to join them on hunts and expeditions, wrote journalist Fredda Dudley in the *Ladies' Home Journal*. As the pinnacle of fan absurdity, Dudley cited the case of one young man who wrote Fred MacMurray a desperate letter. "It's like this, Mr. MacMurray. I know you are a good guy, and regular, and can be trusted, so please write my girl a nasty letter so she'll forget you," he asked. To the movie fan, remarked *Harper's* in 1936, "screen selves and real selves become hopelessly entangled."[23]

Not only were these efforts to interact with stars "ludicrous and pathetic," wrote Dudley, but they could be quite harmful. When fans failed to connect with their idols, they were deeply disappointed. Worse yet, they were devastated if and when they learned that stars were, in real life, different from their characters. "The whole system depends upon the identity of star and role. To the majority of spectators . . . to see [stars] behaving out of character is to see one's universe rock . . . a sensation not unlike going mad," wrote Thorp. Fans had become so deeply immersed in the fantasy, she suggested, that they almost could not bear to face reality.[24]

But was it simply gullibility that caused fans to conflate fantasy and reality? Many critics believed the confusion stemmed from deeper causes—namely, spiritual and emotional failings. Lonely and unfulfilled, fans escaped pain by immersing themselves in the dream world of the screen. They sought salvation in movies and stars, just as others turned to religion. Saddled with a "hungry ego," explained film critic Bosley Crowther in 1942, the average film fan craved a "feeling of personal contact" with his or her favorite star and the fulfillment it brought to "a generally commonplace life." "Indeed," Crowther added, "one may seriously wonder if [fans'] loyalties are to persons who are real or to idealized phantoms which inhabit their own self-identifying dreams."[25]

Everywhere fans looked they were under attack. Magazines and newspapers criticized them; novelists satirized them; even Hollywood, in popular films, poked fun at its most loyal admirers. In RKO's *In Person* (1935) the movie star is pursued not by a single crazed fan but by a violent crowd. After being manhandled at a few chaotic film premieres, the celebrity, played by Ginger Rogers, becomes so terrified of fans that she refuses to go out in public unless disguised. Fans drive the main character of *Honolulu* (1939) so crazy that he flees to Hawaii to avoid them. The star is so satisfied with his peaceful life, free of greedy and frenzied admirers, that he stays in the islands indefinitely.

Some fans may have laughed at the insults. Others might have ignored them. But more than a few were angry—deeply insulted, in fact—and tried diligently to defend themselves from attack. In fan magazines and fan club journals, they assured each other that they were not gullible, not desperate, and certainly not childlike. In an article in *Photoplay* magazine entitled "Are We Morons?," a psychologist commissioned by editor James Quirk assured readers that they were not "morons with the intelligence of a child from eight to twelve," but bright and normal individuals with a healthy love of entertainment. "Intelligent, capable and cultured persons of all ages find relaxation in a movie show. The term moron, as applied to [fans] has been widely abused," he explained. "Don't classify fans as children and unintelligent men and women!" wrote fan club president E. M. Orowitz in a letter to the film industry. "Movie fans know more about pictures than the experts who create them."[26]

Many fans tried explicitly to distance themselves from the aggressive, swooning men and women who had given fandom such a bad name. In his monthly club journal, the *Movie Fan,* Orowitz attacked those fans who "pester screen stars for photos and autographs." "We do not carry those kind of fans on our membership rolls," he bragged. One fan club leader in the 1930s warned club presidents not to participate in a popular "chain letter scam": "Fan clubs and their leaders especially should not do things like sending these letters on. People will form the wrong opinion of fan clubs. We want to prove to the public that we stand for fair play." The president of the Bette Davis club denied that fans were disreputable as they were portrayed. "Articles have been written about the shameful conduct of fans towards stars, but they are grossly exaggerated," she explained. "I've belonged to fan clubs for years and have met members from New York and other parts of the country and have found them to be well-mannered, intelligent, and able to converse upon many subjects other than their main interest, the movies."[27]

But perhaps the most ingenious and effective method to combat the attacks, fans discovered, was to turn the critics' own arguments against them. Yes, fans admitted, they did use the movies as an escape, but the effects were wholly positive. The movies were an important, refreshing, and *temporary* respite from reality, one that helped them cope with life's difficulties. As fan Marian Rodgers explained in a letter to *Photoplay* magazine,

> To the movies I owe a debt of gratitude. During my hardest years they offered me respite and escape. When life is pretty thick, money scarce, clothes shabby, just slip into the grateful darkness of the movie theater for a couple of hours. I remember one occasion in particular. After nursing the kids and their father through a siege of flu, cold packs, hot packs, aspirin, orange juice and the rest, I had them at last safely convalescent and slipped out to a show. It was a romance as picturesque as an old tapestry. And did I enjoy it! I walked home in the rain with new energy to tackle my job.[28]

"A nurse has to have some pretty steady nerves and plenty of patience," wrote Olga Miller. "If she didn't go to a theater once or twice a week—where she can sit in peace and relax and enjoy a good picture—why, she wouldn't last for long." Rather than escape permanently into Hollywood's fantasy world, these people used the movies to enrich their everyday lives.[29]

Moreover, fans explained, the movies were not only a fantasy, they taught them a good deal about reality. Many fans proudly confessed to fan magazines that they "used the movies" to learn about news, manners, and contemporary culture. "My cousin," wrote one woman to *Photoplay,* "has gained a certain poise through watching the screen people. Her manners are improving daily. The effect of the movies is entirely beneficial." One self-described "farm woman" thanked the movies for keeping her "in touch with the right fashions, the proper setting of furniture, and right etiquette." But moviegoers did not imbibe cinematic images unquestioningly. As fans repeated, they copied only the best styles and mannerisms and rejected those they thought unattractive or contrived. One woman dreamed about creating her own unique style, based on a composite of several popular stars: she aspired to "the glamor of Garbo, Connie Bennett's poise, dress like Shearer and legs just like Dietrich's."[30]

The critics of film fandom, claimed one woman, "are denouncing something they know nothing about." "I would like someone to try to tell me that I am demoralized," snapped another. Even though many fans tried to defend themselves from attack, others retreated. Fearing association with immaturity and pathology, many movie magazine readers and fan letter writers denied that they were really fans. Several prefaced their letters to stars and studios with disclaimers: "Although I'm not really a fan letter writer, I've wanted for some time to write," confessed one admirer to Gloria Swanson. In a letter to producer David O. Selznick, a man explained, "This is the first time I have ever written to any producer or any film star so I am *not* a movie struck fan." In particular, fans were concerned that their attempts at correspondence might be interpreted as juvenile. "I am 33 and just a bit too mature to be writing fan mail," explained one fan to Swanson. One man began his letter with a somewhat ironic defense: "Before I go any further than the first sentence of this letter may I say that this is not a fan letter in the usual sense of the word— I am a 25 year old Virginian and my wife is of the same age. We are not in the least bit of the stretch of the imagination two young persons who are given to the practice of taking the time to sit around and write a letter of appreciation to someone in the profession of the arts." Of course, he and his wife *were* writing a letter of appreciation to Gloria Swanson, but his age and maturity, he believed, prevented him from being a "true movie fan."[31]

The fear of being associated with children was well founded. Traditionally linked with immaturity and gullibility, fans were often assumed to be childlike—if not in age, at least in mentality. In the late 1930s and early 1940s, however, the connection between the movies and youth grew even stronger. Children and adolescents, always major participants in movie fan culture, appeared to be joining fan clubs in droves. Moreover, youth culture had become increasingly movie-centered; as sociologist Herbert Blumer noted, teens in the 1930s not only went regularly to the cinema but created elaborate games and rituals built around imitating film stars. More than ever, fandom seemed like a children's activity, and one well-publicized event confirmed it. The Columbus Day Riot of 1944 convinced many Americans that movie fans were no better than screaming, swooning adolescents.

THE SLAVES OF SINATRA

Although adolescents were active film fans, it was adults who most often led and organized fan clubs, read fan magazines, and wrote literally millions of fan letters each year. Americans reading the headlines in the early 1940s, however, may have received a different impression. In magazines and newspapers were warnings of a new fandom menace—not the middle-aged washouts described by Nathanael West in *The Day of the Locust,* but a breed of younger, more enthusiastic, more aggressive star-worshipers. They were called bobbysoxers, and they would reinforce the connection between fandom, immaturity, and violence.

Accounts of bobbysoxer misdeeds were legion. As newspapers frequently reported, these aggressive teenagers (often girls, dressed in skirts and short bobbysocks) screamed, swooned, and insistently pursued their screen idols. When Ingrid Bergman was shopping in a New York store in the early 1940s, she turned around and found 200 or more young fans following her. "Crowding close to her, they pulled her hair, tore her dress, and were so unmannerly that the management had to call the police," read one report. Other teenage fans camped out in front of actors' homes, screaming or pounding on the doors. One 14-year-old bellhop, reported newspapers in July 1944, even attacked actress Jeanette MacDonald in her hotel room. "I hid in a closet and when she got near, jumped out and tried to blind her with a blanket," confessed the boy, who hoped to steal from her a handkerchief or other souvenir. It seemed that fans, particularly young fans, were becoming more brazen than ever before. Was it the war that caused them to behave so desperately? asked critics. Was it the absence of so many fathers? Or was it, as the *New Republic* suggested, "a hunger for heroes"? Did young people feel neglected in a culture that had become so busy "making things and selling things"?[32]

Speculation and sympathy, however, turned to outrage when thousands of New York fans took to the streets. On the morning of

October 12, 1944, 10,000 fans, including many teenagers, lined up in front of New York's Paramount Theater, hoping to buy tickets to see singing star (and novice film actor) Frank Sinatra. Over 20,000 more clogged Times Square, blocking the area entirely. The 150 policemen assigned to the event seemed helpless as frenzied fans destroyed the ticket booth, smashed shop windows, and trampled onlookers. Those who did make it into the performance behaved with similar abandon. Women and girls, in particular, screamed and fainted, prompting fears that Sinatra, like Valentino, would spark the downfall of American womanhood. Even after the show, claimed reports, "girls hid in his dressing rooms, in hotel rooms, in the trunk of his car. After the girls discovered where he lived in New Jersey, they camped outside day and night." "We don't want this thing to go on," said a terrified police commissioner to the *New York Times*. "We can't tolerate young people making a public display of losing their emotions."[33]

Not unlike the Valentino escapade, the Columbus Day Riot, as it was dubbed in the press, led to disgust and bewilderment. Although Sinatra was not a movie star, his admirers' antics prompted many of the same strong reactions reserved for film fans. The frenzy over Sinatra was a terrifying "phenomenon of mass hysteria that is seen only two or three times in a century," reported the *New Yorker.* It was "escapism and substitution," claimed one psychologist; "mass frustrated love," said another. Like the critics of film fandom, many writers suggested that the Sinatra fans had been "hypnotized" by the singer, if not by his voice, then by his celebrity status. Built up by publicity agents, continually described as if larger than life, Sinatra placed viewers in a trance (a "Sinatrance," joked some commentators) as deep and hypnotic as the spell seemingly induced by film stars.[34]

Hollywood, too, was appalled. In an article in *Photoplay* magazine, gossip queen Louella Parsons condemned not only the Sinatra swooners, but the wave of "mob violence that seems to be spreading across our nation wherever stars appear." Those who attacked stars for autographs and invaded their privacy "are not real fans," she claimed. "Our boys and girls who make up the true admirers of the stars . . . suffer as much from these badly-bred uncouth mobs as do the stars." Film producer Dore Schary echoed similar sentiments. Fans would be fine if they "knew their place, which is sitting on a seat in a darkened theater looking at a movie, or maybe talking about the picture afterwards. A few steamed up bobby-soxers are moviedom's perpetual headache," he told *Movieland* magazine.[35]

In spite of its criticism, Hollywood also tried to milk the phenomenon for a few laughs. *The Youngest Profession* (1943) poked fun at the bobbysoxers with the tale of an aggressive yet comical teenage autograph collector who tracks down celebrities in railroad stations and hotels. *The Bachelor and the Bobby-Soxer* (1947) lampooned high school girls who developed crushes on older men. Not everyone, however, found the adolescent hysteria humorous. One psychologist thought the adolescent obsession with stars a cause of juvenile delinquency. Others blamed it for an increase in truancy. And to thousands of film fans, the association with screaming teenagers was yet another blow to the public image of fandom. "We aren't bobby soxers, we're grown men and women!" explained one fan to the *New York Times* in 1947. The previous year a group of 750 adult movie fans, calling themselves "The Senior League," banded together in San Francisco to denounce the bobbysoxers and the distorted image of film fandom that they projected. They were tired of being linked with "puppy love and teenage emotions," they explained, and planned a campaign to change Hollywood's perception of film fandom. By writing letters to studios requesting serious films and mature screen heroes, they hoped to convince the film industry that movie fans were mature, responsible adults. According to the *Los Angeles Times,* similar organizations were springing up across Southern California, and "telegrams from [fans] in Salt Lake City and Miami promised to take up the cudgels there, too."[36]

In letters to movie magazines, fans similarly defended themselves from accusations of immaturity and hysteria. "No, I'm not a bobby socker, not a teenage swooner," wrote one woman to *Photoplay* in 1944. One long-time Sinatra fan complained,

> I've never been able to find a single statement about the plain, everyday undemonstrative Sinatra fan. Since I happen to be of this type, perhaps I'm justified in taking this opportunity to express our views. It seems that no matter how marvelous we think Frankie to be, we've never thrown ourselves prone on a theater floor in unbearable ecstasy, nor have we trampled innocent women and children in our efforts to be near "The Voice."

"Although we've not indulged in this sort of thing," she concluded, "we're still fans and I honestly think we're the best kind." "Newspapers and magazines have frequently carried stories of stars being jostled about and even injured by crowds. Such incidents cast a bad reflection on the mental and emotional balance of all fans as a whole," warned another fan. "So as one fan to all other fans, the next time you see that favorite star of yours, prove your admiration and regard for him by respecting his rights as a human being."[37]

As these comments make clear, many fans found the link with bobbysoxers insulting and demoralizing. It may also have been a self-fulfilling prophecy—that is, the more fandom was associated with teenagers, the more actively and vigorously teenagers participated in fan culture. During the late 1940s and the 1950s, adolescent membership in fan clubs flourished. Thousands of teenagers created new organizations or joined existing clubs; they sponsored conventions, held parties, and even created their own language—autographed photos were "snaps" and screen idols "faves." Movie magazines, sensing the transformation, quickly adjusted their content to include articles and columns aimed at adolescents, who had become a promising new consumer base. This change, not surprisingly, had a significant impact on adult fans, who seemed to back away from film fandom. Threatened by the influx of teens, many adult fans appeared to have dropped out of clubs in the 1950s. Others hid their fan activity, insisting that they were not "real fans." In the words of one fan club president, they became "closet fans," lying "awake at night for fear that [they] might be discovered." The constant association between fandom and immaturity that had developed in the early years of films and had been reinforced in subsequent decades may have at last taken its toll.[38]

A NATION OF FANS

In the 1950s, after years of observing and analyzing film fans, social critics, psychologists, and journalists had reached a conclusion: fans were not to be trusted. The typical fan, they said, was aggressive and violent, unintelligent and unrealistic, simple-minded and immature, and at the very least, naive. "The average fan," proclaimed writer Morton Hunt in 1950, "believes what he sees on the screen and thinks it's all good." According to journalist John Maynard, who made a study of several actors' fan mail, most fans were "homely, thwarted, and shy" and sought comfort in an imaginary screen world "indescribably warmer and fuller than their own. . . . The house lights go up, the show is over, but not the spell," he explained. "The baffled, the unwanted, have found a powerful, vicarious identification, and the cleavage from reality is blurred." The irony, of course, is that fans were probably more concerned with reality than the average spectator. Fans tried continually to learn about actors' private lives, the filmmaking process, and the offscreen world inhabited by the stars. They worked constantly to link, but not merge, screen images with real life.[39]

Accusing fans of conflating the screen and life is also ironic given the growing influence of Hollywood on American culture. At the very same time that critics in the 1930s and 1940s escalated their attack on film fandom, the movies were in many ways *becoming* reality. By the 1930s, the escapades of film stars were constantly reported in the mainstream press. Actors dined with bankers, met with royalty, and conferred with presidents. Perhaps even more important, they shaped the ways that millions of Americans conducted their lives. Fashions, colloquialisms, and mannerisms in the movies quickly made their way into popular culture. After watching Myrna Loy crinkle her nose onscreen, claimed one reporter, thousands of women went home and imitated the habit in front of their mirrors. Men throughout the nation copied Gary Cooper's swagger and James Cagney's rebellious snarl. In the way that they actively copied star styles, in the way that they took home the messages in the movies, average American moviegoers were really no different from fans.[40]

In many ways, the average American by the time of World War II *was* a movie fan. In 1945, over 100 million movie tickets were sold each week; 20 million Americans perused the more than 25 fan magazines in circulation; and millions followed Louella Parsons's and Hedda Hopper's daily columns, which appeared in hundreds of newspapers throughout the country. From 1910 through 1930, following celebrity news, reading fan magazines, and going to the movies regularly were considered fan activities; by the 1940s, they were mainstream pursuits. No longer the marginalized, working-class institution that it had been forty years earlier, the motion picture theater had become a central and vital part of American popular culture.[41]

Not surprisingly, the "Hollywood-ization" of America deeply disturbed social critics. "The long arm of Hollywood," lamented author Leo Rosten in 1940, "reaches into every part of the manners and mores of our time." Not only did Americans base their looks and habits after the stars, he claimed, but they were turning to the movies for education and moral guidance. Rather than learn their values from "the church, school and family," moviegoers took them from Hollywood, which preached spending over saving, pleasure over piety, and recklessness over restraint. Adolescents, too, wrote Robert and Helen Lynd in 1937, were patterning their lives not on traditional authority figures but "on the sharp figures of the silver screen which present gay and confident designs for living." Because the movies posed such a threat to established social institutions, because they were such a powerful influence, argued philosopher Mortimer Adler, "they are more than any other art the social and political problem of our day."[42]

Given these attitudes, it is hardly surprising that fans became a target of attack. Passionate about the cinema and deeply devoted to popular stars, fans were the most visible manifestation of the motion picture's tremendous social power. Though actually somewhat morally conservative, fans were frequently accused of idealizing the glamorous, sexually adventurous lifestyles of the stars and were thus linked with the liberalization—or according to critics, the downfall—of traditional social and sexual ethics. Rising juvenile delinquency in the 1930s and 1940s, greater public frankness about sexual issues, higher rates of teenage pregnancy—all, said critics, could be traced to the fans who glorified Hollywood stars.

Fans also reminded critics of the tremendous impact of the mass media on American culture. Film fans, scholars claimed, lacked what normal spectators possessed: the maturity and intelligence to separate the screen and life. Yet, as they had to admit, even educated mature adults could not distinguish between the mass media and reality in many circumstances. As media experts knew well, exaggerated propaganda films during both world wars swayed public opinion; re-enactments of events, broadcast over the radio, were often so convincing that they seemed to be real. When actor Orson Welles broadcast H. G. Wells's tale of Martian invasion, "The War of the Worlds," over a New York radio station in 1938, mass hysteria ensued. Believing the report that Martians were invading the East Coast to be real, thousands took to the road. In a 1939 study, Princeton scholar Hadley Cantril discovered that many highly educated men and women, contrary to his hypothesis, believed the broadcast. Whether mature or immature, old or young, educated or uneducated, wrote Cantril, Americans seemed to lack the "critical ability . . . to distinguish between reality and fiction." Movie fans, then, represented the tremendous power of the mass media to distort and alter public perception. They reminded critics that truth and illusion, for millions of Americans, were no longer distinct; that the radio and the movies had created a world in which simulated realities often substituted for authentic reality.[43]

Ever since the beginning of the twentieth century, the movies and movie fans have been at the center of a heated national debate over modernity, mass communication, and social change. Fans, argued critics, were the ultimate victims of the modern mass media: seduced by the cinema's powerful illusion of reality, they swooned over actors, wasted hours on fan activities, and mimicked what they saw in films, all with harmful consequences. Though critics frequently couched their comments in the language of reform, worrying about fans and trying to minimize the harm fans inflicted on themselves and others, the real target of their condemnation was a force far greater than fandom or the movies. Underneath the attacks on film fandom lay profound discontent with the tremendous cultural changes—the revolution in manners, morals, and social behavior—that had accompanied Americans into the modern age.

CONCLUSION

The history of film fandom between 1910 and 1950 is a story of passion, admiration, and intense curiosity. As Americans went to the movies night after night, as they fell in love with the images on the screen, they tried to reconcile their enthusiasm with pressing questions. What were film actors really like?, they wondered. How could they trust what they saw? Was it possible to become directly and personally involved with mass, commercial entertainment? To address these concerns, moviegoers in the early years of film created a flourishing culture, movie fan culture, that would endure throughout the rest of the century.

Though often criticized as frivolous, movie fandom was actually a serious attempt by fans to understand and to come to terms with the motion picture—with its seductive images, its powers of realistic representation, and its growing influence on American culture. For many moviegoers, fan activities—writing scripts, joining fan clubs, sending suggestions to studios, collecting facts about Hollywood— were more than just casual pastimes. They were valuable techniques that enabled fans to fulfill three important objectives: to connect personally with the movies, to influence the filmmaking process, and to verify the authenticity of cinematic images. More than just film buffs or celebrity watchers, fans dreamed of taking a knowledgeable, meaningful, active role in their favorite form of entertainment.

The story of film fandom, then, is the story of a vision and a challenge. It is the story of the way that fans explored the boundaries of mass culture and probed many of the themes, messages, and limitations inherent in modern commercial entertainment. Fans learned about the world behind the screen not only because they were curious, but because they questioned the cinema's ability to accurately represent reality. Fans joined clubs and wrote fan letters not only to praise their idols but to become individually involved in what seemed like a distant, impersonal form of mass entertainment. Fans barraged studios with advice and suggestions not merely out of selfishness but from a firm conviction that they were valued Hollywood consumers whose opinions deserved to be acknowledged. Hard workers and great dreamers, fans tried diligently to create a democracy of entertainment in which audiences, as much as studios, had a say in the filmmaking process.

They were successful to an extent. As we have seen, fans determined important production and publicity decisions, casting choices, and even stars' personalities. They out-scooped journalists, revealed media inaccuracies, and skillfully uncovered the truth about their favorite actors. But in the end, as even the most die-hard fans had to admit, it was the film industry that truly controlled Hollywood. Though powerful studios such as MGM and Warner Brothers were often swayed by fans' comments, they ultimately decided who and what appeared on the screen. The story of film fandom is the story of an education: how fans learned to exert their power as activists and consumers, but also to accept the limitations of their influence. Fans learned how to revel in their victories over Hollywood, and at times, how to graciously concede.

But to extend the metaphor of battle too far would be inaccurate, for film fans did far more than struggle with Hollywood. From their love for the movies sprang meticulously organized fan clubs, elaborate national conventions, and lasting friendships. Fans penned scripts, corresponded with actors, and developed expert knowledge of the filmmaking process; they gained strength from their idols, inspiration from films, and companionship and identity from their fan communities. Creative and determined, fans transformed the movies from images on a screen into an activity with great personal meaning.

Moreover, although fans complained about the film industry and its profit-seeking motives, they were also its most loyal and enthusiastic cheerleaders. Fans were the backbone of the film audience; they went to the movies weekly, if not nightly, and religiously attended their favorite stars' films. They fantasized about popular actors, eagerly read fan magazines, and, much to the film industry's delight, patterned their purchases on the recommendations of the stars. Fans may have contested the studios' right to control casting and publicity decisions, but when it came to consumption, they often complied with Hollywood's wishes. With the help of publishers, manufacturers, and advertisers, the film industry sold fans cosmetics and clothing, dreams and lifestyles, and, of course, films.

Hollywood also sold fans the virtues of modernity. With its charismatic stars and its celebration of wealth and leisure, the cinema encouraged and legitimated many of the cultural changes that transformed American society in the early twentieth century. Within each film lay a powerful affirmation of modern manners, lifestyles, and values: conspicuous consumption, youth, glamour, and sensual and sexual expression. By the 1920s, many fans had learned to see the movies as valuable teachers, providing important lessons in style, etiquette, and the art of modern living. The story of film fandom is the story of the way that fans transformed the movies and movie stars from mere entertainers into cultural authorities. Encouraged by advertisers and studios, fans vested stars and films with the power to create fashions, set trends, and influence the habits and lifestyles of millions.

And in doing so, fans changed America. By imitating actors' styles, by copying their mannerisms, by purchasing the products they endorsed, fans fueled a powerful Hollywood cult of celebrity that would dominate twentieth-century American culture. Film fandom, too, became a phenomenally popular national pastime. By the 1930s, millions of Americans belonged to fan clubs, sent fan letters, wrote to studios, and purchased fan magazines. In fact, many activities once associated exclusively with fans had become a part of mainstream culture. On the eve of World War II, Americans across the nation attended the movies weekly. They developed crushes on popular stars, discussed the movies with their friends, and followed the gossip columns that described the world behind the scenes. For countless Americans, enjoying the movies meant not only watching films but actively addressing issues of truth, reality, and authenticity, the same questions that had first been pursued by film fans. The story of film fandom is the story of the way that fans set in motion a revolution in popular culture, and the effects can still be felt.

The story of film fandom is far from over. Movie fandom and movie star fan clubs continue to flourish. Some fan clubs are dedicated to past stars—Harold Lloyd, Clara Bow, Clark Gable, Judy Garland—while others honor contemporary celebrities. Many were formed in recent years; others, like the Jeanette MacDonald International Fan Club, have existed for more than a half-century. Even though today's movie fans face a much different world than their predecessors—the studio system has vanished, fans converse over the internet, and boosting means petitioning television stations to run old films—many of their motives and intentions remain the same. They still want to celebrate and appreciate their idols. They still want to forge contact with fellow fans. They are still curious about what film actors are really like. And they are still, more than ever, movie crazy.

NOTES

INTRODUCTION

1. Nathanael West, *The Day of the Locust* (New York: Bantam, 1959), 131.
2. West, *Locust,* 130.
3. For recent scholarship on fandom, see Henry Jenkins, *Textual Poachers: Television Fans and Participatory Culture* (New York: Routledge, 1992); John Fiske, *Understanding Popular Culture* (New York: Routledge, 1995); Jackie Stacey, *Star Gazing* (New York: Routledge, 1994); Janice Radway, *Reading the Romance* (Chapel Hill: University of North Carolina, 1991); Joshua Gamson, *Claims to Fame: Celebrity in Contemporary America* (Berkeley: University of California Press, 1994); Georganne Scheiner, "The Deanna Durbin Devotees," in *Generations of Youth,* ed. Joe Austin and Michael Nevin Willard (New York: New York University Press, 1998); Lisa Lewis, ed. *The Adoring Audience: Fan Culture and Popular Media* (New York: Routledge, 1993); Cheryl Harris and Alison Alexander, eds., *Theorizing Fandom: Fans, Subculture, Identity* (Creekskill, N.J.: Hampton Press, 1998).
4. According to historian Daniel Boorstin, we demand the mass media's simulated realities because they fulfill our insatiable desire for glamour and excitement. To cultural commentator Richard Schickel, they create an "illusion of intimacy," a sense of security and connection in a society of strangers. Ian Mitroff and Warren Bennis have gone as far as to claim that Americans are living in a self-induced state of unreality. "We are now so close to creating electronic images of any existing or imaginary person, place, or thing . . . so that a viewer cannot tell whether . . . the images are real or not," they wrote in 1989. At the root of this passion for images, they claim, is a desire for stability and control: "If men cannot control the realities with which they are faced, then they will invent unrealities over which they can maintain control." In other words, according to these authors, we seek and create aural and visual illusions—television, movies, recorded music, computers—because they compensate for the inadequacies of contemporary society. If we scratch the surface of this "culture of

unreality," however, we will see an audience that is not desperate, passive, and gullible, but concerned, active, and skeptical. See Daniel Boorstin, *The Image: A Guide to Pseudo–Events in America* (New York: Atheneum, 1975), 3, 240; Richard Schickel, *Intimate Strangers: The Culture of Celebrity* (New York: Doubleday, 1986); Ian Mitroff and Warren Bennis, *The Unreality Industry* (New York: Carol Publishing, 1989), 6, 9.

CHAPTER ONE

1. Eileen Smith to Florence Lawrence, March 13, 1911, Florence Lawrence Collection (FL), Seaver Center for Western History Research, Natural History Museum of Los Angeles County (NHMLAC); Tessie Cohen, December 26, 1911, Bison Archives.
2. "They Can't Fool the Public," *Photoplay*, June 1922, 110.
3. Charles Musser, *The Emergence of Cinema: The American Screen to 1907* (Berkeley: University of California Press, 1990), 104, 162, 125.
4. Edward Wagenknecht, *The Movies in the Age of Innocence* (New York: Ballantine, 1971), 20; Musser, *Emergence of Cinema,* 128.
5. Musser, *Emergence of Cinema,* 118, 201-2. Although the film was actually advertised as "Reproduction of the Corbett and Fitzsimmons Fight," many audiences seem to have ignored or misunderstood the title's implications.
6. Musser, *Emergence of Cinema,* 205-6.
7. *New York Dramatic Mirror,* May 7, 1898, quoted in Robert Allen, *Vaudeville and Film 1895–1915: A Study in Media Interaction* (New York: Arno Press, 1980).
8. Barton Currie, "Nickel Madness," *Harper's Weekly,* August 24, 1907, 1246-7; "The Random Shots of a Picture Fan," *Moving Picture World,* October 21, 1911, 198.
9. Tom Gunning, *D. W. Griffith and the Origins of American Narrative Film* (Chicago: University of Illinois Press, 1991). Also see Joyce Jesionowski, *Thinking in Pictures* (Berkeley: University of California Press, 1987).
10. *Variety,* April 3, 1909, 13; *Moving Picture World,* June 19, 1909, 834; both quoted in Gunning.
11. "Tricks of the Moving Picture Maker," *Scientific American,* June 26, 1909, 476-7.
12. "How Miracles are Performed in Moving Pictures," *Current Literature,* September 1908, 329; William Allen Johnston, "The Silent Stage," *Harper's Weekly,* November 13, 1909, 8-9.
13. George Ethelbert Walsh, "Moving Picture Drama for the Multitude," *Independent,* February 6, 1908, 206.
14. *Moving Picture World,* September 21, 1907, 29; Marjorie Rosen, *Popcorn Venus* (New York: Avon Books, 1973), 21.
15. Both Richard DeCordova and Anthony Slide find little evidence that the policy of anonymity was instituted by actors. As Slide has written, "Did these so called legitimate actors really care that much (about their reputa-

tions)? I doubt it. The majority of actors who accepted screen roles were thankful not only for the work, but for the fame it promised them." Other accounts, however, insist that the policy was initiated by actors concerned with their reputations. In 1910, *Moving Picture World* explained that "Actors are glad to play the parts, but all of them try to shield their identity. They have an undisguised impression that the step from the regular productions to the scenes before the camera is a backward one." As silent film actress Viola Dana agreed, "You never let it be known that you did the 'flickers' in the summertime just to make a few dollars." According to Linda Arvidson, director D. W. Griffith's wife, the motivation behind the Biograph studio's policy of secrecy was the fear that stardom would lead to higher salaries. For these conflicting accounts, see Richard DeCordova, *Picture Personalities: The Emergence of the Star System in America* (Urbana: University of Illinois Press, 1990), 77-8; Anthony Slide, *Aspects of Film History Prior to 1920* (Methuen, N.J.: Scarecrow Press, 1978), 3; "Photographs of Moving Picture Actors," *Moving Picture World*, January 15, 1910; Linda Arvidson, *When the Movies Were Young* (New York: E. P. Dutton, 1935), 187.

16. To Florence Lawrence, May 26, 1911, FL, NHMLAC; "The Motion Picture Field," *New York Dramatic Mirror*, January 15, 1910, 13.

17. On the shift from histrionic to verisimilar acting styles, see Roberta Pearson, *Eloquent Gestures* (Berkeley: University of California Press, 1992).

18. Eileen Smith to Florence Lawrence, March 13, 1911; Mabel Hilton, November 24, 1911; from Portland, Oregon, December 7, 1911; all FL, NHMLAC.

19. Edith Crutcher to Lawrence, April 14, 1910; Mrs. T. L. Wheelis, December 21, 1911; FL, NHMLAC.

20. J. R. Manning to Lawrence, July 30, 1911; Elmer Jones, January 31, 1912; Vertical File 211, Academy of Motion Picture Arts and Sciences (AMPAS); May Woelfel, February 16, 1910, NHMLAC.

21. Stephen Horsky to Florence Lawrence, April 15, 1910; Leland Ayres, December 7, 1909; FL, NHMLAC.

22. Etta Ward to Lawrence, 1916, FL, NHMLAC.

23. "The Motion Picture Field," *New York Dramatic Mirror*; *Moving Picture World*, May 14, 1910, 825.

24. *Moving Picture World*, March 12, 1910, 365. To his death, Laemmle insisted that he had no hand in the publicity stunt. Laemmle claimed that the report of Lawrence's death was planted by a rival organization, the Edison Film Trust; he simply used the opportunity provided by the false announcement to publicize the actress. But the aggressiveness with which Laemmle pursued publicity for Lawrence suggests that the film executive had planned the scheme from the start. For Laemmle's own account of the event, see John Drinkwater, *The Life and Times of Carl Laemmle* (New York: G. P. Putnam, 1931), 140.

25. "The Imp Leading Lady," *Moving Picture World*, April 2, 1910, 517; Rose Saalmueller to Lawrence, April 11, 1910, FL, NHMLAC; A. W. Dustin to Lawrence, March 7, 1910, Vertical File 211, AMPAS; Florence Lawrence with Monte Katterjohn, "Growing Up With the Movies," *Photoplay Magazine*, February 1915, 144; Drinkwater, *Life and Times of Carl Laemmle*, 141.

26. Edith Crutcher to Lawrence, April 14, 1910; Elsie Miller, July 11, 1910; Virginia Kramer and Helen Wood, August 31, 1911; all FL, NHMLAC.

27. George Armstrong to Lawrence, August 30, 1911; Dick Shields, March 6, 1916; FL, NHMLAC.

28. Advertisement for the IMP studio, *Moving Picture World,* February 26, 1910, 323.

29. Advertisement for the IMP studio, *Moving Picture World,* February 3, 1912.

30. "Observations by our Man About Town," *Moving Picture World,* September 9, 1911, 706; Lux Graphicus, "On the Screen," *Moving Picture World,* October 8, 1910.

31. Cyril W. Beaumont, *Fanny Elssler* (London: C. W. Beaumont, 1931), 26; Neil Harris, *Humbug: The Art of P. T. Barnum* (Chicago: University of Chicago Press, 1973), ch. 5; Ivor Brown, "Edwardian Idols of My Youth," in *The Rise and Fall of the Matinee Idol,* ed. Anthony Curtis (New York: St. Martin's Press, 1974), 33; David Carroll, *The Matinee Idols* (New York: Arbor House, 1972), 15.

32. My conclusions about theater fans are drawn from dozens of books and articles, including "A Personal Interview with 'The Virginian,'" *Theater,* October 1906; "Letters to Actors I Have Never Seen," *Theater,* October 1904, 182; "Noted Young Men of the American Stage," *Cosmopolitan,* December 1900, 421; "The Brutality of the Matinee Girl," *Lippincott's,* December 1907, 687; Frederick Wemyss, *Twenty Six Years in the Life of an Actor and Manager* (New York: Burgess and Stringer, 1847); William Wood, *Personal Recollections of the Stage* (Philadelphia: H. C. Baird, 1855); Theodore Dreiser, *Sister Carrie* (Cleveland: World Publishing, 1946), ch. 5.

33. See Gaylyn Studlar, *This Mad Masquerade* (New York: Columbia, 1996), ch. 3, for stories of fans who tried to see their idols in person.

34. "Letters to the Spectator," *New York Dramatic Mirror,* November 11, 1911, 28; "Inquiries," *Moving Picture World,* December 2, 1911, 738. Frank Woods later claimed that "Is Broncho Billy married?" was "the first question ever asked by any publication about any film player." See *Photoplay,* December 1917, 108.

35. Most writing on theatrical stars had also avoided the personal. In the last quarter of the nineteenth century, publishers issued a wave of books devoted to the major roles and performances of popular actors. Books like *Stage Favorites* and *The Stage and Its Stars* chronicled stars' professional careers, but never mentioned their offstage lives; families and spouses were discussed only when they played a role in an actor's rise to fame. By the turn of the century, writers toyed with the idea of investigating actors' home lives—a 1901 article from *Cosmopolitan* magazine (Burr McIntosh, "Actresses at Leisure," October 1901, 586) for example, described what famous leading ladies did on their days off—but the vast majority of theatrical writing continued to focus on their onstage roles and performances. Even works like *Eminent Actors in Their Homes,* by Margherita Arlina Hamm (New York: James Pott and Company, 1902) examined the ways in which sophisticated interiors reflected the serious professionalism of their celebrity occupants. Also see Lewis C. Strang, *Famous Actors of the Day* (Boston: L. C. Page,

1899); *Stage Favorites* (New York: Minton, 1894); Howard Paul, ed. *The Stage and Its Stars* (Philadelphia: Gebbie and Company, ca. 1890).

36. "Notes of the Picture Players," *Motion Picture Story Magazine,* April 1911, 129; January 1912, 121.

37. "Those ???," *Motion Picture Story Magazine,* June 1912, 138.

38. "Answers to Inquiries," *Motion Picture Story Magazine,* October 1911, 142.

39. "Florence Lawrence," *Photoplay,* October 1912, 105; "Interview with Owen Moore," *Photoplay,* December 1912, 100.

40. Wilma Bright, "Interview with George Periolat," *Photoplay,* January 1913, 118; Pearl Gaddis, "Taking Tea with Alice Hollister," *Photoplay,* July 1915, 87.

41. "Chats with the Players," *Motion Picture Story Magazine,* December 1911, 132; Mabel Condon, "The Real Perils of Pauline," *Photoplay,* October 1914, 60; *Photoplay,* October 1912, 55. According to film scholar Richard DeCordova, because so many fan magazine articles between 1910 and 1913 described the similarity between actors and their characters, stars essentially had a professional identity, one that was derived entirely from their onscreen roles. Stars, he writes, were portrayed by magazines as "just like the characters they played, but unlike those characters, they were real." DeCordova characterizes this information as unimportant or trivial, particularly when contrasted to the more revealing facts about stars' private lives that were released in the 1920s. Even though fans may have learned relatively little about stars' private lives in the previous decade, I argue that what they did learn was of great importance. Stars appeared to be living versions of the roles they played on screen. And to many moviegoers, that simple fact was profoundly reassuring. The image they adored had a basis in reality. See DeCordova, *Picture Personalities,* 86-92.

42. "Will You Take Your Star Married or Single," *Chicago Tribune,* February 6, 1914; "Rocks and Roses," *Photoplay,* July 1915, 151; "The Ideal of the Screen," *Photoplay,* November 1915, 130.

43. "The Film Comedian Off Duty," *Literary Digest,* January 1, 1916, 33.

44. Richard Koszarski, *An Evening's Entertainment* (Berkeley: University of California Press, 1990), 193.

45. "Musings of the Photoplay Philosopher," *Motion Picture Story Magazine,* October 1912, 135-6; Koszarski, *Evening's Entertainment,* 193; Gaylyn Studlar, "The Perils of Pleasure: Fan Magazine Discourse as Women's Commodified Culture in the 1920s," in *Silent Film,* ed. Richard Abel (New Brunswick, N.J.: Rutgers University Press, 1996), 264.

46. *Motion Picture,* February 1915, 86.

47. "His First Show," *Motion Picture Story Magazine,* October 1911, 140.

48. To Betty Marsh, July 4, 1917, Vertical File 32; Linna Dutchers to Buster Collier, August 9, 1916, Buster Collier Collection, Folder 1; both AMPAS.

49. Cecil Wood to William S. Hart, 1917; F. Stake, 1917; anonymous fan, n.d.; all William S. Hart Collection (WH), NHMLAC.

50. Charles Carter, "Letter Writing Lunacy," *Picture Play,* November 1920, 3.

51. "They Can't Fool the Public," *Photoplay,* June 1922, 110.

52. Myrtle Gebhart, "Myrna, Are You Real?," *Picture Play,* November 1926, 74; advertisement for *Pictorial Review* in *Motion Picture Classic,* June 1923, 77.

53. Angelina Kovez to Florence Lawrence, 1916; Mrs. T. L. Wheelis, 1911, FL, NHMLAC; Mrs. J. J. Smothers to William S. Hart, 1919, WH, NHMLAC.

CHAPTER TWO

1. *Motion Picture Story Magazine,* January 1912, 117; Richard Koszarski, *An Evening's Entertainment* (Berkeley: University of California Press, 1990), 25-6.

2. *Moving Picture World,* editorial, January 16, 1909, 1; "The Variety of Moving Picture Audiences," September 25, 1909, 406.

3. Barbara Stones, *America Goes to the Movies* (North Hollywood: National Association of Theater Owners, 1993), 28.

4. Robert Sklar, *Movie-Made America* (New York: Vintage, 1994), 44-6.

5. *Motion Picture Story Magazine,* October 1912, 131.

6. B. H. Smith, "Nervy Movie Lady," *Sunset,* June 1914, 1323; "The Real Life Perils of Pauline," *Literary Digest,* December 5, 1914, 1148.

7. Louella Parsons, "Seen on the Screen," *Chicago Herald,* October 15, 1915, Scrapbook 1, Louella O. Parsons (LOP) Collection, Margaret Herrick Library, Academy of Motion Pictures Arts and Sciences (AMPAS).

8. Ad for Pompeian skin cream, *Motion Picture,* November 1916; Kathryn Fuller, *At The Picture Show* (Washington: Smithsonian, 1996), 157-8; Eileen Whitfield, *Pickford: The Woman Who Made Hollywood* (Lexington: University of Kentucky Press, 1997), 132.

9. Lary May, *Screening Out the Past* (Chicago: University of Chicago Press, 1983), 164.

10. Mlle. Pilar Morin, "The Value of Silent Drama, Or Pantomime in Acting," *Moving Picture World,* November 3, 1909, 682; Roberta Pearson, *Eloquent Gestures* (Berkeley: University of California Press, 1992), 22.

11. "Blanche Sweet," *Weekly Movie Record,* May 17, 1915, 1.

12. "Public Opinions of Popular Plays and Players," *Motion Picture,* March 1915, 122; "Letters to the Editor," April 1915, *Motion Picture,*168.

13. "Blanche Sweet"; "Popular Player Contest," *Motion Picture Story Magazine,* July 1913, 117.

14. Herbert Howe, "They Can't Fool the Public," *Photoplay,* June 1922, 47.

15. Orison Swett Marden, *Pushing to the Front* (New York: Thomas Crowell, 1894), 76; Warren Susman, "Personality and the Making of Twentieth Century Culture," in *Culture as History* (New York: Pantheon, 1984), 271-85.

16. "The Secret of Making People Like You," *Film Fun,* December 1919. For other perspectives on the modern self-as-performance (in particular, a performance aimed at pleasing others) see Erving Goffman, *The Presentation of Self in Everyday Life* (New York: Anchor, 1959).

17. Advertisement for the Gentlewoman Institute; advertisement for Ralston University correspondence course in personality, both in *Motion Picture,* 1921.

18. French Strother, "Cut Loose and Give Your Personality a Chance," *American Magazine,* February 1928, 43.

19. Imogene Wolcott, *Personality as a Business Asset* (New York: G. P. Putnam, 1925), 243.

20. "Picture Personalities," *Moving Picture World,* September 23, 1910, 680; December 24, 1910, 1462.

21. "What Makes Them Stars?," *Photoplay,* November 1923, 48; Joan Cross, "Name Her and Win $1,000," *Movie Weekly,* May 28, 1925, 5. The marriage of personality and acting was not only limited to motion pictures. In the first quarter of the century, the stage was also swept by a craze for personality. Traditionally told to disguise their own qualities by immersing themselves in their roles, actors were now urged to infuse their personal charisma into each of the characters they played. By 1910, the trend had become so widespread that one critic lamented, "It is the personalities we go to see, not the actors and sometimes not the play." Actress Ethel Barrymore, in particular, deplored the direction the theater had taken. Personality was useful, she explained in 1911, but could never substitute for experience and ability. "Many people on the stage have a great deal of personality but little talent, and they do not go far," she claimed.

    Barrymore worked tirelessly to restore talent and training to the art of acting. But even she had to admit that audiences preferred personality to ability. In 1917, *Film Fun* wrote a scathing review of Barrymore's first appearance in motion pictures. Why was her performance so dull and unimpressive? "Ethel Barrymore completely lacks screen personality," the magazine explained. See Ethel Barrymore, "How Can I Be A Great Actress," *Ladies' Home Journal,* March 15, 1911, 6; Benjamin McArthur, *Actors and American Culture, 1880–1920* (Philadelphia: Temple University Press, 1984), ch. 7; *Film Fun,* April 1917, 32.

22. Helen Hancock, "Is Impersonation a Lost Art in America?," *Filmplay Journal,* August 1922, 36; Esther Lindner, "How to Be Your Own Publicity Manager," *Motion Picture,* April 1918, 129.

23. "Brickbats and Bouquets," *Photoplay,* June 1923, 10; "What the Fans Think," *Picture Play,* September 1922, 8; January 1924, 11; January 1926, 10.

24. To Billie Dove, Billie Dove Collection, AMPAS; "What The Fans Think," *Picture Play,* April 1922, 104; "Brickbats and Bouquets," *Photoplay,* April 1927, 128; to William S. Hart, 1917, William S. Hart Collection, Natural History Museum of Los Angeles County.

25. Betty Rosser, "To Mary Pickford, the Recollections of her Number One Fan," Mary Pickford Collection, AMPAS; Herbert Blumer, *Movies and Conduct* (New York: Macmillan, 1933), 40; "Brickbats and Bouquets," *Photoplay,* May 1928, 10; Charles Dolista, "Terrible Consequences," *Movie Weekly,* December 10, 1921, 27.

26. *Motion Picture,* June 1923, 56; "Brickbats and Bouquets," *Photoplay,* July 1926, 10; May 1927, 123; Betty Rosser, "To Mary Pickford, the Recollections of her Number One Fan."

27. "The Best Known Girl in America," *Ladies' Home Journal,* January 1915, 9; *New York Review,* November 28, 1914, quoted in Whitfield, *Pickford,* 126; Nicholas Vachel Lindsay, "To Mary Pickford," *Photoplay,* December 1914, 102.

28. Between 1890 and 1930, the proportion of women in the workforce rose from 19 to 25 percent. See May, *Screening Out,* 201.

29. May, *Screening Out,* 119, 142. In 1920, Pickford earned the remarkable income of one million dollars a year.

30. *Motion Picture,* January 1923, 56; Cari Beauchamp, *Without Lying Down: Frances Marion and the Powerful Women of Early Hollywood* (New York: Scribner's, 1997), 53.

31. "Lillian Russell's Beauty Secrets," *Chicago Tribune,* September 3, 1914; *Essanay News,* June 15, 1914.

32. "Mary Pickford's Daily Talks," *San Francisco Bulletin,* January 16, 1916, 14; December 21, 1915, 8.

33. "Daily Talks," *San Francisco Bulletin,* December 13, 1915, 14; May, Screening Out, 125-6.

34. "Daily Talks," *San Francisco Bulletin,* March 7, 1916, 15.

35. "Daily Talks," *San Francisco Bulletin,* December 2, 1915, 14. Pickford was so popular, claimed *American Magazine,* that she received more mail each day than President Wilson. Edwin Carty Ranck, "Mary Pickford—Whose Real Name is Gladys Smith," *American Magazine,* May 1918, 34-5.

36. Richard Schickel, *His Picture in the Papers* (New York: Charterhouse, 1973), ch. 1-4.

37. "What the Fans Think," *Picture Play,* January 1924, 88; Douglas Fairbanks, *Youth Points the Way* (New York: D. Appleton, 1924), introduction.

38. Douglas Fairbanks, *Laugh and Live* (Britton Publishing Company, 1917), 47.

39. Wallace Reid, "Get the Smiling Habit," *Photodrama,* September 1921, 3; ad for the Gentlewoman Institute, *Motion Picture,* May 1920, 109.

40. May, *Screening Out,* 202.

41. May, *Screening Out,* 201-2; Roland Marchand, *Advertising the American Dream* (Berkeley: University of California Press, 1985), 6-7.

42. On the origins of "psychological advertising" see Marchand, *Advertising,* 10-13.

43. Dorothy Spensley, "What Is It?," *Photoplay,* February 1926, 33.

44. Mark Larkin, "What Is 'It'?," *Photoplay,* June 1929; Alice M. Williamson, *Alice in Movieland* (New York: D. Appleton, 1928), ch. 4.

45. On changing sexual ethics in the 1920s see Nancy Cott, *The Grounding of Modern Feminism* (New Haven: Yale University Press, 1987), ch. 5; Paula S. Fass, *The Damned and the Beautiful* (New York: Oxford, 1977), ch. 6.

46. "They Say," *Motion Picture Classic,* March 1927, 6; Blumer, *Movies and Conduct,* 36-7, 43.

47. James Quirk, "Close Ups and Long Shots," *Photoplay,* November 1928, 1.

48. Gene Brown, *Movie Time* (New York: Macmillan, 1995), 99.

CHAPTER THREE

1. Anna Steese Richardson, "Filmitis: The Modern Malady," *McClure's*, January 1916, 12.
2. "Dress and the Picture," *Moving Picture World,* July 9, 1910, 73; Barton Currie, "Nickel Madness," *Harper's Weekly,* August 24, 1907, 1246; "Nickel Theaters Crime Breeders," *Chicago Tribune,* April 13, 1907, 3. In 1920, the *New York Times* reported that 60 percent of film audiences were women; in 1927, *Moving Picture World* claimed that 83 percent of viewers were female—see Richard Koszarski, *An Evening's Entertainment* (Berkeley: University of California Press, 1990), 30.
3. "Dress and the Picture," *Moving Picture World,* July 9, 1910, 73; *The Fashion Review,* April 27, 1912, 342; Gardner Wood, "Magazines and Motion Pictures," *Moving Picture World,* July 7, 1914, 194.
4. "What Motion Pictures Mean to Me," *Photoplay,* June 1920, 78.
5. "What It Means to Be Movie Struck," *Film Fun,* February 1919, 26. During the 1920s, a quarter of employed women worked in factories and nearly 40 percent in clerical, managerial, sales, and professional positions. Nancy Cott, *The Grounding of Modern Feminism* (New Haven: Yale University Press, 1987), 130.
6. "Mary Pickford's Daily Talks," *San Francisco Bulletin,* December 2, 1915, 14.
7. Betty Melnick to Florence Lawrence, July 4, 1910; Rose Forte to Lawrence, 1911, Florence Lawrence Collection (FL), Natural History Museum of Los Angeles County (NHMLAC); to Lawrence, October 8, 1914, Vertical File 211, Margaret Herrick Library, Academy of Motion Picture Arts and Sciences (AMPAS).
8. "Getting into a Picture Company," *Motion Picture Story Magazine,* February 1912, 147; "Owed to the Ambitious," *Photoplay,* January 1917, 136.
9. Lux Graphicus, "On the Screen," *Moving Picture World,* March 19, 1910, 420; Patrick Donald Anderson, *In Its Own Image: The Cinematic Vision of Hollywood* (New York: Arno, 1978), 79-80.
10. "Should Moving Pictures Be Censored?," *Current Opinion,* May 1921, 653.
11. "Ethel Barrymore's Advice to Stage Aspirants," *Cosmopolitan,* December 1906, 661; "As An Actor Sees Women," *Ladies' Home Journal,* December 1906, 26.
12. The fact that prostitutes often plied their trade in the notorious third tier of many theaters only strengthened the connection between the stage and sex. "What It Means to Be a Chorus Girl," *Ladies' Home Journal,* March 1910, 58.
13. Beatriz Michelena, "Friendly Talks With Screen-Struck Girls," *San Francisco Examiner,* May 7, 1916, 24; clipping, 1915, Scrapbook 1, Louella Parsons Collection (LOP), AMPAS.
14. Richard Griffith, ed., *The Talkies* (New York: Dover, 1971), xvi.
15. "Breaking Into the Game," *Photoplay,* August 1914, 131; Elizabeth Peltret, "The Girl Outside," *Photoplay,* July 1917, 29-31.
16. *Moving Picture World,* October 1913, quoted in Kathryn Fuller, *At the Picture Show* (Washington, D.C.: Smithsonian, 1996), 126.

17. "How Twelve Famous Women Scenario Writers Succeeded," *Photoplay,* August 1923, 31.

18. Terrence Eugene Ramsay, "Finding the Ten-Thousand-Dollar Girl," *Photoplay,* April 1915; "The $250 Prize Awarded," August 1914, 153; "A Fortune for an Idea," January 1917, 34.

19. Elaine Sterne, "Writing for the Movies as a Profession," *Photoplay,* September 1914, 156; Monte M. Katterjohn, "Thumbnail Biographies," *Photoplay,* October 1914, 166; H. Z. Levine, "In the Moving Picture World," *Photoplay,* March 1912, 37.

20. Lawrence Quirk, "Quirk of Photoplay," *Films in Review,* March 1955, 97-107. From 1890 to 1930, the number of women in the workforce rose from 19 to 25 percent. The greatest rise occurred among married women: the proportion of married women in the workforce doubled between 1900 and 1930, increasing at six times the rate of unmarried women. Lary May, *Screening Out the Past* (Chicago: University of Chicago Press, 1983), 201; Cott, *Modern Feminism,* 129.

21. Vivian Barrington, "Laura Leonard, Heart Specialist," *Photoplay,* October 1914, 136.

22. Elizabeth Peltret, "On the Lot with Lois Weber," *Photoplay,* November 1917, 89; "The Million Dollar Girl," *Photoplay,* October 1923, 63; "How Twelve Famous Women Scenario Writers Succeeded."

23. Elizabeth Peltret, "Frances Marion, Soldieress of Fortune," *Photoplay,* November 1917, 31-3; Cari Beauchamp, *Without Lying Down: Frances Marion and the Powerful Women of Early Hollywood* (New York: Scribner's, 1997).

24. Dorothy Spensley, "You Are So Pretty—You Should Go In Pictures," *Photoplay,* April 1926, 28.

25. John H. Blackwood, "Author, Author!" *Photoplay,* February 1916, 27-9; Gordon Brooke, "Coming! The Million Dollar Scenarioist," *Picture Play,* July 1920, 56-7.

26. Irving Shulman, *Harlow* (New York: Dell, 1964), 72.

27. "Gullible Girls Seeking Fame," *Literary Digest,* February 1921.

28. Marilyn Conners, *What Chance Have I in Hollywood?* (Hollywood: Famous Authors, 1924), 11.

29. "Report Girl Missing," *Moving Picture World,* July 10, 1920, 192.

30. "Studio Club Founded for Benefit of Girls in Picture Studios," *Hollywood Citizen,* December 29, 1916, 1; "$150,000 Studio Club Planned," December 19, 1922; Elizabeth McGaffey, "The Studio Club," *Photoplay,* September 1917, 83-8; Laurance L. Hill and Silas E. Snyder, *Can Anything Good Come Out of Hollywood?* (Hollywood: Snyder Publications, 1923), 2-3.

31. Jessica Lawrence and Mrs. Cecil B. DeMille to Will Hays, May 18, 1923, in *The Will Hays Papers,* ed. Douglas Gomery (Frederick, Md.: University Publications of America), Reel 10; Ruth Waterbury, "The Truth about Breaking Into the Movies," *Photoplay,* December 1926, 32-3.

32. Rudy Behlmer, *Hollywood's Hollywood* (Secaucus, N.J.: Citadel Press, 1974), 104; Hollywood Chamber of Commerce to Agnes O'Malley, May 28, 1927, Box 71, Folder 1150, Mack Sennett Collection, AMPAS.

33. Ruth Waterbury, "Don't Go to Hollywood!" *Photoplay,* March 1927, 28.

34. Walter DeLeon, "The Hollywood Extra," *Saturday Evening Post,* June 1926; Ruth Waterbury, "The Truth About Breaking Into the Movies," *Photoplay,* February 1927, 40; Cedric Belfrage interviewed in *Hollywood: Single Beds and Double Standards* (London: Thames Television, 1980).

35. Kay Carewe, "Vignette of a Blonde," *Photoplay,* December 1916, 86. In a 1949 interview, Will Hays thanked Quirk for his efforts in dealing with the extra-girl crisis and star scandals of the 1920s: "He worked with me to clean up the abuses in the film world. . . . He tried to protect Hollywood and raise its sights." See Lawrence Quirk, "James Quirk: An Appreciation."

36. "Miss Talmadge Says," *Photoplay,* June 1922, 78.

37. Carolyn Van Wyck, "Poise, Clothes and Grooming," *Photoplay,* November 1922, 52.

38. Advertisement, *Motion Picture,* July 1918.

39. Advertisement, *Motion Picture,* October 1925; *Photoplay,* June 1925.

40. Fuller, *Picture Show,* 159.

41. Fuller, *Picture Show,* 159-61.

42. Metro-Goldwyn-Mayer publicity manual for *Chained,* Metro-Goldwyn-Mayer Collection, University of Southern California; Charlotte Cornelia Herzog and Jane Marie Gaines, "Puffed Sleeves Before Tea Time," in *Stardom,* ed. Christine Gledhill (New York: Routledge, 1991), 78. A chain of competing Cinema Fashion Shops, run by Bernard Waldman, also offered inexpensive imitations of star fashions. Studios sent Waldman photographs of dresses that were to appear in upcoming films. The dresses were then mass manufactured and would appear in the shops at the same time as the film's release.

43. Herbert Blumer, *Movies and Conduct* (New York: Macmillan, 1933), 31-2; "Brickbats and Bouquets," *Photoplay,* October 1931, 6. For a study of the way that female fans in the 1940s and 1950s selectively incorporated stars' styles into their own identities, see Jackie Stacey, *Star Gazing: Hollywood Cinema and Female Spectatorship* (New York: Routledge, 1994).

CHAPTER FOUR

1. "The Confessions of Edwin August," *Motion Picture Story Magazine,* June 1914, 83; "Greenroom Jottings," February 1914, 113. Between 1911 and 1915, the magazine was known as *Motion Picture Story;* in 1915 its title was changed to *Motion Picture.*

2. To Florence Lawrence, dated August 31, 1912; from Quebec, 1916; Etta Ward to Lawrence, 1916, Florence Lawrence Collection (FL), Natural History Museum of Los Angeles County (NHMLAC).

3. Alexander Walker, *Stardom* (New York: Stein & Day, 1970), 111; Rudolph Valentino, "I'm Tired of Being a Sheik," *Collier's,* January 16, 1926.

4. Gladys Hall, "The Photoplayers," *Motion Picture Story Magazine,* June 1914, 113; Patricia Foulds, "Such is the Life of a Popular Movie Star," *Motion*

Picture Classic, September 1917, 70; "Brickbats and Bouquets," *Photoplay,* June 1927, 10.

5. E. K. McMullen, "Are You Movie Wise," *Photoplay,* August 1925, 71; Martin Levin, ed., *Hollywood and the Great Fan Magazines* (New York: Arbor House, 1970), 63; advertisement for *Stars of the Photoplay, Photoplay,* June 1931, 151.

6. Advertisement for "The Barretts of Wimpole Street," *MGM Studio News,* August 16, 1934; Christopher Finch and Linda Rosencrantz, *Gone Hollywood* (New York: Doubleday, 1979), 274.

7. "Information Desk," *Modern Screen,* September 1936, 66. As film critic Richard Schickel has observed, sound films revolutionized the relationship between audiences and stars. "The psychological distance between stars and their audience was radically shortened with the coming of sound. What seemed to be their last significant secret, their tones of voice, was now revealed." See Richard Schickel, *Intimate Strangers: The Culture of Celebrity* (New York: Doubleday, 1986), 99-100.

8. Anthony Slide, *The Idols of Silence* (South Brunswick, N.J.: A. S. Barnes, 1976), 109-18; David Stenn, *Clara Bow: Runnin' Wild* (New York: Doubleday, 1988), 120-5; Adela Rogers St. Johns, *The Honeycomb* (New York: Doubleday, 1969), ch. 8; ad for Realsilk hosiery, *Photoplay,* March 1932.

9. Thomas Wood, "The First Lady of Hollywood," *Saturday Evening Post,* July 15, 1935, 9.

10. Louella Parsons, *The Gay Illiterate* (New York: Doubleday, 1944), 8.

11. "Seen on the Screen," *Chicago Record Herald,* October 15, 1915, Scrapbook 1, Louella O. Parsons Collection (LOP), Margaret Herrick Library, Academy of Motion Pictures Arts and Sciences (AMPAS).

12. "Flickerings from Films," *New York American,* August 5, October 25, 1925, Scrapbook 12, LOP, AMPAS; Neal Gabler, *Winchell: Gossip, Power, and the Culture of Celebrity* (New York: Knopf, 1994).

13. George Eells, *Hedda and Louella* (New York: G. P. Putnam, 1972), 152-3.

14. John Dunning, *On the Air: The Encyclopedia of Old–Time Radio* (New York: Oxford University Press, 1998), 323-4.

15. Review of *Hollywood Hotel, Washington Post,* n.d., Scrapbook 23, LOP, AMPAS.

16. Clipping from *San Diego Radio News,* n.d.; clipping from *Radio Life,* June 29, 1941; *Los Angeles Examiner,* May 29, 1941, Scrapbook 27, LOP, AMPAS.

17. To Louella Parsons dated February 28, March 27, April 17, 1934, *Hollywood Hotel* Files, LOP, Cinema Television Library, University of Southern California (USC).

18. To Louella Parsons, n.d.; Virginia Hitchcock to Parsons, March 7, 1934; *Hollywood Hotel* Files, LOP, USC.

19. Letters, n.d., *Hollywood Hotel* Files, LOP, USC.

20. "Bunk!" *Photoplay,* January 1921, 1; Frank Ward O'Malley, "Hot Off the Press Agent," *Saturday Evening Post,* June 25, 1921, 56; Mary Pickford, "The Greatest Business in the World," *Collier's,* June 10, 1922, 7.

21. Walker, *Stardom,* 246. During Hollywood's studio era, most actors relied on official studio publicists for their contact with the media. Those actors not

contracted to studios or those who wanted additional publicity hired independent press agents. For the difference between publicists and press agents, see Jane Wilkie, *Confessions of an Ex–Fan Magazine Writer* (New York: Doubleday, 1980), ch. 3.

22. "Tradeviews," *Hollywood Reporter,* June 20, 1934; "Publicity Heads Unite in Plan to Curb Fan Magazines," August 10, 1934; "Fan Magazines Promise to be Good, Will Cut Writers," August 16, 1934; Carl Cotter, "The Forty Hacks of the Fan Mags," *Coast,* February 1939; Murphy McHenry, "Dishing that Fan Mag Guff," *Variety,* September 24, 1936, 51. In addition, writers employed directly by studio publicity departments were assigned to plant articles with newspapers and wire services, which often ran the pieces verbatim. "The planters are the unhappiest men in all Hollywood," explained *Editor and Publisher* in 1939. "They catch hell from everybody—from producers, stars, correspondents, and the Hays office. They're blamed for stories they didn't plant, and when a spicy hunk of scandal begins to get around, they must try to persuade their friends on the paper to kill the story." ("Press Agents Busy as Beavers in Fantastic Hollywood," *Editor and Publisher,* September 23, 1939.)

23. Al DiOrio, *Barbara Stanwyck* (New York: Coward-McCann, 1983), 119; Warren Harris, *Gable and Lombard* (New York: Simon & Schuster, 1974), 98-9; "A Heart to Heart Talk," *Photoplay,* February 1939, in *The Talkies,* ed. Richard Griffith (New York: Dover, 1971), 132.

24. Eells, *Hedda and Louella,* 170.

25. Wood, "First Lady of Hollywood," 9.

26. "Boos and Bouquets," *Photoplay,* June 1938, 8.

27. Letter, n.d.; letter, February 28, 1934; *Hollywood Hotel* Files, LOP, USC; "The Audience Speaks Up," *Photoplay,* June 1932, 12. According to *Modern Screen,* "A great deal of discussion has been aroused with the release of MGM's *Bombshell*. While everybody admits it's grand entertainment, there are those who think it unwise to debunk Hollywood. They claim that there are people who still idolize movie stars, think Hollywood a glamorous place to live, and to them the picture will be a disappointment." *Modern Screen,* January 1934, 37.

28. "Brickbats and Bouquets," *Photoplay,* March 1927, 115; "What the Fans Think," *Picture Play,* September 1926, 10; "Artificial Star Building," *Movie Fan,* December 1936, 5.

29. "What the Fans Think," *Picture Play,* January 1924, 10; "Disillusionment?," *Movie Fan,* July 1936, 4; "Activities of the EMO Movie Club," August 1936, 6.

30. Walker, *Stardom,* 202.

31. "Brickbats and Bouquets," *Photoplay,* July 1927, 16; letter from Tabor, Iowa, March 4, 1934, *Hollywood Hotel* Files, LOP, USC; Faith Service, "What Stars Would You Like to Meet," *Modern Screen,* December 1933, 58; "Between You n' Me," *Modern Screen,* March 1934, 15, 123.

32. "Disillusionment?," *Movie Fan,* 4.

33. Marian Rhea, "Bette Davis in Person," *Screen Book,* June 1936, 31.

34. "Your Fan Club," *Movieland*, November 1948, 74; Patricia Schoonmaker, "A Visit with Gloria," *Deanna's Diary*, First Quarter 1942; "Between You n' Me," *Modern Screen*, July 1936, 68; Wilkie, *Confessions*, vii.

35. Rita Boyd, "Hollywood Premiere," Esther Williams Fan Club Journal, Winter 1952.

36. Herbert L. Strock, "Your Autograph Please," *Modern Screen*, December 1936; Margaret Thorp, *America at the Movies* (New Haven: Yale University Press, 1939), 87-8. The Hollywood star tour dates back to the early 1920s. In 1921, Adela Rogers St. Johns told *Photoplay* readers about her experience on one such tour: the reporter and "fifteen curious sightseers" sat in a rickety bus while the driver yelled to the passengers through a megaphone. "Any minute you may see Mary Pickford standing on some corner, or Bebe Daniels doing a Spanish dance on the sidewalk, or Katherine MacDonald smoking a cigarette," he promised as the bus ambled up Hollywood Boulevard. Adela Rogers St. Johns, "Sight-seeing the Movies," *Photoplay*, April 1921, 30.

37. "One Out of 12 Crashes Barriers Set Up Around Movie Stars," *Washington Herald*, September 6, 1936, Fans Clipping File, AMPAS; *Los Angeles Citizen*, May 14, 1935, Jean Harlow Clipping File, AMPAS.

38. *Deanna's Diary*, Spring 1943, 8; To Billie Dove, July 1, 1939, Billie Dove Collection, AMPAS.

39. "The Audience Talks Back," *Photoplay*, December 1932, 6.

CHAPTER FIVE

1. "The Fan Club Corner," *Photoplay*, November 1934, 86.

2. "To the Hills!" *New York Times*, April 6, 1947, Section 2, 5.

3. *Motion Picture Story Magazine*, May 1912, 131.

4. *Motion Picture Story Magazine*, October 1912, 131; Marjorie Powell Fohn, "A Fan Club Talk," *Picture Play*, January 1922, 16; to William S. Hart, December 12, 1919, William S. Hart Collection, Box 10, Natural History Museum of Los Angeles County (NHMLAC).

5. Irving Shulman, *Harlow* (New York: Dell, 1964), 102.

6. Lora Kelly, "How One Girl Built Up a Fan Club," *Picture Play*, December 1925, 72-5.

7. Fohn, "Fan Club Talk," 16.

8. Kelly, "How One Girl Built," 72-5.

9. "The Fan Club Corner," *Photoplay*, October 1935, 115; February 1935, 121; August 1934, 120. One of the largest motion picture fan clubs of the 1930s honored not a movie star but a cartoon character. The Mickey Mouse Fan Club had two million members in the United States in 1933, "and plans are already on foot for a national convention, with delegates from all over the land," reported *Photoplay*. "The Star of Stars," *Photoplay*, June 1932, 46.

10. "Fan Clubs Costing American Public over $1,000,000 a Year," *Motion Picture Herald*, November 12, 1936; Welty Earnest, president of the Buster Collier

Fan Club, to Buster Collier, November 4, 1928, Buster Collier Collection, Academy of Motion Picture Arts and Sciences (AMPAS); Kelly, "How One Girl Built," 72-5.

11. To Jennifer Jones, n.d., Box 1354, Folder 7, David O. Selznick Collection (DOS), Harry Ransom Humanities Research Center, University of Texas, Austin (UT); Martin Levin, ed., *Hollywood and the Great Fan Magazines* (New York: Arbor House, 1970), 194, 198, 202.

12. Fan Mail Report, November and August 1945, Box 4557, Folder 10, DOS, UT.

13. "Dove Tales," 1931, Billie Dove Collection, AMPAS; Esther Williams Fan Club Journal, Summer 1952, Vertical File 224, AMPAS.

14. "Your Fan Club," *Movieland*, November 1948, 74; October 1948, 80; "Fan Club Corner," *Photoplay*, October 1934, 120.

15. "What Fans Think," *Picture Play*, August 1924, 119.

16. To Florence Lawrence, October 1914, Florence Lawrence Collection, NHM-LAC; "What Fans Think," *Picture Play*, August 1928, 10.

17. "Your Fan Club," *Movieland*, November 1948, 74; "Boosters Band Wagon," Esther Williams Fan Club Journal, Winter 1951.

18. *Gone with the Wind* letters from 1937, Box 3379, DOS, UT.

19. J. Smith to H. Klein, January 27, 1947, Box 3943, Folder 27, DOS, UT.

20. "Let's Do Something to Help Screen's Character Players," *Movie Fan* (newsletter of the EMO Movie Fan Club), September 1936.

21. "An Open Letter to Metro-Goldwyn-Mayer," *Golden Comet*, Winter 1938, 7.

22. "My Fans Saved Me," *Movieland*, August 1951; clipping from *Hollywood Citizen News*, April 26, 1949, Fan Club File, AMPAS.

23. "Your Fan Club," *Movieland*, April 1948, 72; to Gloria Swanson, April 1951, Box 67, Folder 1, Gloria Swanson Collection (GS), UT.

24. Fan Mail Reports, October, November 1945, Box 4557, Folder 10; to Guy Madison, 1947-1948, Box 3943, Folders 4, 27; DOS, UT.

25. Edward Hall to Greta Garbo, n.d., Vertical File 51, AMPAS; to Gloria Swanson, September 22, 1930, November 1, 1929, GS, UT.

26. Catherine Andrews to Billie Dove, March 25, 1929, Billie Dove Collection, AMPAS.

27. Gloria Swanson to Georgina Murray, March 4, 1951, Box 68, Folder 2, GS, UT.

28. "Your Fan Club," *Movieland*, January 1948, 90.

29. *Deanna's Diary*, Volume 5, Number 1, 1941, 3.

30. "Jeanette's Original and Official Invitation Backstage," *Golden Comet*, Spring 1940; *Deanna's Diary*, Spring 1943, 8.

31. "Your Fan Club," *Movieland*, November 1948, 74; note dated September 3, 1982, Box 70, Folder 5, GS, UT.

32. Newsletter of the Esther Williams Club, Summer 1953, Vertical Files, AMPAS.

33. "Dear Friend," *Movie Fan*, April 1936, 1.

34. "Disillusionment?," *Movie Fan*, July 1936, 4; "The Real Age of Shirley Temple," *Movie Fan*, October 1936, 1.

35. Bob Thomas, *Joan Crawford* (New York: Bantam, 1978), 143.

36. *Deanna's Diary,* June 1942, 2; to Gloria Swanson, December 3, 1952, Box 68, Folder 3, GS, UT; Esther Williams Fan Club Journal, Summer 1953.

37. "Your Fan Club," *Movieland,* June 1948, 74; December 1948, 74; Margaret Thorp, *America at the Movies* (New Haven: Yale University Press, 1939), 100.

38. *Hollywood Citizen News,* April 26, 1949, Fans Clipping File, AMPAS.

39. *Bulletin of the Wallace Reid Memorial Club,* May 1926; *Motion Picture,* March 1943, 13; Cameron Shipp, "You are My Favorite Movie Star," *Today's Woman,* October 1947, Fans Clipping File, AMPAS.

40. Joseph J. Barie to Greta Garbo, Feb 10, 1928, Vertical File 51, AMPAS; to Guy Madison, February 1, 1947, Box 4943, Folder 4, DOS, UT.

41. J. Smith to H. Klein, January 27, 1947, Guy Madison fan letters, Box 3943, Folder 27, DOS, UT; Thorp, *America,* 89.

42. Carolyn Whelchel, "Your Fan Club," *Movieland,* August 1947, 18.

43. "Meet One of Our English Members," *Golden Comet,* Summer 1942, 18.

44. "Comet Comments," *Golden Comet,* Spring 1943.

45. Georganne Scheiner, "The Deanna Durbin Devotees," in *Generations of Youth,* ed. Joe Austin and Michael Nevin Willard (New York: New York University Press, 1998); "Movie Cook-coos," *New Movie Magazine,* December 1932, 95; Marian Squire, "Here's What Happens at an Executive Session of a Joan Crawford Fan Club," *Variety,* 1939, Joan Crawford File, AMPAS.

46. "Happenings of the New York Chapter," *Golden Comet,* November/December 1941.

47. Betty Rosser, "To Mary Pickford, the Recollections of her Number One Fan," Mary Pickford Collection, AMPAS.

48. For a discussion of the importance of scrapbooks in movie fan culture, see Georganne Scheiner, "The Deanna Durbin Devotees." Scheiner argues that fan clubs, with their scrapbooks and detailed club journals, produced texts rather than merely consumed those (movies and fan magazines) issued from Hollywood.

49. Mary Dunphy to Jane Smoot, June 1947, Jeanette MacDonald collection, UT.

50. Ruth May Knell, "From Where I Sit," *Golden Comet,* Spring 1962; Ralph Reppert, "Their Melody Lingers On," *Baltimore Sun,* reprinted in *Golden Comet,* Spring 1969.

CHAPTER SIX

1. Fan mail report, 1945, Box 3939, Folder 21, David O. Selznick Collection (DOS), Harry Ransom Humanities Research Center, University of Texas, Austin (UT).

2. "My Fans Saved Me," *Movieland,* August 1951, 65.

3. Alexander Walker, *Stardom* (New York: Stein & Day, 1970), 253.

4. Leo Rosten, *Hollywood* (New York: Harcourt, Brace, 1941), 411. Sometimes fans made it as far as the film set before they were discovered. Greta Garbo,

claims her biographer, had an uncanny ability to spot fans who had hidden among film extras in crowd scenes. "There are people here who do not belong here," she would announce to the director. John Bainbridge, *Garbo* (New York: Holt, Rinehart & Winston, 1955), 217.

5. Bob Thomas, *Joan Crawford* (New York: Bantam, 1978), 112; Irving Shulman, *Harlow* (New York: Dell, 1964), 274-5. "No one is more appreciative than I am of the interest of the fans and if [they] want me to talk to them, I'll be glad to do so," Harlow explained in an official statement to the press. *Los Angeles Citizen,* May 14, 1935, Jean Harlow File, Margaret Herrick Library, Academy of Motion Picture Arts and Sciences (AMPAS).

6. Helen Ogden, "Fan Letters the Stars Appreciate," *Picture Play,* August 1925, 90; "Between You n' Me," *Modern Screen,* November 1936, 12.

7. Walker, *Stardom,* 250; Clive Brook, Vertical File 44; Esther Ralston, Vertical File 66, AMPAS; "What Happens to Fan Mail," *Photoplay,* August 1928, 40, 130.

8. Samuel Marx, *Mayer and Thalberg: The Make Believe Saints* (New York: Random House, 1975), 166.

9. To David O. Selznick, n.d., Box 221, Folder 9, DOS, UT.

10. Fan mail report, September 1945, May 1946; C. Slaughter to Selznick, 1942; to Selznick, 1937; all DOS, UT.

11. Florence Keely to Selznick, January 23, 1948; to Selznick, October 19, 1937; both DOS, UT.

12. David Stenn, *Clara Bow: Runnin' Wild* (New York: Doubleday, 1988), ch. 8; *Lady Killer,* dir. Roy Del Ruth, Warner Brothers, 1933.

13. Marx, *Mayer and Thalberg,* 92; Karen Swenson, *Greta Garbo: A Life Apart* (New York: Scribner's, 1997), 193.

14. David O. Selznick to Daniel O'Shea, December 10, 1942, December 17, 1943, DOS, UT.

15. "Wallace Beery," MGM studio biography, Wallace Beery Files, AMPAS.

16. Antoni Gronowicz, *Garbo* (New York: Simon & Schuster, 1990), 250, 257-8.

17. Niven Busch, "Lana Turner," *Life,* December 23, 1940, 64.

18. Gary Carey, *All the Stars in Heaven* (New York: Dutton, 1981), 258; Jane Ellen Wayne, *Lana: The Life and Loves of Lana Turner* (New York: St. Martin's Press, 1995), 15; "Scrapbook on Lana Turner," *Photoplay,* October 1944, 52.

19. Joan Crawford with Jane Kesner Ardmore, *A Portrait of Joan* (London: Frederick Muller, 1962), 13.

20. Joan Cross, "Name Her and Win $1000," *Movie Weekly,* May 28, 1925, 5; "Joan Crawford is the Winning Name," *Movie Weekly,* September 19, 1925. The prize for the winning name was 500 dollars; the ten runners-up won 50 dollars each.

21. Crawford, *Portrait of Joan,* 67; Alexander Walker, *Joan Crawford, The Ultimate Star* (New York: Harper & Row, 1983), 22; Thomas, *Joan Crawford,* 57.

22. Crawford, *Portrait of Joan,* 59.

23. "Between You n' Me," *Modern Screen,* April 1934, 12.

24. "Joan Crawford," MGM studio biography, Joan Crawford File, AMPAS; "What the Audience Thinks," *Photoplay,* October 1932, 16.

25. Walker, *Joan Crawford*, 22; Thomas, *Joan Crawford*, 79, 143.

26. Crawford, *Portrait of Joan*, 101; "What The Audience Thinks," *Photoplay*, October 1932, 16; Thomas, *Joan Crawford*, 86.

27. Joe Morella and Edward Z. Epstein, *Gable & Lombard & Powell & Harlow* (New York: Dell, 1975), 82.

28. James Quirk, "Why Women Go Crazy About Clark Gable," *Photoplay*, November 1931, reprinted in Richard Griffith, ed., *The Talkies*, 44.

29. Morella and Epstein, *Gable & Lombard*, 24.

30. Marx, *Mayer and Thalberg*, 157; Mordaunt Hall, "The Screen," *New York Times*, February 28, 1931, 15.

31. Quirk, "Why Women Go Crazy About Clark Gable"; Warren Harris, *Gable and Lombard* (New York: Simon & Schuster, 1974), 35.

32. "Clark Gable," studio biography, Clark Gable File, AMPAS; publicity manual for *Chained*, MGM Collection, Cinema Television Library, University of Southern California (USC).

33. Lyn Tornabene, *Long Live The King* (New York: G. P. Putnam, 1976), 129, 141; Walter Ramsay, "What Happened, Gable?," *Modern Screen*, April 1934.

34. Tornabene, *Long Live*, 211, 214-5; Morella and Epstein, *Gable & Lombard*, 55.

35. Harris, *Gable and Lombard*, 37.

36. Audience Preview Cards from *Parnell*, MGM Collection, USC; "What the Audience Thinks," *Photoplay*, September 1937; Tornabene, *Long Live*, 213; "No Beard for Gable," *Movie Fan*, December 1936, 5.

37. Beth Young to David Selznick, April 1937, Box 69, DOS, UT.

38. Dorothy Carter to Selznick, January 9, 1939, DOS, UT; Rudy Behlmer, *Memo from David O. Selznick* (New York: Viking, 1972), 167.

39. "What the Audience Thinks," *Photoplay*, October 1932, 16; Katherine Albert, "Why They Said Joan Was 'High Hat,'" *Photoplay*, August 1931, 112.

CHAPTER SEVEN

1. Carolyn Whelchel, "Your Fan Club," *Movieland*, January 1947, 80.

2. "To the Hills!" *New York Times*, April 6, 1947, sec. 2, 5; *Today's Woman*, October 1947, Fans Clipping File, Margaret Herrick Library, Academy of Motion Picture Arts and Sciences (AMPAS).

3. Morton Hunt, "Our Drooling Movie Fans," *Woman*, September 1950; "Dear Mr. Gable," *McCall's*, February 1949, Fans Clipping File, AMPAS.

4. To Gloria Swanson, n.d., Box 70, Gloria Swanson Collection (GS), Harry Ransom Humanities Research Center, University of Texas, Austin (UT); to David O. Selznick, August 23, 1938, Box 3391, Folder 6, David O. Selznick Collection (DOS), UT.

5. Louis E. Bisch, "How the Screen Hypnotizes You," *Photoplay*, February 1928, 40; P. W. Wilson, "The Crime Wave and the Movies," *Current Opinion*, March 1921, 320-1.

6. "Psychology of the Movies," *Literary Digest*, July 1917, 79; Hugo Munsterberg, *The Photoplay: A Psychological Study* (New York: D. Appleton, 1916), 95.

7. Wilson, "The Crime Wave and the Movies," 320; George Humphrey, "Do the Movies Help or Harm Us," *Collier's*, May 24, 1924, 5.

8. U.S. Congress, House, Committee on Education, Federal Motion Picture Commission: Briefs and Statements filed with the 64th Congress, 1st sess., H.R. 56. Washington: GPO, 1916.

9. Joseph Levenson, "Censorship of the Movies," *Forum*, April 1923, reprinted in James Rutland, ed., *State Censorship of Motion Pictures* (New York: H. W. Wilson, 1923), 83.

10. *Annual Report of the Motion Picture Commission of New York State*, in *Selected Articles on Censorship of the Theater and Moving Pictures*, ed. Lamar T. Beman (New York: H. W. Wilson, 1931), 137; A. T. Poffenberger, "Motion Pictures and Crime," in *The Movies in Our Midst*, ed. Gerald Mast (Chicago: University of Chicago Press, 1982), 204-5; *New York Times*, January 5 and 7, 1921.

11. "Should Moving Pictures Be Censored?," *Current Opinion*, May 1921, 653.

12. A. T. Poffenberger, "Motion Pictures and Crime," *Scientific Monthly*, April 1921, 336-9, in *State Censorship of Motion Pictures*, 59-60.

13. Louis E. Bisch, "What Makes Us Movie Fans," *Photoplay*, April 1928, 74.

14. Humphrey, "Do the Movies Help or Harm Us," 5.

15. "Lays Death to Valentino's," *New York Times*, August 28, 1926, 6.

16. Alexander Woolcott, "The Strenuous Honeymoon," *Everybody's*, November 1920, 36.

17. "Thousands in Riot at Valentino Bier, More than 100 Hurt," *New York Times*, August 25, 1926, 1.

18. Irving Shulman, *Valentino* (New York: Trident Press, 1967), 13.

19. "Crowds Still Try To View Valentino," *New York Times*, August 27, 1926, 3; "Kipling and Valentino," *New York Times*, August 28, 1926. Heywood Broun may have been one of the only members of the press to defend the spectators: "I rather think that some of the reports have been too severe in judging the motives of the crowd. I saw the long lines at a distance in the dripping rain, and it is my belief that if it had been possible for a reporter to look into the hearts of all there he would have found in many . . . a profound emotion." Heywood Broun, "It Seems to Me," *New York World*, August 27, 1926, 11.

20. "Valentino, the Martyr," *Moving Picture World*, September 4, 1926, 19; "What the Fans Think," *Picture Play*, January 1928, 10; May 1928, 10.

21. Margaret Thorp, *America at the Movies* (New Haven: Yale University Press, 1939), 94; Carl Cotter, "The Forty Hacks of the Fan Mags," *Coast*, February 1939, Fans Clipping File, AMPAS.

22. Thorp, *America*, 98; Murphy McHenry, "Dishing that Fan Mag Guff," *Variety*, September 24, 1936, 51.

23. "One Out of 12 Crashes Barriers Set Up Around Movie Stars," *Washington Herald*, September 6, 1936, Fans Clipping File, AMPAS; Fredda Dudley,

"Usually They Want Something," *Ladies' Home Journal*, January 1941, 79; Ruth Suckow, "Hollywood Gods and Goddesses," *Harper's*, July 1936, 189.

24. Dudley, "Want Something," 79; Thorp, *America*, 94.

25. Bosley Crowther, "Those Amazing Movie Fans," *New York Times Magazine*, April 24, 1942, 15.

26. Louis E. Bisch, "Are We Morons?," *Photoplay*, March 1928, 50; "Disillusion-ment?," *Movie Fan*, July 1936, 4.

27. "Activities of the EMO Movie Club," *Movie Fan*, August 1936; "The Fan Club Corner," *Photoplay*, August 1935, 105; "Your Fan Club," *Movieland*, June 1948, 74.

28. Richard Griffith, ed., *The Talkies* (New York: Dover, 1971), 9.

29. "What the Audience Thinks," *Photoplay*, August 1933, 10.

30. "The Opinion of Movie-goers," *Photoplay*, January 1934, 8; "What the Public Thinks," *Photoplay*, September 1933, 15.

31. Hanz Benz to Gloria Swanson, n.d., Box 66, Folder 6; anonymous fan letter, Box 70, Folder 1, GS, UT; to David O. Selznick, August 23, 1938, Box 3391, Folder 6, DOS, UT.

32. Louella Parsons, "They're Human, Too," *Photoplay*, August 1946, 33; clipping, July 17, 1944, Scrapbook 7, Jeanette MacDonald Collection, UT; "The Voice and the Kids," *New Republic*, November 6, 1944, 593.

33. Arnold Shaw, *Sinatra: Twentieth–Century Romantic* (New York: Holt, Rine-hart & Winston, 1968), 47; "Sinatra Fans Pose Two Police Problems and Not the Less Serious Involves Truancy," *New York Times*, October 13, 1944, 20.

34. "The Voice and the Kids," 592; E. J. Kahn, "The Slaves of Sinatra," *New Yorker*, November 1946.

35. Parsons, "They're Human, Too," 33; Dore Schary, "Does Hollywood Think Fans Are Pests," *Movieland*, April 1947, 48. *Variety* suggested that attacks on stars by bobbysoxers may have once been used as a method of studio publicity: "The mobbing of stars by frenzied fans and bobby soxers seeking autographs used to be a convenient means of getting free publicity. But it was overpromoted and now has become the press agents' biggest headache. Mobs of bobby soxers, acting to perfection the part of lunatics, have torn actresses' expensive gowns and knocked down and half stripped screen heroes." Joseph Wechsberg, "Press Agents Star in Making Stars Glitter," *Variety*, June 8, 1947.

36. "To the Hills!" *New York Times*, April 6, 1947; "Bobby Soxers Dynasty Target of 'Frankly 40's'," *Los Angeles Times*, March 10, 1946, 2.

37. "Speak For Yourself," *Photoplay*, October 1944, 118; January 1945, 16.

38. Alan F. Berge, "Fans, Friends, or Foes?," *Taylor Topics*, Spring 1982.

39. Morton Hunt, "Our Drooling Movie Fans," *Woman*, September 1950; John Maynard, "Dear Mr. Gable," *McCall's*, February 1949, 7.

40. Christopher Finch and Linda Rosencrantz, *Gone Hollywood* (New York: Doubleday, 1979), 364.

41. Leo Handel, *Hollywood Looks at Its Audience* (Chicago: University of Illinois Press, 1950), 95; ad in *Variety*, November 8, 1944; George Eells, *Hedda and Louella* (New York: G. P. Putnam, 1972), 12.

42. Leo Rosten, *Hollywood: The Movie Colony, the Movie Makers* (New York: Harcourt, Brace, 1941), 355; Robert S. Lynd and Helen Merrell Lynd, *Middletown in Transition* (New York: Harcourt, Brace, 1937), 169; Adler quoted in Rosten, *Hollywood*, 368.
43. Hadley Cantril, *The Invasion from Mars: A Study in the Psychology of Panic* (New York: Harper & Row, 1966), 204.

BIBLIOGRAPHY

Allen, Robert. *Vaudeville and Film 1895-1915: A Study in Media Interaction.* New York: Arno Press, 1980.

Anderson, Patrick Donald. *In Its Own Image: The Cinematic Vision of Hollywood.* New York: Arno Press, 1978.

Arvidson, Linda. *When the Movies Were Young.* New York: E. P. Dutton, 1935.

Bainbridge, John. *Garbo.* New York: Holt, Rinehart & Winston, 1955.

Balio, Tino. *Grand Design.* Berkeley: University of California Press, 1995.

Beauchamp, Cari. *Without Lying Down: Frances Marion and the Powerful Women of Early Hollywood.* New York: Scribner's, 1997.

Beaumont, Cyril. *Fanny Elssler.* London: C. W. Beaumont, 1931.

Behlmer, Rudy. *Hollywood's Hollywood.* Secaucus, N.J.: Citadel Press, 1974.

————. *Memo from David O. Selznick.* New York: Viking, 1972.

Beman, Lamar T., ed. *Selected Articles on Censorship of the Theater and Moving Pictures.* New York: H. W. Wilson, 1931.

Blumer, Herbert. *Movies and Conduct.* New York: Macmillan, 1933.

Boorstin, Daniel. *The Image: A Guide to Pseudo-Events in America.* New York: Atheneum, 1975.

Braudy, Leo. *The Frenzy of Renown.* New York: Vintage, 1997.

Brown, Gene. *Movie Time.* New York: Macmillan, 1995.

Cantril, Hadley. *The Invasion from Mars: A Study in the Psychology of Panic.* New York: Harper & Row, 1966.

Carey, Gary. *All the Stars in Heaven.* New York: Dutton, 1981.

Carroll, David. *The Matinee Idols.* New York: Arbor House, 1972.

Conners, Marilyn. *What Chance Have I in Hollywood?* Hollywood: Famous Authors, 1924.

Cott, Nancy. *The Grounding of Modern Feminism.* New Haven: Yale University Press, 1987.

Crawford, Joan, with Jane Kesner Ardmore. *A Portrait of Joan.* London: Frederick Muller, 1962.

Curtis, Anthony, ed. *The Rise and Fall of the Matinee Idol.* New York: St. Martin's Press, 1974.

DeCordova, Richard. *Picture Personalities: The Emergence of the Star System in America.* Urbana: University of Illinois Press, 1990.

DiOrio, Al. *Barbara Stanwyck.* New York: Coward-McCann, 1983.

Drinkwater, John. *The Life and Times of Carl Laemmle.* New York: G. P. Putnam, 1931.

Dunning, John. *On the Air: The Encyclopedia of Old-Time Radio.* New York: Oxford University Press, 1998.

Dyer, Richard. "*A Star Is Born* and The Construction of Authenticity." In *Stardom,* ed. Christine Gledhill. New York: Routledge, 1991.

Eells, George. *Hedda and Louella.* New York: G. P. Putnam, 1972.

Fairbanks, Douglas. *Laugh and Live.* New York: Britton Publishing, 1917.

———. *Youth Points the Way.* New York: D. Appleton, 1924.

Fass, Paula S. *The Damned and the Beautiful.* New York: Oxford, 1977.

Finch, Christopher, and Linda Rosencrantz. *Gone Hollywood.* New York: Doubleday, 1979.

Fiske, John. *Understanding Popular Culture.* New York: Routledge, 1995.

Forman, Henry. *Our Movie Made Children.* New York: Macmillan, 1933.

Fuller, Kathryn. *At the Picture Show.* Washington, D.C.: Smithsonian, 1996.

Gabler, Neal. *Life the Movie: How Entertainment Conquered Reality.* New York: Knopf, 1998.

———. *Winchell: Gossip, Power, and the Culture of Celebrity.* New York: Knopf, 1994.

Gamson, Joshua. *Claims to Fame: Celebrity in Contemporary America.* Berkeley: University of California Press, 1994.

Gelman, Barbara, ed. *Photoplay Treasury.* New York: Crown, 1972.

Griffith, Richard, ed. *The Talkies.* New York: Dover, 1971.

Griffith, Richard, and Arthur Mayer. *The Movies.* New York: Simon & Schuster, 1977.

Gronowicz, Antoni. *Garbo.* New York: Simon & Schuster, 1990.

Gunning, Tom. *D. W. Griffith and the Origins of American Narrative Film.* Chicago: University of Illinois Press, 1991.

Halttunen, Karen. *Confidence Men and Painted Women.* New Haven: Yale University Press, 1982.

Handel, Leo. *Hollywood Looks at Its Audience.* Chicago: University of Illinois Press, 1950.

Harris, Cheryl, and Alison Alexander, eds. *Theorizing Fandom: Fans, Subculture, Identity.* Creekskill, N.J.: Hampton Press, 1998.

Harris, Neil. *Humbug: The Art of P. T. Barnum.* Chicago: University of Chicago Press, 1973.

Harris, Warren. *Gable and Lombard.* New York: Simon & Schuster, 1974.

Herzog, Charlotte Cornelia, and Jane Marie Gaines. "Puffed Sleeves Before Tea Time." In *Stardom,* ed. Christine Gledhill. New York: Routledge, 1991.

Hill, Laurance L., and Silas E. Snyder. *Can Anything Good Come Out of Hollywood?* Hollywood: Snyder Publications, 1923.

Jenkins, Henry. *Textual Poachers: Television Fans and Participatory Culture.* New York: Routledge, 1992.

Jensen, Joli. "Fandom as Pathology." In *The Adoring Audience: Fan Culture and Popular Media,* ed. Lisa Lewis. New York: Routledge, 1993.

Klaprat, Cathy. "The Star as Market Strategy: Bette Davis in Another Light." In *The American Film Industry,* ed. Tino Balio. Madison: University of Wisconsin Press, 1976.

Koszarski, Richard. *An Evening's Entertainment.* Berkeley: University of California Press, 1990.

Levin, Martin, ed. *Hollywood and the Great Fan Magazines.* New York: Arbor House, 1970.

Lewis, Lisa, ed. *The Adoring Audience: Fan Culture and Popular Media.* New York: Routledge, 1993.

Lynd, Robert S., and Helen Merrell Lynd. *Middletown in Transition.* New York: Harcourt, Brace, 1937.

Marchand, Roland. *Advertising the American Dream.* Berkeley: University of California Press, 1985.

Marden, Orison Swett. *Pushing to the Front.* New York: Thomas Crowell, 1894.

Marx, Samuel. *Mayer and Thalberg: The Make Believe Saints.* New York: Random House, 1975.

May, Lary. *Screening Out the Past.* Chicago: University of Chicago Press, 1983.

McArthur, Benjamin. *Actors and American Culture, 1880-1920.* Philadelphia: Temple University Press, 1984.

Mitroff, Ian, and Warren Bennis. *The Unreality Industry.* New York: Carol Publishing, 1989.

Morella, Joe, and Edward Epstein. *Gable & Lombard & Powell & Harlow.* New York: Dell, 1975.

Munsterberg, Hugo. *The Photoplay: A Psychological Study.* New York: D. Appleton, 1916.

Musser, Charles. *The Emergence of Cinema: The American Screen to 1907.* Berkeley: University of California Press, 1990.

Noble, Peter. *Bette Davis.* Great Britain: Citizen Press, 1948.

Parsons, Louella. *The Gay Illiterate.* New York: Doubleday, 1944.

Pearson, Roberta. *Eloquent Gestures.* Berkeley: University of California Press, 1992.

Powdermaker, Hortense. *Hollywood: The Dream Factory.* New York: Grosset & Dunlap, 1950.

Radway, Janice. *Reading the Romance.* Chapel Hill: University of North Carolina, 1991.

Rosen, Marjorie. *Popcorn Venus.* New York: Avon Books, 1973.

Rosten, Leo. *Hollywood: The Movie Colony, the Movie Makers.* New York: Harcourt, Brace, 1941.

Rutland, James, ed. *State Censorship of Motion Pictures.* New York: H. W. Wilson, 1923.

Scanlon, Jennifer. *Inarticulate Longings.* New York: Routledge, 1995.

Scheiner, Georganne. "The Deanna Durbin Devotees." In *Generations of Youth,* ed. Joe Austin and Michael Nevin Willard. New York: New York University Press, 1998.

Schickel, Richard. *His Picture in the Papers.* New York: Charterhouse, 1973.

———. *Intimate Strangers: The Culture of Celebrity.* New York: Doubleday, 1986.

Shaw, Arnold. *Sinatra: Twentieth-Century Romantic.* New York: Holt, Rinehart & Winston, 1968.

Shulman, Irving. *Harlow.* New York: Dell, 1964.

———. *Valentino.* New York: Trident Press, 1967.

Sklar, Robert. *Movie-Made America.* New York: Vintage, 1994.

Slide, Anthony. *Aspects of Film History Prior to 1920.* Methuen, N.J.: Scarecrow Press, 1978.

———. *The Idols of Silence.* South Brunswick, N.J.: A. S. Barnes, 1976.

St. Johns, Adela Rogers. *The Honeycomb.* New York: Doubleday, 1969.

Stacey, Jackie. *Star Gazing: Hollywood Cinema and Female Spectatorship.* New York: Routledge, 1994.

Stenn, David. *Clara Bow: Runnin' Wild.* New York: Doubleday, 1988.

Stine, Whitney. *Mother Goddam.* New York: Berkley, 1980.

Stones, Barbara. *America Goes to the Movies.* North Hollywood: National Association of Theater Owners, 1993.

Story, Margaret. *How to Dress Well.* New York and London: Funk & Wagnalls, 1924.

Studlar, Gaylyn. "The Perils of Pleasure: Fan Magazine Discourse as Women's Commodified Culture in the 1920s." In *Silent Film,* ed. Richard Abel. New Brunswick, N.J.: Rutgers University Press, 1996.

Susman, Warren. "Personality and the Making of Twentieth Century Culture." In *Culture as History.* New York: Pantheon, 1984.

Swanson, Gloria. *Swanson on Swanson.* New York: Pocket Books, 1980.

Swenson, Karen. *Greta Garbo: A Life Apart.* New York: Scribner's, 1997.

Thomas, Bob. *Joan Crawford.* New York: Bantam, 1978.

Thorp, Margaret. *America at the Movies.* New Haven: Yale University Press, 1939.

Tornabene, Lyn. *Long Live The King.* New York: G. P. Putnam, 1976.

Turk, Edward Baron. *Hollywood Diva.* Berkeley: University of California Press, 1998.

Wageknecht, Edward. *The Movies in the Age of Innocence.* New York: Ballantine, 1971.

Walker, Alexander. *Joan Crawford, The Ultimate Star.* New York: Harper & Row, 1983.

———. *Stardom.* New York: Stein & Day, 1970.

Wayne, Jane Ellen. *Lana: The Life and Loves of Lana Turner.* New York: St. Martin's Press, 1995.

West, Nathanael. *The Day of the Locust.* New York: Bantam, 1959.

Whitfield, Eileen. *Pickford: The Woman Who Made Hollywood.* Lexington: The University of Kentucky Press, 1997.

Wilkie, Jane. *Confessions of an Ex–Fan Magazine Writer.* New York: Doubleday, 1980.

Williamson, Alice. *Alice in Movieland.* New York: D. Appleton, 1928.

Zierold, Norman. *Garbo.* New York: Stein & Day, 1969.

INDEX